Unequal Burden

UNEQUAL BURDEN

*Economic Crises,
Persistent Poverty,
and Women's Work*

edited by

LOURDES BENERÍA &
SHELLEY FELDMAN

Cornell University

WESTVIEW PRESS
Boulder • San Francisco • Oxford

Copyright © 1992 by Westview Press, Inc.

Published in 1992 in the United States of America by Westview Press, Inc., 5500 Central Avenue, Boulder, Colorado 80301-2847, and in the United Kingdom by Westview Press, 36 Lonsdale Road, Summertown, Oxford OX2 7EW

Library of Congress Cataloging-in-Publication Data
Unequal burden : economic crises, persistent poverty, and women's work
  / edited by Lourdes Benería, Shelley Feldman.
    p. cm.
  Includes bibliographical references and index.
  ISBN 0-8133-8229-7 — ISBN 0-8133-8230-0 (pbk.)
  1. Structural adjustment (Economic policy)—Developing countries.
2. Poor women—Developing countries. 3. Women—Employment—
Developing countries. 4. Households—Developing countries.
I. Benería, Lourdes. II. Feldman, Shelley.
HC59.7.U266 1992
331.4′09172′4—dc20   92-2873
                                                         CIP

Printed and bound in the United States of America

 The paper used in this publication meets the requirements
of the American National Standard for Permanence of Paper
for Printed Library Materials Z39.48-1984.

10   9   8   7   6   5   4   3   2   1

Contents

Preface

The decade of the 1980s left profound changes on the world's economic and political landscape. It also left us with many questions about the long-term significance of these changes, which, for a large proportion of the world's population, involved high costs of adjustment and survival. The most serious difficulties have been experienced in countries suffering from the devastating consequences of the foreign debt crisis, but problems of survival and adjustment have not been exclusive to these areas. In industrialized countries like the United States, the 1980s witnessed a drastic polarization of incomes and living standards. The prosperity of some sectors of the population grew parallel to the increased deterioration or stagnation of others, giving rise to a new set of social problems such as homelessness, the drug culture, and increasing urban crime.

As the 1980s proceeded, some of the problems generated by the debt crisis and the policies that followed became increasingly apparent. Studies about the negative effects of the standard IMF-style structural adjustment policies for dealing with the crisis began to emerge by the middle of the decade. The pioneer work of UNICEF in investigating the effects of the crisis on child and human welfare resulted in the publication of *Adjustment with a Human Face* in 1987.[1] The book is a collection of country studies documenting the devastating effects of structural adjustment on the most vulnerable sectors of the population, particularly in Africa and Latin America. It also represents a plea for a more humanitarian approach to adjustment along the lines of a liberal model.

What the initial UNICEF studies did not have was a focus on the unequal distribution of the burden of the debt within households that included a gender dimension in the analysis. Yet, it was becoming increasingly obvious and had been emphasized as early as the 1985 UN Decade for Women Conference held in Nairobi that women were confronting a very heavy burden in the process of adjustment. UNICEF's own Office for Latin America and the Caribbean, in fact, began to deal with this issue with the publication of three case studies.[2] With the objective of continuing this effort and deepening the discussion, the then newly created Program on International Development and Women (PIDW) at Cornell University organized a workshop entitled "Economic Crises, Household Strategies, and Women's Work" held on September 2–5, 1988. Attended by participants from a variety of Third World and high-income countries, its main goal was to shift the discussion of these issues beyond the UNICEF approach at the time by taking the analysis to the level of the household so as to understand in more detail the distribution of the burden of adjustment among household members.

More specifically, the objectives of the workshop were manifold, deriving from the need to: (a) understand the ways households have coped with crises so as to best design empowering actions and policies; (b) analyze the role of gender in determining women's role in the adjustment process, including ideological factors defining women's "proper location" in society; (c) compare the experiences of different countries, including those from the industrialized world; (d) analyze class differences in the processes of adjustment; (e) locate the microprocesses of adjustment, such as those at the household level, within the wider framework of macroeconomic adjustment policies; and (f) explore alternatives and avenues beyond "survival strategies" by empowering those involved and by further defining alternative policies and actions at the micro- and macrolevel.

Faithful to the original project, this volume includes a major proportion of the original papers discussed at the workshop plus three additional ones. To the extent possible, all of the chapters have been updated to reflect new questions emerging under a rapidly evolving domestic and international situation. The basic facts, however, have not changed. In countries suffering from the burden of foreign debt, the social costs of adjustment have been staggering. Thus, a debt often incurred by nondemocratically elected governments has fallen mostly upon citizens who had no input in the process. The IMF model of adjustment, a practically standardized set of policies applied to countries whose problems are often different, has so far not succeeded in promoting growth and reversing the predominant trends of the past decade. In the industrialized high-income countries, the hegemonic neoliberal model has resulted in new inequalities and polarization of incomes, which have intensified the problems of the marginalized sectors. We have, therefore, witnessed a decade of increasing inequalities within countries and between countries, with the flow of resources from the poorer to the richer countries.

It is, in fact, ironic that as the world's capacity to produce and meet the basic needs of its population has reached unprecedented heights with modern technologies and economic globalization, some of the most basic human problems remain unresolved or have even deteriorated. Perhaps one of the worst legacies of the 1980s is that we are left without clear alternatives to the hegemonic and seemingly triumphant neoliberal model. Given women's instrumental role in solving the problems of daily life, we believe that they have an important contribution to make toward thinking through and implementing such alternatives. In describing what has been, this volume raises many useful questions about what could be and points toward some avenues for change.

This project would not have been possible without a collective effort. The financial support of the Ford Foundation was instrumental both for the initial workshop and the book project; many thanks to Michele Heisler for her support and active participation. At Cornell we received encouragement and help from faculty and students, particularly from those associated with the Program on International Development and Women. In particular, we thank Wendy McFarren for her work in organizing the details of the workshop and colleagues at the Center for International Studies, Women's Studies, and the Department of City and Regional Planning and Rural Sociology for their institutional support. Special thanks are also due Betty Van Amburg for her careful organization and typing of the manuscript. Finally, our thanks to all workshop participants for their work, their spirit, and their contribution to a discussion and a project that has by far not ended.

Lourdes Benería
Ithaca, NY

NOTES

1. Giovanni A. Cornia, Richard Jolly, and Frances Stewart (eds.). *Adjustment with a Human Face.* Vol. 1. New York: UNICEF/Clarendon Press, 1987.

2. UNICEF. *The Invisible Adjustment: Poor Women and the Economic Crisis.* New York: UNICEF, 1987.

1

Crises, Poverty, & Gender Inequality: Current Themes & Issues

❧ SHELLEY FELDMAN

The Third World debt crisis and the global economic changes of the past decade have restructured nation-based macroeconomic policies, community resources, and intrahousehold divisions of labor in many parts of the world. Although some areas of the world economy have been relatively protected from a general deterioration of living standards, recognized as one consequence of this crisis, the persistence and expansion of rural and urban poverty represent the living conditions of an increasing proportion of the world's population. The reallocation of national resources, in concert with policies that liberalize the economy, for example, have swelled the ranks of the unemployed, the poor, and the malnourished. Women, in particular, have been especially affected by the debt crisis and processes of restructuring because they represent a disproportionate share of the world's poor, are increasingly represented among low-wage workers, and are forced to balance wage work with subsistence and domestic production in meeting household needs. Women also represent a growing proportion of de jure and de facto household heads who have the sole responsibility for meeting household reproduction costs, that is, maintaining the household over a long period.

This volume, through country-based studies of the debt crisis and persistent poverty, provides a rethinking of the consequences of the economic crisis and the debt crisis from the point of view of changing state practices, household and family organization and patterns of negotiating resource endowments, and women's work. The book examines the diverse ways in which communities, households, and intrahousehold relations are being transformed in light of the reallocation of national, local, and household resources. It also identifies the ways in which extant

1

social relations structure national policy formation and mediate the expression of the crisis within specific national contexts. The comparative-historical perspective employed in the case studies included in the volume illuminates the recursive relations that shape the interaction between different levels of social organization and between policy changes and the creation of new behavioral practices. The intrahousehold division of labor and the division of labor in the workplace are especially salient in the case studies as these divisions are recast during times of crisis and change. The empirical chapters also examine how new normative behaviors and the ideology that is used to legitimate appropriate female interactions are re-created during times that place new demands on people's lives.

THE INTERNATIONAL CONTEXT

Profound changes in the global production and exchange of agricultural commodities, manufactured goods, and services have forged new relations of interdependence among countries, resulting in the creation of a highly interconnected, unevenly developed, and highly unstable international system. This system is manifest in the transition from the postwar period of high levels of employment and rapid rates of growth of national income and trade to increasing levels of unemployment, rising prices, declining wages, and reduced standards of living, particularly striking in selected countries and regions of the world.

The combined and uneven development of this complex global system reveals the ways in which international relations and national ones shape how processes of accumulation and legitimacy are negotiated and reproduced over time. As MacEwan and Tabb (1989:7–20) suggest, conflicts of the 1950s and 1960s have undermined U.S. hegemony and ushered in an era of relative stagnation and new relations among international capitalists. These changes have created new conditions of national productive capacity and new ties of dependence among countries. For example, the shift from import substitution to export production and an increased dependence on international financial resources among countries has legitimated new policy demands placed on national governments by multilateral lending institutions. For example, the demands put forward by the structural adjustment programs of the International Monetary Fund (IMF) and the World Bank have significantly recast the economic and political environment of nations dependent on multilateral financing. The policy proscriptions required by these lending institutions have shaped the relocation and fragmentation of production on a global scale and have reorganized labor markets and labor processes in the industrialized West as well as in the Third World.

Cross-national comparisons of macroeconomic policy initiatives suggested by international lending institutions point to the importance of trade liberalization and the shift in national development strategy from import substitution to export-led growth. Structural adjustment policies also include reductions in public sector employment, limitations on food and agricultural subsidies, the denationalization of public sector enterprises, and reductions in public expenditure that are envisioned to increase global competition. The commitment to globalize production and integrate productive sectors across nations is also visible in the policies suggested to promote private investment. These policies include not only credit incentives to stimulate productive capacity but also tax holidays and trade and tariff reforms to encourage export production. Small-scale entrepreneurial activity is also encouraged through a decentralization of credit extension.

Implicit in this approach is the assumption that increasing productive capacity will generate employment for those increasingly dispossessed of both land and other productive resources and thus set the conditions for stable economic growth. The initiatives that have been suggested represent neoliberal assumptions about the long-term growth potential of capitalism and a reintegration of the global economy. However, although these alterations in development strategy are thought to enable long-term growth with equity, the short-term costs of the crisis are slowly being recognized as bearing disproportionately on the poor (Cornia, Jolly, and Stewart 1987).

In response to reductions in public sector employment, rising commodity prices, declines in social services, and other "belt tightening" policies, development agency programs organized by the United Nations Children's Emergency Fund (UNICEF), the World Bank, the United Nations Development Programme (UNDP), and the World Food Program, among others, have addressed the immediate needs of those most affected, primarily women and children. Their interventions, as Elson (in Chapter 2) reminds us, are "protecting the vulnerable" rather than challenging the conditions that create a significant proportion of a nation's impoverished masses.

The demands of the multilateral and bilateral lending institutions have generated a range of nation-based policy initiatives that have challenged contemporary development strategy and set the context for new patterns of global integration. These national policy reforms have also mediated the demands of lending institutions and have conditioned new patterns of capital accumulation and new relations shaping global political hegemony. As such, international demands for economic restructuring and changes in state practices need to be examined as recursive relations that are affected by, and also affect, the particular consequences of economic integration and structural adjustment processes as these shape everyday life.

Indeed, some nations have been relatively protected from deteriorating living standards, recognized as one significant consequence of economic restructuring, but others have had limited maneuverability with regard to the range of political strategies they are able to deploy to mediate the effects of the debt crisis and more general changes brought about by the restructuring of production.[1] For example, countries without a natural resources base with which to barter on the international market may have only limited maneuverability in negotiating the policy reforms required by multilateral lending institutions. This limitation is because the demands to privatize production and expand export production are often preconditions for loans or credit and, with only limited exports of high demand, bargaining between nations and lending institutions will disproportionately favor the lending community. Notwithstanding these unequal bargaining relations, the long-term nature of the global economic crisis suggests that the success of the IMF and the World Bank in managing national debt problems is more a strategy of "debt containment" than a transformation of contemporary conditions (Wood 1989:305).

THE NATIONAL CONTEXT

Despite differences in how countries shape their national policies, there are similarities in the ways in which nations restructure their labor market, reorganize production, set wage and price controls, and condition the lives of different segments of their population. In addition to the differential effects of the economic crisis for international relations, in other words, is the unequal distribution of the effects of economic change within nations. In this context, it is worthwhile to point out that poor nations do not necessarily imply a totality of poor people. In fact, the distinction between poor nations and poor people draws attention to the importance of examining who benefits from, and who bears the cost of, selected policy reforms that restructure the production environment and transform public expenditures. For what segment of the population do belt-tightening policy initiatives mean more limited access to food, social services, and employment? For whom do they represent opportunities for increased access to credit, tax holidays, and incentives to expand production and thus increase accumulation and profit-making opportunities? These differential class effects are critically important to disaggregate for economies and regions as well as for communities and households if we are to understand the unequal impact of global change and economic crisis on various constituencies.

The effects of global restructuring on national economies have come under the scrutiny of policy analysts, development agency planners, and scholars. Policy analysts and development planners, particularly those employed by the international lending institutions, have generally been concerned with reshaping the policy environment within countries to enhance productive capacity. These writers assume that a reorganization of national economies will enable countries to meet their debt service payments and create an economic environment to enhance private investment and private accumulation. This literature draws attention to the patterns of slow economic growth or stagnation that are the assumed symptoms of the crisis and emphasizes the costs of declining rates of profit for capital (MacEwan and Tabb 1989:7-20, 23-43).

Not surprisingly, country responses to demands from the lending community and the reorganization of global production have transformed relations between various productive sectors and producers. Within countries these changes have transformed relations among producers and between production sectors. For example, the globalization of the food system initiated by the postwar policies of comparative advantage has transformed agricultural production and reshaped how, with what resources and methods, and under what labor regimes production takes place. This transformation, in turn, has generated conditions promoting new relations of interdependence among countries for modern inputs, expertise, and agricultural commodities. It has also promoted a diversification of the rural as well as the urban economy, an increase in rural to urban migration, and a reorganization of the household as a unit of production and consumption. Rural diversification brought changes in petty commodity production that generated new relations of production and new patterns of resource and labor control. In some countries there is also a structural reorganization of intrahousehold kin relations, which include the shift from extended to more nucleated forms as well as new networks of family interaction as households diversify income and employment opportunities.

As new patterns of intrahousehold divisions of labor emerge, they alter the norms and values that guide everyday life in both the private domain of the household and the public domain of the workplace. In both the household and the workplace a new gender division of labor may generate contradictory outcomes. On the one hand, these outcomes may entail new relations of inequality, subordination, and exploitation for women. On the other hand, they may provide opportunities for greater independence and resource control for all household members.

Many national economies have embraced the reorganization of social life outlined above despite the short-term costs of structural adjustment for those most negatively affected by its policy consequences. In response to declines in food availability and increasing unemployment, subsidized feeding programs and rural reconstruction schemes such as Food for Work programs have been organized for those deemed most vulnerable: women and children. Little attention, however, has been given by policy analysts and development agency planners to how households, families, and individuals strategize to maintain social life under conditions of economic and social insecurity.[2]

The scholarly community, by contrast, has recently begun to address issues raised by the long-term impact of the debt crisis and structural adjustment lending on the organization of global production and on the internationalization of the labor market and labor force.[3] This literature has focused on macroeconomic issues and increasingly on a reconsideration of the ways in which units of social organization, including the household and the community, as well as gender relations are being transformed by new demands required for social survival (MacEwan and Tabb 1989). Especially important is a feminist theoretical and conceptual interpretation of the differential impact of the crisis and of the reforms proposed for women (Stichter and Parpart 1990). Scholars have also begun to explore how social movements have responded to the changing world order (Amin et al. 1990).

ISSUES AND ARGUMENTS

Below are a number of salient themes drawing this book together and indicating the ways in which it contributes to a critique of contemporary analyses of the uneven development of the global economy, the debt crisis, persistent poverty, and patterns of inequality between and within nations, social classes, and households. First, the contributors depart from studies addressing the debt crisis or the costs of economic restructuring as a generalizable phenomenon and instead show that because of the resource bases and historical conditions of different nations, countries respond to their conditions of dependence in specific and contingent ways. Highlighting contingency helps us to recognize that there are important distinctions in the responses of communities, households, and individuals to economic declines. Contingency also helps us to recognize that nation-based crises of debt dependency and accumulation, brought about by the global restructuring of production and labor as well as financial and trade institutions, have created conditions in Asia and the industrialized West similar to those in Latin America and Africa, although responses to changes differ in important ways.

Particular responses to the debt crisis and aid dependence, resulting in the reallocation of resources away from public expenditures to private sector development, have been shaped by how a country is presently integrated into the global economy, the diversity of its resource base, and the nature of its aid and trade regime. To illuminate these differential effects, the book includes contributions from countries in Latin America, the Caribbean, and Africa (Benería, Safa and Antrobus, McFarren, Pérez-Alemán, Tripp) where indebtedness to private banks has been a major determinant of the crisis; from Asia where growing and persistent poverty not alleviated by aid dependence has shaped the nature of the crisis (Feldman); and from Italy (Saraceno) where services and special state subsidies have limited the costs of labor market restructuring for a segment of formal sector workers.

Second, national political stability and the extent to which selected populations protect their own interests are salient issues in understanding how people organize their everyday lives. The strategic plans, policies, and practices employed by the state to ensure its hegemony have intended as well as unintended and contradictory consequences. For example, as the state seeks to maintain its hegemony, new relations of control may be deployed that challenge existing patterns of negotiation between government and bureaucratic authorities and local constituencies. It is therefore important to examine the mechanisms regimes employ to secure their own hegemony and to explore the extent to which previously organized forms of resistance to exploitation have been co-opted, made illegal (such as the case of trade unionism), or viewed as limited because the intensification of labor has required that all available time and energy be spent on the short-term goal of daily maintenance. What trade-offs do regimes negotiate to secure their own survival? Between military expenditures and public expenditures? Between rural social programs and urban employment schemes?

Alternatively, how have various constituencies responded to limits on their political organization? How have new state strategies created new collective opportunities for organizing and negotiating for resistance and change? In the book, examples from Britain and the United States as well as the Third World are drawn upon to establish the basis for what Diane Elson suggests is the shift from "survival to transformative strategies."

These themes provide the context within which the chapters collectively explore how the debt crisis, growing inequality, and persistent poverty shape and are shaped by the gender division of labor and household and family organization in countries suffering most profoundly from the debt crisis, such as Mexico (Benería), as well as those where aid dependence has resulted in conditions of persistent poverty and growing inequality, such as Bangladesh and India (Feldman, Agarwal). Also included in this volume are chapters that cover industrialized countries (Saraceno), where the resource base differs markedly from conditions in the Third World and where crises of production have transformed labor relations and generated crises of employment and social survival.

A third theme concerns the role of the community and the household as arenas of mediation, exchange, and negotiation. A focus on these institutional settings emphasizes the importance of mediating structural contexts in shaping responses to economic crises. The attention the chapters give to collectivities as important units of social analysis highlights organizational sites for planning and for restructuring existing patterns of resource use and social reproduction (McFarren). Moreover, a comparative framework (Saraceno, McFarren) that highlights regional differences within and between countries acknowledges the significance of these mediating structures and differences in regional resource endowments for shaping household resource availability and ultimately resource use.

Fourth, this volume indicates the limitations of research employing national indicators of poverty to identify economic crises and to explain the diverse responses households and individuals make to forestall disaster. As we will elaborate below, studies that use national census data to identify patterns of work, migration, and consumption are theoretically and methodologically distinct from the effort to construct the processes by which people make choices to mediate the costs of economic change and to organize efforts to restructure control of production and consumption. These choices are made through interaction with a range of social institutions and individuals that represent competing and conflicting as well as shared interests. These various social relations highlight processes of social reproduction that, broadly speaking, refer to the means by which the daily lives of people are maintained and perpetuated. It is useful here to recall the important distinction among processes of reproduction drawn by Edholm, Harris, and Young (1977), which include biological reproduction, the reproduction of the labor force, and reproduction of the institutions of social life. The latter two processes of reproduction include the basic subsistence needs of food, clothing, and shelter as well as the basic social needs provided by the institutional infrastructure, such as education and training, health care, and social welfare.

Fifth, this volume also departs from studies limited to only the most vulnerable sectors of the population and from proscriptions and outcomes that depend on various forms of state intervention to reshape production and consumption strategies. The collection draws attention to how various constituencies respond to and shape creative ways of managing changes in their financial and social security. Two important processes are thus illuminated. The first is how individual and collective action shape and structure social outcomes and alternatives as people respond to challenges to their everyday lives. Second, a focus on collective action highlights how various constituencies employ differential resources to develop income and employment diversification strategies. Identifying class differences in the way people mediate economic change invites attention to how different resource packages enable and constrain survival strategies. How important, for example, are technical resources such as education in mediating access to employment? What role does home ownership or permanent employment play in shaping the choices households and individuals make in mediating economic decline? How are kin and social networks used to create opportunities for housing or employment among different segments of a nation's population? What comparisons can be drawn among responses to economic decline across countries?

A COMPARATIVE-HISTORICAL APPROACH TO HOUSEHOLD STRATEGIES

Studies that rely on secondary data to interpret the consequences of economic change on the social organization of the state and community generally underestimate the relations of interdependence between policy formation and policy outcomes and between changes in the economy and in household relations. For example, those who employ secondary data to examine the consequences of particular policy changes on social action often examine a particular behavior, such as migration, and assert its connection to a change in policy. The links between a policy change and increased migration might be incentives given to farm households to mechanize agricultural production, which, in turn, may reduce the demand for rural labor, increase rural unemployment, and create the push to secure employment elsewhere. Studies limited to describing patterns of migration, however, can only *assert* migration as a policy outcome or an individual/household strategy engaged in as a response to incentives to agricultural producers. The use of the term *strategy* in this case results in the assessment of a form of behavior embracing neither negotiation nor choice. As such the term *strategy* omits the actual processes involved in choosing among a range of possible options that a household or individual might use in the face of changing employment circumstances.

Moreover, this use of the concept of strategy does not invite attention to how state policies are contested by sectors of the state or segments of the population in shaping their response to changing social conditions. This view also distinguishes between arenas of social life so that the household, the workplace, and the state/government respond differently to policy initiatives rather than each arena engaging with others to shape policy and behavioral outcomes. It is not surprising then that survival strategies are examined as the outcome of individual or household behavior rather than as processes of negotiation over a diverse set of social and technical resources. This operationalization of responses to economic change, in other words, fails to appreciate the processes by which households and individuals make choices, generate opportunities, and reorganize existing resources, including labor, to meet household subsistence needs. This view also fails to recognize how regional and community differences may shape resource availability, and how household characteristics, including but not limited to demographic and life cycle differences, shape resource accessibility.

Finally, this conventional approach exemplifies a nonconflictual view of the household and its diverse organizational forms and relations that structure and are structured by the choices people make in response to changing circumstances. Recent scholarship on the household, however, has begun to reexamine the household and retheorize the household as a social unit by identifying new assumptions about intrahousehold relations (Folbre 1986; Hartmann 1981; Dwyer and Bruce 1988; Sen 1990). The "new household economics," for example, explaining the gender division of labor in the household and the workplace, argues that women have a comparative advantage in reproductive (domestic, child care, and childbearing) activities and thus are disadvantaged relative to men in the labor market. This argument, premised on biological determinism and economic efficiency, implies that a sharing of social roles and obligations is less efficient than a division of labor between home and work. Human capital theorists argue that need determines the different behaviors of men and women. But, as Folbre (1986) notes, this does not explain intrahousehold inequities by age and sex regarding training and skill development.

Marxist and socialist-feminist theorists also have critically examined the household as a unit of production and consumption drawing special attention to the intrahousehold gender division of labor. Addressing a broad range of issues such as the domestic labor debate of the early 1970s, these theorists have encouraged a more nuanced theoretical, empirical, and political discussion of household work, noncapitalist commodity production, unpaid wage labor, and the ways in which the unrecognized labor of women subsidizes capital (Seccombe 1974; Gardiner 1975; Dallacosta and James 1975; Himmelweit and Mohun 1977). Although these explanations for the sexual division of labor draw attention to the household and to social reproduction more broadly, they do not fully appreciate how intrahousehold relations and relations of production are socially constructed.

Recent social constructionist analyses of intrahousehold relations provide a more recursive view of family–labor market interactions. Whether the household economy is viewed as autonomous from the generalized mode of production or integrated within the capitalist economy (Bennholdt-Thomson 1984; Long 1984), it is envisaged as a contested terrain representing diverse and conflicting interests. From a methodological view, an analysis of the intrahousehold division of labor as a construction of different, changing, and negotiated interests cannot be adequately understood by employing available census data. Poverty indicators do little to illuminate the effects of the debt crisis on daily life or to enable one to construct how families strategize in the face of economic decline. Census data do not provide the information necessary to understand the household as a socially constructed and historically specific division of labor or to elucidate the processes that household members employ to create options to manage change with the resources available to them. Strategies interpreted with the use of census data offer little more than patterns of behavior imputed by the analyst with meaning and choice.

An important methodological contribution of this volume, then, is an understanding of how households and families negotiate existing resources to create daily survival strategies. Each chapter attempts to broaden our present understanding of the resource constraints and obligations of people and the specific cultural and historical processes shaping their daily lives. This means that the arguments developed by the contributors are grounded in the activities and practices of those whose lives are being transformed by the contemporary debt crisis and patterns of persistent poverty.

This methodological commitment highlights the importance for the authors of "social agency" and the emphasis the authors place on the creative mechanisms employed differentially by households and household members to generate alternative production and consumption patterns to ensure survival. These mechanisms include new patterns of community organizing and inter- and intrahousehold patterns of support as well as processes of family and household dissolution. They also include new relations of work; new patterns of integration among wage, exchange, and domestic labor; new configurations of household membership; and new patterns of migration. Secondary data provide contextual information, but the contributions in this volume draw primarily on primary data collected by means of various qualitative research designs and field research techniques, including in-depth interviewing, participant observation, and ethnographic methods. Researchers discussed with respondents how they conceived of their economic situation, how their situation differed from previous circumstances, and how they negotiated for resources during times of increasing impoverishment. Rather than ex post facto interpretations, the contributors asked people to discuss in concrete detail how they actually negotiate their changing resource base to ensure everyday survival. In this way the authors focus not simply on outcomes and observed behavior but rather on the processes by which people respond to and create their conditions.

Diane Elson's contribution sets the broad context for the case studies that follow and offers an interpretation of economic crisis and how women can and do play key roles in the transformation of everyday life. From a global perspective, Elson reviews conventional interpretations of global economic restructuring, illuminating how changes in production, exchange, and finance have intensified the work of the wage labor force, restructured the organization of production, and destroyed previously constructed forms of worker resistance. These changes have transformed relations among countries, the national policy environment through structural adjustment lending requirements, and relations among different segments of the population. The contemporary economic crisis, she argues, is not simply "a turning point for capital accumulation . . . but a turning point for a whole range of social institutions and practices."

A central theme of Elson's contribution is her identification of the transformational possibilities inherent in periods of crisis. Although structural adjustment policy responses to the contemporary crisis generally ignore or exacerbate the demands on women's time and energy, the new social relations that emerge can actually serve as catalysts for radical change. Such change can be the consequence of increasing women's control over resources or of the new patterns of mobilization and organization that evolve as women and households create new production and consumption strategies. Change can also be the consequence of new organizational and living arrangements, new relationships between family and work, and new forms of community organization that structure social life.

Elson conceptualizes the current economic crisis as a period of transition characterized by stagnation, instability, and restructuring, which may ultimately develop into a new form of capital accumulation. Under these conditions, new consumption relations within the household can be developed. Additionally, these new conditions may provide the context for "transforming the organization of the public sector so as to put more resources at women's disposal and enhance women's dignity, autonomy, and bargaining power." As Elson notes so eloquently:

Restructuring opens up new opportunities . . . (as) change creates conditions for new forms of struggle. . . . (Out) of the crisis may come some progressive transformation of the conditions of struggle of oppressed and disadvantaged groups, and the forging of new links between them. . . . In short, an economic crisis may produce new political configurations (understanding "politics" in a very broad sense), new alliances and new demands, with some potential for changing the terms of the social and economic restructuring necessitated by the crisis in a way that is more favorable to oppressed and disadvantaged groups.

Thus, in addition to examining how structural adjustment programs have forced women to assume a greater share of work as austerity measures have been put into place, Elson identifies potential opportunities to generate alternative ways of organizing social life.

Another important theme Elson addresses is the male bias in structural adjustment policies. As she notes, there is an explicit lack of consideration of unpaid labor, where women carry most of the burden of the nonremunerated reproduction and maintenance of human resources, and a shifting of costs from the paid economy to the unpaid economy. The invisibility of women's labor expended in meeting household responsibilities, including child care and domestic chores as well as childbearing, is made possible by a homogeneous view of the household that ignores the contradictory responsibilities and interests shaping household relations. This consensual view of the household also ignores the household as a site for the subordination of women and the structuring of patriarchy. Elson also argues for a disaggregated view of the public sector, where women's labor is less valued than men's and where forms of exploitation can be transformed through collective organization.

CASE STUDIES

This section identifies the salient themes of each contribution by drawing on the central issues noted above. The chapter by Helen I. Safa and Peggy Antrobus, for example, provides an intraregional perspective on the economic crisis in the Caribbean, focusing particular attention on Jamaica and the Dominican Republic, which are the two countries in the region most severely affected by the crisis. Their chapter highlights the shift of responsibility from the state to the household and the increasing burden faced by women, who maintain primary responsibility for meeting household needs. This study identifies how Caribbean countries have been integrated into the global economy as well as how dependent development has differentially shaped country-specific responses to the crisis. For example, while unemployment rates increased in both the Dominican Republic and Jamaica, differences in the sex composition of the labor force and the higher proportion of female-headed households in Jamaica have generated country-specific demands and created country-specific opportunities for women.

Especially interesting is the finding by Safa and Antrobus that in both countries there have been only low levels of collective action in response to the contemporary economic crisis. Moreover, comparison of household responses to the crisis reveals that Jamaican and Dominican households, as well as the Mexico City households examined by Benería, have not engaged in the community-based organizational efforts identified in McFarren's study of Bolivian households or in the collective initiatives taken to meet consumption needs found in studies of other Latin American countries (Sara-Lafosse 1987).

Safa and Antrobus also emphasize the cultural heterogeneity of the region and the ways in which different state policies and practices shape the resources available to people in each country. Finally, these contributors highlight the alternative resources and strategies deployed by nongovernmental agencies within each country and how their initiatives have helped to shape household responses to economic crises.

Chapter 4, by Lourdes Benería, centers on the impact of structural adjustment policies in Mexico on the distribution of resources and on living standards for different classes of urban households. She gives particular attention to three changes in the policy environment: the process of devaluation with its corresponding effects on prices, wages, and standard of living; the austerity program that severely cut social services; and the process of economic restructuring that liberalized the economy and shifted the model of accumulation from one based on the domestic market to one oriented toward the international market.

Benería highlights the importance of household relations as these mediate the effects of structural adjustment policies among different classes in Mexico City. She also emphasizes the ways that household members deploy diverse strategies to meet their survival needs and draws special attention to the ways in which urban middle-class households renegotiate their consumption patterns in light of declining family resources. Rather than focus solely on labor and employment strategies, Benería describes the variety of ways that urban households renegotiate their budget allocations and consumption patterns, thus drawing attention to the importance of what Elson refers to as "consumption politics."

Especially interesting is the attention Benería gives to the increased significance of the family as the primary source of support and as the arena in which household members negotiate strategies for survival. She examines the contradictory and paradoxical relations characterizing families in Mexico City and how intrafamilial relations represent new patterns of increased solidarity. Among her sample, Benería describes the virtual absence of community and collective initiatives as the privatized, nuclear, middle-class household in Mexico City faces the crisis on its own, pooling whatever resources it can. Households sharing limited resources tend to respond to economic crises with a protective strategy that increases intrahousehold dependence. This has resulted in mistrust and hostility toward outsiders and has generated new tensions within and between households. Increasing familial interdependence has increased both women's participation in the labor market and the intensification of women's domestic work, making gender asymmetries within the household more visible.

Increasing familial interdependence in response to economic declines differs markedly from collective efforts such as the Peruvian *comedores populares* and from the collective struggles in Bolivia identified by McFarren. The communal response to economic decline, which characterizes squatter communities in Bolivia, developed in the context of networks shaped by patterns of urban migration. These networks provide important vehicles for building community solidarity among households.

The specific opportunities and constraints faced by the declining resource base of the middle class are also highlighted by Shelley Feldman, who examines new employment opportunities available to educated middle-strata rural women in Bangladesh. However, unlike the earlier studies in this volume, which focus on responses to the debt crisis of the 1980s, this chapter explores the economic crisis in Bangladesh as a consequence of the specific aid and trade regime that has shaped persistent poverty and continuing declines in household income. Floods, famines, and cyclones have continued to plague Bangladesh since its independence in 1971, and the country's inability to buffer the costs of these disasters can partially be explained by the way it has been incorporated into the global economy and the economic development choices that have been made in the context of structural adjustment lending.

Feldman suggests that the structural adjustment initiatives required by countries dependent on public financing, as distinct from private bank financing, have had effects similar to those where private capital has shaped domestic policy reform. For example, as Safa and Antrobus and Benería argue for debt-dependent countries, allocations to expand support for the military and to increase private sector production in Bangladesh have grown significantly since 1975, while the distribution of resources to health care, social welfare, and education have decreased. Overall declines in public expenditure demanded by the World Bank and International Monetary Fund, and their request to expand export production through the creation of an export-processing zone, have shaped national policy priorities in countries depending on financial and technical assistance from public lending institutions as well as those whose debt to private banks has legitimated international intervention.

For Bangladesh, aid dependence has forced the government to accept a liberalization of the economy and has drawn on the country's comparative advantage as a source of cheap female wage labor to increase foreign earnings. The establishment of export-processing enclaves, which could draw on low-wage female workers, has created a demand for women previously denied access to the labor market. The demand for female workers thus has created an opportunity to constitute a labor force from among middle-strata rural families able to secure education for their daughters. This opportunity challenges the proscriptions of female behavior that were shaped by a variant of Islamic doctrine and Bengali culture and that, in the past, severely limited women's access to education and employment. Although the numbers of women employed represent only a small proportion of those demanding work, almost overnight a labor force of approximately 180,000 young, unmarried, educated girls between the ages of twelve and twenty-one emerged in Dhaka City. This rapid expansion in the female work force has reshaped the urban labor market in the capital city and restructured the demand for urban housing and transportation. It has also made visible a growing number of young unchaperoned women previously absent from the buses, thoroughfares, and movie theaters in the city.

Women's increased access to and participation in the labor force has also required a reinterpretation of family status and has generated new patterns of status construction for rural middle-strata Bangladeshi families who once were among those most likely to limit their daughters' participation in the labor force. It has also challenged the ideological hegemony that had heretofore legitimated patterns of female exclusion. Identifying how new behavioral patterns are constructed by new definitions of appropriate female behavior, comportment, and male-female interactions and by changes in the demand for women workers illuminates how female workers help to define their own appropriate behavior. A constructionist view of women's changing access to the labor market also invites attention to how the state, through policy reforms and state subsidies to private sector development, shapes how Islamic ideology can be employed to maintain a gender division of labor in the workplace. That is, through the use of Islamic proscriptions of appropriate female behavior, the propriety of women has been used to shape the recruitment practices of urban entrepreneurs, maintain a segmented labor market where women work in the lowest paying occupations, and leave unchallenged the responsibilities women continue to have for family maintenance.

Most importantly, the chapter signals the importance of ideological and cultural transformations as these work in concert with changing material conditions to shape new family and work relations. For example, state policies and capital investment help to create a labor market of workers once excluded from access to employment and to reshape interpretations of women's behavior. Yet, the new conditions under which women work and the shift from home-based activities to factory production have contradictory consequences for women. On the one hand, these new conditions create opportunities for women to meet other women, gain increased access to public resources, and initiate new relationships with male friends, including marrying for love rather than by arrangement. On the other hand, these conditions create new relations of inequality and intrafamilial dependence that limit women's resource control and decision-making authority. Finally, this study highlights the salience of kin networks and migration flows in shaping recruitment strategies and patterns of social obligation and patriarchal control.

Wendy McFarren illustrates the importance of migration streams and forms of community organization in her comparison of two migrant communities on the outskirts of La Paz, Bolivia, in the peripheral city of El Alto. This case study examines the consequences of the privatization of the state sector, particularly the tin industry, in shaping patterns of unemployment and migration. McFarren identifies the important militant tradition that has characterized miners and their wives' interpretations of the adjustment plans put forward by President Paz Estenssoro. Her sensitivity to the dynamic relation between the Federated Syndicate of Mining Workers and government illustrates the range of alternatives that could inform development planning should the voices and interests of those most affected by the crisis be embraced in the development planning process.

McFarren's study provides a major contribution to our understanding of survival strategies among mining households by addressing the question: How did the transition from economic dependence on the mines to economic autonomy affect mining households and the response and experience of women leaders to declining resources and employment opportunities? She demonstrates the importance of development projects, including self-help housing and public works initiatives, in constructing the quality of everyday life in migrant communities. She also emphasizes the importance of prior organizing experience and processes of empowerment among those living on the margins of cities and controlling only minimal resources for shaping how social and kin networks and community organizations are used. McFarren's focus on immigrant mining households also draws attention to the importance of labor market networks and the salience of existing social relations in forming the strategies women and household members have employed to creatively manage declining family resources. She focuses attention on the differing views of male leaders concerning women's independent actions and thus to the gender and political ideologies that mediate household responses to relocation and changing employment opportunities.

Chiara Saraceno's study in Italy also draws attention to the significance of mediating structures in shaping the consequences of the economic crisis for households, families, and women's work. Saraceno points to the significance of regional distinctions in creating the variety of public and private income sources available to different households. The comparisons between the industrialized north, the underdeveloped south, and the "third Italy" help to identify different regional labor markets and the varying importance of informal and service-sector employment for adult women with family responsibilities. As she notes, during the 1950s and 1960s women tried to maintain their living standards by intensifying their domestic labor. During the 1970s, and particularly during the 1980s, a combination of paid and unpaid work became the buffer against economic crisis and declining living standards. Married women who lose their jobs, however, tend to make less use of the commercial services engaged during their employment, which suggests that "women feel justified in being partially replaced in their capacity as family workers only insofar as their time is occupied by paid work."

Through her case study of FIAT in Turin, Saraceno also identifies both the costs and opportunities for households receiving different state subsidies. For example, a large-scale state program, Cassa Integrazione Guadagni (CIG), provided social security to more than 200,000 workers laid off by FIAT. This financial gain, however, also had profound personal costs as these unemployed workers were cast into ambivalent social positions that generated conflicting perceptions of their status as workers as well as of their rights to an income. Worker alienation and the resulting hopelessness seriously challenged established patterns of family interaction. Saraceno's chapter graphically illustrates the costs of unemployment for families of different compositions, age grades, and life cycles and emphasizes the point that the costs of unemployment are not simply tied to the loss of income. Although social security can prevent destitution during times of unemployment, the loss of status within the household that accompanies unemployment often hinders a redefinition of the family division of labor and the establishment of more egalitarian family social relations.

With rising underemployment and unemployment in Europe, North America, and the Third World, Saraceno's study draws attention to the growing importance of income schemes as a means to ensure subsistence for a growing proportion of the world's population. The costs of these schemes, however, would differ by the resource base of national economies and mitigate against their possible success in countries without a sufficient tax base to ensure implementation. Moreover, the lack of experience with welfare/income schemes in some countries would limit the ability of some governments to secure hegemony under conditions demanding significant reallocations of resources among classes. Lastly, and most poignantly addressed in Saraceno's study, are the costs of a scheme that challenges a basic connection between work and income. The Protestant ethic and individualism are central concepts framing notions of social responsibility under capitalism. Challenging this concept of social responsibility requires new state-society relations and a significant transformation of democratic forms of social organization.

In Chapter 8, Bina Agarwal also emphasizes the mediating effects of region in understanding the coping strategies of households with different assets. Regional differences in patterns of land inheritance, income earning among women as illustrated through labor force participation rates, access to communal resources, and kin support systems are given particular attention in identifying how rural women bargain for and utilize resources. As Agarwal notes, rural women have a much higher bargaining strength in Kerala than elsewhere in South Asia. In northwest India, women have limited bargaining strength, especially in the household and the labor market. Sex ratios are one extreme indicator of intrafamily gender differentials in the distribution of subsistence resources, especially for food and health care. However, gender inequalities need not manifest themselves in higher female-to-male mortality, a primary characteristic of gender relations in northeast India. An examination of the various regional differences shaping the culture as well as the practice of intrahousehold negotiation and resource control offers an important modification for studies that force generalizations about countries and national populations.

In addition to the important contribution Agarwal makes to understanding regional patterns of gender inequality is her broadened view of economic crisis to include questions of ecological changes brought about by seasonality and calamitous events such as famine. Centered on a discussion of food insecurity associated with seasonal changes in the agricultural production cycle, Agarwal elaborates Amartya Sen's entitlement approach to the study of famine. Sen stresses the salience of women's access to employment and other income-earning possibilities, and women's ownership and/or control of assets, usually land. Agarwal highlights the significance of traditional rights to communal resources and external social-support networks as these help to define a person's negotiating position during times of crisis. Her operational principle is that the greater the ability of a person to draw on extrafamilial resources, the greater a person's bargaining position within the household.

This principle helps us to understand why it is that men generally fare better than women in mediating declines in household resources during times of crisis. It also helps us to understand why women who are better able to control communal resources and draw on extrafamilial social networks are in a more secure bargaining position within the household than women for whom *purdah* and exclusion from public sector resources and networks define their appropriate behavior. Agarwal's identification of communal resources and extrafamilial social networks extends the heuristic distinction often drawn between public and private space and the control of public versus private resources, especially as these characterize societies where the division of labor is gender segregation between the household and the market.

What is so interesting in the Agarwal contribution, therefore, is the way in which she illuminates the connection between public resources and private ones in shaping processes of negotiation among household members. Three general conclusions frame her findings. First, she concludes that intrahousehold cooperation among men, women, and children is critical in enabling poor households to mediate seasonal troughs. Second, women from poor households are in a weaker bargaining position than men because they have more limited access to productive resources and income, lower skills levels and lower wages, and greater fluctuations in employment and earnings. Within poor households, in particular, women continue to bear the brunt of domestic responsibilities. Third, for all classes of household, women are likely to bear more of the burden than men in relation to the coping mechanisms employed to stave off the most dire costs of food insecurity and persistent poverty.

The case study of Tanzania by Aili Mari Tripp also highlights the importance of intrahousehold negotiation in shaping patterns of consumption and production and emphasizes the growing importance of income from informal sources as a proportion of total household income. Tripp builds on the theoretical contributions that form the critique of the new household economics (Folbre 1986; Hartmann 1981; Dwyer and Bruce 1988) to provide valuable insights into how definitions and patterns of work shape household economies and national planning initiatives. This study of urban life contains two important themes: The first identifies the range of ways women contribute to household incomes and the effect of women's projects or informal work on household survival. The conceptual shift from "women's projects" to "informal work" highlights the second important contribution. Tripp's study thus shows the growing importance of female employment and wages for household consumption practices and demonstrates as well how this contribution may result in a transformation in the household division of labor. As she notes, between 1976 and 1988 wages as a proportion of total household income declined from 77 percent to 10 percent. Between 1971 and 1988, urban self-employed women in her sample increased from 7 to 66 percent, indicating the extent to which women make a financial contribution to the family in addition to their extensive role in agriculture and in meeting child care and housework responsibilities.

Tripp also highlights the declining objection to women's expanding control of household income as men come to appreciate and depend on women's incomes. She invites us to rethink the complementarity of informal and formal employment in meeting household needs by showing that informal activities have not merely supplemented male wage employment but have been necessary for sustaining the entire urban economy throughout the years of unprecedented hardship.

The growing importance of informal work has also resulted in workers' energies being focused on increasing off-the-job wages rather than on mobilizing for pay increases in government-regulated sectors. This focus indicates a recognition of the economic decline that appears to prohibit raising the minimum wage. It also recognizes that industrial restructuring and the promotion of small-scale and informal enterprises are long-term consequences of processes of global restructuring that need to be included in nation-based industrial policy formation. The inclusion of the growing number of small-scale producers in the planning process will need inevitably to incorporate the increased dependence on women's labor for improved productivity rates in the country.

As we have seen, the intrahousehold gender division of labor—as this influences both production and consumption practices and responses to changing policy initiatives and patterns of adjustment—is a central theme in many of the chapters. The study by Paola Pérez-Alemán also addresses this theme in her exploration of how the pre-Chamorro Nicaraguan state, under conditions of war and economic crisis, sought to maintain economic viability but at the cost of increasing the burden on women to meet the costs of everyday life. The result has been a challenge to traditional gender relations and a reorganization of public sector resources and the labor market.

To meet the objectives of the development policies supported by the Sandinista government, efforts were initially made to expand public and social services, including 39 percent of state expenditures to meet the combined needs of health, education, and housing. Pérez-Alemán elegantly ties together the commitment to meet the basic needs of the population with the growing aggression against the Sandinista regime and the profound effect this has had on the national economy and all the communities and households seeking to manage everyday life. The major impact of the crisis was a drastic drop in real incomes, reductions in government spending on social programs, and the elimination of consumer and producer subsidies. In concert, these changes forced households to both increase their participation in the labor market and diversify their sources of household income.

The Nicaraguan case, in other words, couples a structurally weak economy inherited from the Somoza era with a war that caused thousands of men to fight in the struggle for national autonomy. These conditions, which included an increasing number of male migrants who seek employment in the United States, Canada, and Mexico, resulted in a growing number of de facto female-headed households forced to rely primarily on female labor. Unlike the example from Bolivia where households have migrated to urban locales as a social unit, Pérez-Alemán highlights how male migration has meant an increased burden for women as they must meet the employment, informal income, and domestic responsibilities and needs of their families.

In this context the economic crisis has driven an unprecedented number of women and younger family members into the labor force as well as increased their domestic responsibilities. Low wages have made those employed in the formal sector particularly vulnerable to declines in real wages, to inflation, and to currency devaluation, and has forced a growing number of people into an expanding informal labor market. Paralleling the findings of Tripp's study of Tanzania, Pérez-Alemán provides a view of the informal sector that highlights its primary rather than secondary contribution to employment and household income. In the Nicaraguan case we find an instance where formal sector income provides a means of obtaining state-supplied benefits and in-kind resources (food exchanges, health sources, and so on) rather than a means to secure sufficient wages for family maintenance.

An important outcome of the growing burden on women's time is women's increased individual and collective consciousness and their participation in struggles to meet their immediate survival needs. For example, in addition to their participation in existing union activity, women are key actors in neighborhood organizations seeking to lower food costs, clean up neighborhoods, and maintain public schools. These efforts have forced unions and political parties to include these issues on their agendas. However, these struggles have yet to directly confront forms of oppressive gender relations or what Pérez-Alemán refers to as long-term strategic objectives to emancipate women.

Said another way, the fight for what Maxine Molyneux calls "practical gender interests" has yet to directly challenge patterns of gender oppression and subordination. Nonetheless, these collective initiatives provide the organizational and communication networks that can become vehicles to fight for "strategic gender interests" (Molyneux 1986). As Diane Elson notes in Chapter 2, these collective efforts provide an opportunity for the development of transformative strategies of political change. The creative energies required for survival by the crisis in Nicaragua, in other words, have unleashed new opportunities for struggle and challenge. In addition to new forms of community solidarity most clearly identified by Pérez-Alemán and McFarren, Elson identifies the opportunities for building international solidarity among workers and for constructing authentic, representative, and participatory democratic politics in the future.

In sum, the central themes of this volume highlight the effects of economic restructuring and the debt crisis on individual countries and the differential impact of persistent poverty on regions, communities, and households. Rather than focusing exclusively on the debt crisis, which has shaped intranational conditions and international relations in a number of countries in Latin America and Africa, these contributors argue that specific aid and trade regimes dependent on financial resources from the World Bank, the IMF, and bilateral lending institutions have also brought demands for economic restructuring and declines in public expenditures that disproportionately affect the poorer populations of these countries.

A second theme in this volume is the importance of a comparative approach to analyses of economic change and responses to declines in economic resources. An examination of the household as a contested terrain of contradictory interests invites attention to the ways that women's work has remained invisible despite demands for policy reform and changing labor-market demands placed on women. The various case studies also emphasize the ways that women negotiate the demands of their private contribution to household work in the form of unpaid family labor and unwaged commodity production and their public contribution through informal sector activities and formal sector employment. This emphasis draws attention to changes in men's behavior in that they are more willing to accept women's increased control of women's own wages but less willing to share household labor.

Finally we find in a comparative reading of the chapters the consistently vibrant responses of households, families, and women as they meet the challenges of economic crisis at the level of the family and workplace and how these arenas of work and activity intersect to reshape gender relations and patterns of inequality. The responses of these women differ and in some ways are contradictory. Seen another way, however, such differences demonstrate the varied and rich ways that women respond and resist forms of class and gender oppression. This book is dedicated to the courage and consistent effort of these countless thousands of women who employ a myriad of ways to turn disaster into transformation.

NOTES

1. "Relatively protected" refers to the degree to which an individual country negotiates the ways in which it restructures its production environment and organizes its labor force.

2. For a partial exception to this see Cornia, Jolly, and Stewart 1987 and UNICEF 1987.

3. There has been a wealth of research on the reorganization of production, industrial restructuring, and flexible specialization (Fröbel, Heinrichs, and Kreye 1980; Jenkins 1984; Piore and Sabel 1984; Elson and Pearson 1989; Elson 1991) but this work was not linked to the debt crisis per se.

REFERENCES

Amin, Samir, Giovanni Arrighi, André Gunder Frank, and Immanuel Wallerstein. 1990. *Transforming the Revolution: Social Movements and the World-System.* New York: Monthly Review Press.

Bennholdt-Thomson, Veronika. 1984."Subsistence production and extended reproduction." Pp. 41–54 in Kate Young, Carol Wolkowitz, and Roslyn McCullagh (eds.), *Of Marriage and the Market.* Boston: Routledge and Kegan Paul.

Cornia, Giovanni A., Richard Jolly, and Frances Stewart (eds.). 1987. *Adjustment with a Human Face.* Vol. 1. New York: UNICEF/Clarendon Press.

Dallacosta, MariaRosa, and Selma James. 1975. *The Power of Women and the Subversion of the Community.* 3rd edition. Bristol, U.K.: Falling Wall Press.

Dwyer, Daisy, and Judith Bruce. 1988. *A Home Divided: Women and Income in the Third World.* Stanford: Stanford University Press.

Edholm, Felicity, Olivia Harris, and Kate Young. 1977."Conceptualising women." *Critique of Anthropology* 3 (9/10):101–130.

Elson, Diane. 1991. "Male bias in macro-economics: The case of structural adjustment." Pp. 164–190 in Diane Elson (ed.), *Male Bias in the Development Process.* Manchester, U.K.: Manchester University Press.

Elson, Diane, and Ruth Pearson (eds.). 1989. *Women's Employment and Multinationals in Europe.* London: Macmillan.

Folbre, Nancy. 1986. "Hearts and spades: Paradigms of household economics." *World Development* 17 (7):979–991.

Fröbel, Folker, Jurgen Heinrichs, and Otto Kreye. 1980. *The New International Division of Labor.* New York: Cambridge University Press.

Gardiner, Jean. 1975. "Women's domestic labour." *New Left Review* 89:47–58.

Hartmann, Heidi. 1981. "The family as the locus of gender, class, and political struggle." Pp. 109–134 in Sandra Harding (ed.), *Feminism and Methodology.* Bloomington: Indiana University Press.

Himmelweit, Susan, and Simon Mohun. 1977. "Domestic labour and capital." *Cambridge Journal of Economics* 1:15–31.

Jenkins, Rhys. 1984. "Divisions over the international division of labour." *Capital and Class* 22:28–57.

Long, Norman. 1984. *Family and Work in Rural Societies: Perspectives on Non-Wage Labour.* London: Tavistock.

MacEwan, Arthur, and William K. Tabb (eds.). 1989. *Instability and Change in the World Economy.* New York: Monthly Review Press.

Molyneux, Maxine. 1986. "Mobilization with emancipation? Women's interest, state, and revolution." Pp. 280–302 in R. Fagen et al. (eds.), *Problems of Third World Socialism.* New York: Monthly Review Press.

Piore, Michael J., and Charles F. Sabel. 1984. *The Second Industrial Divide*. New York: Basic Books.

Sara-Lafosse, Violeta. 1987. "Communal kitchens and low-income neighborhoods in Lima." Pp. 90–204 in M. Schmink and J. Bruce (eds.), *Learning about Women and Urban Services in Latin America*. New York: The Population Council.

Seccombe, Wally. 1974. "The housewife and her labour under capitalism." *New Life Review* 83 (January–February):3–24.

Sen, A. K. 1990. "Gender and co-operative conflicts." In Irene Tinker (ed.), *Persistent Inequalities: Women and World Development*. New York: Oxford University Press.

Stichter, Sharon, and Jane L. Parpart. 1990. *Women, Employment and the Family in the International Division of Labour*. London: Macmillan.

UNICEF (United Nations Children's Emergency Fund). 1987. *The Invisible Adjustment: Poor Women and the Economic Crisis*. New York: UNICEF.

Wood, Robert E. 1989. "Debt crisis update: 1988." *Socialist Review,* No. 80/3 (July–September):103–115.

2

From Survival Strategies to Transformation Strategies: Women's Needs & Structural Adjustment

🌫 DIANE ELSON

Insofar as development policymakers today pay any attention to the specificity of gender, they tend to conceptualize women as a resource for development (Moser 1989). In the context of economic crisis and structural adjustment, women are particularly valued for their ability to devise and implement survival strategies for their families, using their unpaid labor to absorb adverse effects of structural adjustment policies (Elson 1989). This chapter presents a critical evaluation of contemporary structural adjustment processes and the "survival" role that women are envisaged to play in these processes. It argues for a gender-aware approach to economic policy and to the household, and it suggests that strategies adequate to women's needs must focus beyond economic restructuring to a restructuring of the social relations constraining women. A way of moving from survival strategies to transformation strategies through the development of a *politics* of consumption is tentatively explored.

ECONOMIC CRISIS AND STRUCTURAL ADJUSTMENT

Economic crisis is best understood as a turning point or period of transition. Antonio Gramsci described it as a situation in which the old is dead and the new is not yet born. What is dead is the long boom of the capitalist world economy—the high levels of employment creation and rapid rates of growth of national income and international trade in the capitalist and industrialized world from the early 1950s to the early 1970s. What is not yet born is a new mode of capital accumulation that leads to a return to high and stable growth rates in the world capitalist economy. We are in the middle of a period of stagnation, instability, and restructuring.[1]

Certainly the incidence of the crisis is uneven. Some parts of the capitalist world economy continue to enjoy rapid growth and high levels of employment: Sweden and Austria in Europe, for instance, and Singapore and South Korea in Asia. Other parts of the capitalist world economy have suffered absolute falls in per capita income, particularly in Latin America and sub-Saharan Africa. Yet other countries such as the United Kingdom (UK) have recently been experiencing increased output at the same time as stagnation of employment.

Certainly the current period has seen extensive and significant changes in the organization of production (Kaplinsky 1989): the internationalization of production, the growing mobility of capital, the increasing "casualization" or "informalization" of work in the industrial countries, the use of new technologies of flexible specialization, and new ways of organizing links between different stages of production as well as the link between production and the market (Child Hill 1989; Elson 1989; Fernández-Kelly 1989).

Some people see this restructuring of production as establishing the basis for a new phase of renewed capital accumulation, often labeled the "post-fordist" phase or mode of production (Hall and Jacques 1989). However, a renewal of stable expansion of capitalist accumulation requires not just a restructuring of industrial production; it requires a restructuring of the conditions of international trade and finance. Exchange rates continue to be unstable; stock markets are volatile; international trade is a source of friction between the industrialized countries; in many countries real interest rates are at a historic high. As MacEwan and Tabb point out, "Without stability, the basis for investment is seriously undermined. Sharp fluctuations in exchange rates, trade balances, and financial movements, either directly or through their influence on government policies, are bound to generate periods of rising unemployment, inflation, and slow and unstable economic growth" (MacEwan and Tabb 1989:32). Multinational firms can restructure their own production processes, but they are powerless to restructure the international system of trade and finance.

The build-up of debt, both international debt and debt within countries, is symptomatic of the unresolved nature of the current transition. The resolution of a crisis of capitalist accumulation requires destruction before construction can properly get under way. In particular, it requires destruction of accumulated capital so as to clear the ground for new investment. Typically in capitalist economies this is not accomplished through a planned decommissioning of capital but through bankruptcies and through mass unemployment, which destroys the previously constructed forms of workers' resistance to exploitation through trade unions. The mass unemployment facilitates an intensification of work on the part of those remaining employed in paid work and a restructuring of the organization of the labor process. This, in turn, helps to restore the profitability of investment in real assets. But investment in real assets is relatively risky, and investors are likely to prefer liquid financial assets. An overhang of financial assets is both a symptom of crisis and a barrier to successful restructuring. The piling up of debt is a way of postponing the crisis when profitability of investment in real assets is declining. The existence of a debt mountain also acts as a barrier to new real accumulation. Typically, in the past, crisis resolution has entailed the destruction of accumulated debt through defaults and financial crisis.

Today, the crisis of the international capitalist economy is a prolonged malaise rather than a sharp turning point precisely because only real capacity utilization and employment are being destroyed while the debt mountain is perpetuated. To be sure, the major banks that lent to Third World countries are making massive provisions for loss against loans to the Third World—and enjoying tax advantages in so doing—and there are plans for debt reduction through securitization (the transforming of debt into financial securities such as bonds). But the loss provisions of the banks do not imply debt forgiveness; securitization simply changes the forms of the liability of Third World countries but does not reduce the pressure upon them to generate more foreign exchange. Policy coordination between central bankers and debt management coordination by the International Monetary Fund (IMF) have prevented the financial crisis that seemed imminent in 1982 (when Mexico suspended debt service) and 1987 (when stock markets crashed). The absence of a destructive financial crisis serves to stretch out the transition period rather than provide the basis for a new stable mode of capital accumulation.

A crisis of accumulation does require structural adjustment for its resolution. But what we are seeing today is a one-sided structural adjustment involving the destruction of real economic activity as well as attempts to construct new forms of production but without a corresponding destruction of financial capital and without a reconstruction of international financial systems and international financial flows.

The approach to structural adjustment embodied in IMF and World Bank programs does not get to the heart of the matter. It does not take adjustment far enough. It is based on the belief that soon, next year, maybe, or the year after, the world economy will return to "normal"—

that is, to the conditions of the 1950s and 1960s. It assumes that what is required is a piecemeal, country by country, adjustment of internal economic structures, focusing on the reallocation of real resources. The structural adjustment of the international financial system is not seriously on the agenda. It is true that some governments (for example, Japan, France, UK, Canada) have begun to make proposals for writing off official debt of poor sub-Saharan African countries and there is the Brady Plan for debt reduction, but this involves changing the form of the liabilities of Third World countries rather than wiping them out. What no government of a developed country has yet dared to place on the agenda is a structural adjustment of the private international financial system, which now dwarfs both the central banks and the IMF (Epstein 1989).

Until there is a fundamental restructuring of international debt and finance, the long drawn-out crisis is unlikely to be resolved, and high rates of growth and international trade will not be restored. Of course, some areas of the global economy will enjoy local minibooms (often through piling up of yet more debt—witness the case of the United States) and will be relatively protected from the general deterioration of production and living standards. National policies can modify the effect of deterioration of the international economic environment. But without corresponding international changes, the room for maneuver in many countries is very constrained. Conditions of economic crisis are thus likely to persist for the foreseeable future in many parts of the world, particularly in Latin America, the Caribbean, and Africa.

An economic crisis is not just a turning point for capital accumulation. It is also a turning point for a whole range of social institutions and practices. Restructuring opens up new opportunities as well as closing old opportunities. Oppressed and disadvantaged groups find that change creates conditions for new forms of struggle. Trying to resist the tide of change and to preserve precrisis social relations rarely works. A more creative approach that tries to influence the terms of restructuring, to restructure not just production but also social relations, and to create new institutions and organizations of and for oppressed and disadvantaged groups may have more chance of success.

It would be overoptimistic to expect such an approach to fully protect oppressed and disadvantaged groups from the adverse effects of a crisis. But out of the crisis may come some progressive transformation of the conditions of struggle of oppressed and disadvantaged groups and the forging of new links between them. For instance, the international restructuring of production produces new opportunities for building links between workers in different countries and for exploring the possibilities of international solidarity. In short, an economic crisis may produce new political configurations (understanding "politics" in a very broad sense), new alliances, and new demands, with some potential for changing the terms of the social and economic restructuring necessitated by the crisis in a way that is more favorable to oppressed and disadvantaged groups. Out of the crisis of the 1930s in the United States came the New Deal; in Europe came the welfare state; and in many parts of the Third World came nationalist and liberation movements.

So, although we should painstakingly record and vigorously protest the devastating effects of the prolonged stasis in the capitalist world economy upon the oppressed and disadvantaged, we should also recall the dialectic of crisis and look for new steps being taken in challenging the conditions that perpetuate oppression and disadvantage and consider how these beginnings can be strengthened. The very poorest people, on the barest margins of survival, may be unable to do more than desperately seek to adapt to the adverse conditions through existing strategies; and even in this they may fail, as rising rates of infant mortality and child deaths testify (Cornia, Jolly, and Stewart 1987:30). But for those able to survive there may be the possibility of strategies going beyond survival to transformation of existing social relations of oppression and disadvantage.

THE HOUSEHOLD AND
STRUCTURAL ADJUSTMENT POLICIES

A response to economic crisis in many Third World countries has been the introduction of structural adjustment policies as a condition for obtaining loans from the IMF and World Bank. The policies might be summarized as deflation, devaluation, decontrol, and privatization. The aim is to reduce the balance-of-payments deficit by increasing exports and reducing imports while at the same time restructuring the economy so as to move it to a new growth path. Typically this involves cuts in public expenditure, reductions in public sector employment, higher prices for food and other crops, and reduction in the role of government intervention in the economy. A key objective is to switch resources from the production of goods and services that are not *internationally* tradeable (nontradeable) to those that are *internationally* tradeable (tradeable).

Structural adjustment policies are not explicitly conceptualized in terms of the operations of households. The national budgeting process is certainly a focus of macroeconomic thinking and policymaking; but economists engaged in this know little or nothing about household budgeting processes. The designers of structural adjustment programs are explicitly concerned with the switching of resources, including labor, from the production of nontradeables to the production of tradeables. They rely on economic models in which switching resources from nontradeable to tradeable is a costless operation (Elson 1990). This reliance might be criticized as a patently unwarranted assumption totally at odds with the difficulty of reallocating real resources. But it is possible to rationalize this assumption in terms of an implicit assumption about the capacity of households to absorb real costs of reallocation with no implications for the monetary economy. A macroeconomist could argue that he[2] was justified in ignoring the costs of resource reallocation because these were absorbed by households in ways that had no repercussions for the monetary economy. In other words, an increase in unpaid labor in the household made it possible to treat the switching from one form of paid labor to another as costless. So long as households absorbed the costs of resource reallocation without any implications for the monetary variables (wages, prices, balance of payments, gross national product [GNP], etc.) then resource reallocation could be treated as costless.

Thus a macroeconomist could argue that he has no need to explicitly consider the household unless it can be shown that households are unable to absorb the costs of resource reallocation in ways that have no repercussions for the variables with which he is concerned. An argument that there are repercussions for variables of concern to the macroeconomist forms part of the United Nations International Children's Emergency Fund (UNICEF) case for "adjustment with a human face." This is the argument that the extra burdens on households absorbing the costs of restructuring will have long-term repercussions for the rate of growth of GNP because of a deterioration in the quality of human resources (Cornia, Jolly, and Stewart 1987:141–142).

This is not, however, the dominant argument made by Cornia, Jolly, and Stewart for "adjustment with a human face." The emphasis is on an appeal to humanitarian values (which we may suppose to be shared by macroeconomists). The argument is that the costs of adjustment are too great—that poor households are unable to absorb them, leading to absolute declines in the living standards, including irreparable damage to children through malnutrition. It is further argued by these authors that structural adjustment policies could be redesigned so that the costs to poor households are reduced and their capacity for survival during periods of economic crisis is enhanced.

There has been some response by the World Bank to criticisms of the impact of structural adjustment programs on poor households (World Bank 1987; Addison and Demery 1986). The process of structural adjustment has been likened to "crossing the desert"—a short period of hardship preceding arrival in the land of plenty. The favorite World Bank recipe for avoiding excessive costs to poor households appears to be supplementary feeding programs and public works programs that can be added on to the existing format of structural adjustment programs. The possibility that some countries may get lost and wander round in circles in the desert or that the boundaries of the desert may be expanding is not seriously entertained. However, it is by no means certain that conventional structural adjustment programs will lead to sustained growth. Bienefeld (1988) argues that although there are some economies that are already relatively strong and in which structural adjustment programs may, after a period of hardship, lead to a positive response, there are other, weaker, economies in which structural adjustment programs are instead likely to invoke a negative response of inflation, social conflict, and increased uncertainty. One recent, careful evaluation of World Bank structural adjustment lending for the period 1980–1987 found that, taken as a whole, the sample of countries receiving such lending did not show any significant impact from such loans on gross domestic product (GDP) growth rates; indeed such loans appeared to have adversely affected investment, though they did improve the short-run balance-of-payments position. However, there was considerable variation within the sample, and in some countries there was a positive effect on growth (Harrigan and Mosley 1989).

The World Bank and the United Nations Development Program (UNDP) have published a much more optimistic report, *Africa's Adjustment and Growth in the 1980s,* but this has been subject to widespread criticism about its selective use of data (Economic Commission for Africa 1989a). World Bank and IMF structural adjustment programs are, in fact, "high risk" programs because they increase a country's exposure to the unstable international market. They are not perceived as such by their designers because of the overoptimism that prevails in both the Bank and the Fund about the future course of the international economy, particularly about the terms of trade of Third World countries (ODI 1988). Recovery to "normal" conditions is believed to be just around the corner; and adjustment can proceed on a case-by-case basis, with ad hoc measures to protect the poor. The main measures envisaged by the World Bank for protecting the poor would also increase the dependence of the poor. The Bank would do nothing to tackle the structures of oppression and disadvantage that have put poor households at risk in the first place. Empowering the poor does not figure strongly in World Bank thinking despite some nods in the direction of land reform (Addison and Demery 1986).

But neither is empowering the poor the main focus of the alternative offered by UNICEF. The advocates of "adjustment with a human face" prefer to talk about "protecting the vulnerable." No doubt this is a far more acceptable concept to the majority of governments in both developed and developing countries. There are things to commend in the UNICEF approach, for it does emphasize that structural adjustment has an international dimension and cannot simply be achieved on a country-by-country basis. However, it supposes that more expansionary macroeconomic policies are the answer, together with better sectoral priorities and more international policy coordination. It does not situate structural adjustment within the context of global restructuring of capital accumulation.

The national dimension of adjustment is presented in the UNICEF work almost entirely in terms of improved policies from enlightened governments. As with all approaches emanating from international agencies, it is unable to explicitly confront the question of what happens if governments are not enlightened. Households are viewed in this approach as objects of policy more than potential actors in political processes through which social relations of oppression and disadvantage may be restructured. The UNICEF approach is concerned with protection, survival, and adjustment, but not with transformation. Public expenditure is to be restructured and better targeted but the social relations of the state are not discussed. The state is not problematized by "adjustment with a human face." In contrast, the state is problematized by the World Bank/IMF programs but in the wrong way, as merely a problem of the overextension of the state to be tackled by rolling back the state rather than transforming it.

"Adjustment with a human face" is a desirable goal but the strategy advocated to achieve it never really confronts the question of the relation between adjustment and the social relations of capitalism; it never addresses the question of profit. If the objective is simply the restoration of high rates of capital accumulation and growth with basically unchanged social relations of production and reproduction, then there is inevitably a destructive aspect to the restructuring necessary to secure a higher profitability of real investment. To the extent that the destruction of financial assets is blocked, there is likely to be a greater destructive impact on real assets and, hence, on the lives of the poor. If the objective is the restoration of higher growth rates and the creation of a more humane society, then this requires some degree of transformation of social relations of production and reproduction. "Adjustment with a human face" thus has to be linked with strategies for struggle as well as for survival. Indeed, struggle (demands, campaigns, institution building, mobilization) is the way from survival strategies to transformation strategies.

MALE BIAS AND
STRUCTURAL ADJUSTMENT POLICIES

Structural adjustment policies, whether put forward by the World Bank and IMF or by UNICEF, are presented in a language that appears to be gender neutral, but that masks an underlying male bias (Elson 1990). World Bank/IMF analysis of structural adjustment is couched in macroeconomic concepts such as GNP, balance of payments, tradeables and nontradeables, efficiency and productivity—all of which appear to have no gender implications. Women are not "visible" in this analysis; but then, neither are men. It is a depersonalized analysis dealing only with abstract suppliers and consumers of resources. However, this abstract analysis has a hidden agenda that covers the process of the reproduction and maintenance of human resources. This process is not explicitly included in macroeconomic thinking. Indeed, the macromodels appear to treat human resources as a nonproduced means of production like land. Of course, macroeconomists know that labor supplies are maintained and reproduced through shopping, cooking, housework, child care, and care for the sick and elderly; but they could argue that they are justified in treating labor as if it were like land and not considering the work required for its maintenance and reproduction because that work is unpaid, and hence, in their view, has no repercussions for the macroeconomic variables with which adjustment programs are concerned.

This lack of explicit consideration of unpaid labor is an example of male bias because it is women who carry most of the burden of the nonremunerated reproduction and maintenance of human resources. It is the work that is, above all else, considered as "women's work" that is excluded from consideration. Indeed, it may be argued that it is precisely because it is women's work that it is excluded; there are other forms of unpaid labor that may be undertaken by men, and, on the whole, much more effort is put into enumerating men's unpaid work and including it in GNP.

One important implication of the form of male bias that excludes the unpaid work that women do in the home is a bias in the definition of terms like "productivity" and "efficiency" that are frequently used in connection with structural adjustment. What is regarded by economists as an increase in productivity or efficiency may instead be a shifting of costs from the paid economy to the unpaid economy. Take an example from health care. Efforts to make hospitals more efficient may lead to earlier discharge of patients who still need time for convalescence. This transfers the burden of looking after them from paid hospital staff to unpaid female relatives in the home.

The male bias in the UNICEF approach is more subtle. The proponents of "adjustment with a human face" do pay considerable attention to the maintenance and reproduction of human resources. Women are visible in this approach, appearing, along with children, as a "vulnerable" group. But the social relations through which human resources are maintained and reproduced are not discussed. The discussion of adjustment at the household level (Cornia, Jolly, and Stewart 1987: Ch. 4), though an improvement over anything published so far by the World Bank or IMF, still treats the household as a unit. Here the male bias lies in not disaggregating the household to examine the different positions of women and men in the household, thus ignoring the implications of the household as a site for the subordination of women. There is now a wealth of evidence from feminist anthropological, sociological, historical, and economic studies that reveals the household as a site of tension and conflict as well as of cooperation—a site of inequality as well as mutuality (Dwyer and Bruce 1988). Here I will not review all the evidence but simply illustrate the point with an example of industrial home workers in Mexico City (Benería and Roldan 1987:122).

> The description of distribution patterns [of income within the household] makes it clear that none of the assumptions regarding the monolithic household/family are valid in our sample strictu sensu. Husbands and wives differ in the definition of the basic necessities of the family complex, their consumption priorities, the way in which income should be distributed, and the proportion to be allocated for the common fund, if there is one. We do not find, therefore, the household to be a collective entity adopting decisions on allocative patterns according to a single corporative interest; instead we find main control points, all along the allocative circuits, and it is through these mechanisms that the majority of husbands impose the basic features of the household's survival.

However, as the study also makes clear, though the women are not in control of household resources, they have the obligation and duty to manage household resources so as to feed, clothe, house, and educate the rest of the household. This responsibility for making ends meet without control over resources is a source of constant problems and anxiety for poor women. It is they who have to devise household survival strategies, but it is their husbands who control access to major resources.

These relations of male domination and female subordination that characterize the household as a social institution have enormous implications for conceptualizing household responses to structural adjustment. For instance, it cannot be assumed that households will react to structural adjustment by reducing expenditures on luxuries so as to maintain expenditures on necessities. There is evidence to show that in both developed and developing countries, through a wide spectrum of class positions and even in very poor households, men tend to maintain a personal allowance largely spent on luxuries such as alcohol, cigarettes, gambling, and socializing in beer halls and cafés (Dwyer and Bruce 1988; Hart 1989). The wife acting alone has no power to reduce household consumption of these luxuries so as to be able to afford higher food prices.

Surprising though it may seem, neglect of gender is also common in documents produced by official agencies with a specific concern for women. An example is a recent report: "The Impact of the Economic Crisis on the Vulnerable Groups in African Societies: Women" (African Training and Research Centre for Women 1988). This report treats women as an isolatable group and provides no analysis of the relations between women and men in the household. Lots of familiar policy recommendations are made that would indeed benefit women, were they to be introduced. Most of them require more resources to be directed to women—but there is no discussion of where these resources are to come from nor of the barriers that have prevented these policies, long advocated, from being introduced in the past. There is reluctance to face the fact that more resources for women, especially in a context of economic stagnation or decline, means fewer privileges for men. An analysis that does not say anything about male privilege and male power over women and about strategies for reducing these is ultimately biased toward men.

WOMEN'S NEEDS

An approach adequate to women's needs thus requires not simply to make women visible and call for resources to be directed to women. It requires an analysis of how male privilege and power over women can be reduced. This does not mean that calls for gender equality and the liberation of women can be expected to be effective in mobilizing demands for the majority of women around the world. Women will quite rationally focus on their immediate and pressing practical needs, especially needs for resources to ensure household survival and a better future for their children. But the fulfillment of these practical gender needs is not totally disconnected from strategic gender needs (Moser 1989). A fully satisfactory meeting of women's practical gender needs implies also some improvement in meeting women's strategic gender needs; that is, their needs for a diminution of their subordination to men, for "an alternative, more equal and satisfactory organization of society than that which exists at present, in terms of both the structure and nature of relationships between men and women" (Moser 1989:1803). The needs of women for resources of their own to discharge their duties as household managers cannot be adequately met without some reduction of women's dependence on men, some move toward greater gender equality in the control of resources.

Thus, a gender-aware approach does not neglect women's practical gender needs and focus only on women's strategic gender needs. Rather it begins from the immediate needs that women themselves express and analyzes the interconnection between those needs and strategic gender needs. The needs of poor women for more resources of their own cannot be adequately campaigned for in terms of abstract demands for equality. But there is a connection between greater resource availability for poor women and greater equality between women and men and between greater resource availability for poor women and the empowerment of women.

GENDER, THE MARKET, AND THE STATE

The market and the state are social institutions of particular relevance to the transformation of gender relations. They have been seen as institutions with the capacity to enable women to be more independent with more control over resources.

Liberals, in particular, have emphasized the beneficial effect of participation in the market for women. The market appears to treat women as individuals in their own right. If women can sell their labor or their products and get a decent cash income of their own, this lessens their economic dependence upon men, increases their economic value, and may increase their bargaining power within the household. Access to a decent income of their own tends to be highly valued by women, not only for what it buys but also for the greater dignity it brings. (Participation in the market does not, however, guarantee a decent income—a point taken up in the next section.)

However, so long as women carry the double burden of unpaid work in the reproduction and maintenance of human resources as well as paid work producing goods and services, then women are unable to compete with men in the market on equal terms. Legislation for equal pay and opportunities and diminution of "traditional" barriers to women working outside the home cannot by themselves free women from domestic burdens and expectations. Access to markets has benefits for women, but those benefits are always limited, even if markets are entirely free from gender discrimination. Benefits are limited because the reproduction and maintenance of human resources is structured by unequal gender relations and because the reproduction and maintenance of human resources cannot be directly and immediately responsive to market signals, so long as human beings are regarded as having an intrinsic and not merely instrumental value.

Women with high incomes can reduce their disadvantage in the market relative to men by buying substitutes for their own unpaid work— employing cleaners, maids, nannies, and cooks. But even this does not obliterate their disadvantage, as they still have responsibility for household management. All other women who are not in the highest income groups do not have this option and must undertake a "double day" of work.

Of course, women would be able to gain more from markets if the sexual division of labor in the household were to change, with men doing more domestic tasks. But it would be idealistic to rely on this. Exhortations to men to share more of this load do not work, as the experience of several socialist countries shows. The problem is precisely that unpaid domestic tasks are private rather than social, and because they are both unpaid and private, there is no social system of incentives, of rewards and penalties, to encourage a change. In the household, it is an individual woman confronting an individual man, and in the politics of housework, the cards are stacked in favor of the man (Mainardi 1970).

If most women are to gain from access to markets, they also need access to public sector services, such as water supplies, electricity, sanitation facilities, public transport, health care and education, which will lighten the burden of their unpaid work and enable them to acquire the skills they need to enter the market. For all but well-off women, there is a complementarity between state provision of services required for human resource development and the ability to make gains from participation in the market. For most women, the choice is not between dependence on the state and independence, but between dependence on the state and dependence on a man.

However, the state does not always operate in the interests of women. The state frequently plays a major role in perpetuating social, economic, and ideological processes that subordinate women (Agarwal 1988). Women are frequently treated as dependents of men in legal and administrative procedures rather than as persons in their own right. The state frequently upholds patriarchal family forms in which women do not have the same access to resources as men. Examples abound of public sector projects and programs that ignore the needs of women and direct resources toward men.

But the deficiencies of the state do not mean that women can rely on the market. Rather than more of the market and less of the state, which is a major feature of IMF/World Bank structural adjustment programs, women have an interest in restructuring and transforming both the public sector and the private sector to make them both more responsive to women's needs and contributions as both producers and reproducers.

It is necessary to disaggregate the public sector and the private sector. In the public sector, we need to distinguish different categories of expenditure and agency: social services; transport and energy; police, legal system, and armed forces; and state-owned factories, farms, and marketing and distribution facilities—often called parastatals. Within each category we need to examine exactly what is being supplied (primary health care or open-heart surgery, for example) and to identify who is benefiting from these activities. We need to examine the relation between producers and users of public sector goods and services. How responsive are producers to the needs of users? What mechanisms are there for users to influence the allocation of resources in the public sector? The structural adjustment required in the public sector is not so much a reduction in expenditure and costs, but a change in its priorities and in its relation to users of services, so that users have a voice in deciding priorities and forms of service.

The private sector needs disaggregating into categories: the formal sector and the informal one; foreign-owned and locally owned enterprises; large and small enterprises; those employing wage labor and those employing family labor; joint-stock companies and cooperatives; farmers, traders, manufacturers; activities directed by women and activities directed by men. If greater reliance is to be placed on private enterprise, we need to ask whose enterprise: the enterprise of the woman farming or trading on her own account or the enterprise of agribusiness and merchants with monopoly power? The enterprise of a women's cooperative or the enterprise of a multinational corporation? The mobilization of women's enterprise in activities that provide a decent income and a basis for sustained economic growth requires support from state agencies, particularly in the provision of credit and training and in services that meet children's needs and free women's time from domestic duties.

This, in turn, requires a diminution in male privilege: Resources will have to be redistributed from men to women in either relative terms (when there is growth) or absolute terms (when there is stagnation or economic decline). Restructuring to meet women's needs is thus a political issue, and some thought has to be given to the politics of this redistribution. Such redistribution in favor of a socially subordinated group is likely to be facilitated (though it cannot, of course, be guaranteed) by the emergence of democratic politics and the replacement of military dictatorships and authoritarian governments by democratically elected governments. A campaign for democratic politics is thus an important component of a strategy of restructuring the state to meet women's needs and has the advantage of being a campaign in which strategic alliances may be made and some men persuaded of the desirability of a redistribution of resources to women. There is growing recognition among activists and intellectuals in the Third World that a campaign for democratic politics is at the heart of a transformatory approach to structural adjustment (Thomas 1989; ECA 1989b). More thought needs to be given to the particular forms that political democracy can take and the way that it is integrated with grass-roots struggle so as to ensure that democracy is not defined in male terms.

GENDER RELATIONS AND
SURVIVAL STRATEGIES

Gender relations, like all other social relations, are not static. They are subject to change, particularly at moments of crisis. The current crisis is no exception: For instance, there is evidence in many parts of the Third World of a widespread rise in female participation in paid labor (Standing 1989). This is interpreted by some to be evidence of an increase in women's status (Joekes 1987). However, such rising participation rates may represent distress sales—women being forced as a last resort to work long hours for a pittance because they are desperate for cash (Elson 1988). When women's pay is very low, it has only limited impact on their bargaining position in the household (Benería and Roldán 1987). Moreover, it is essential to distinguish forms of participation in paid labor: The position of women workers in electronics factories in Singapore is quite different from that of women doing industrial homework in Mexico City. The extent to which rising rates of female participation in paid labor decompose[3] existing forms of women's subordination depends primarily on the level of remuneration that women receive and the opportunities that the organization of paid work provides for collective action of various kinds. In the case of most forms of female participation in the urban informal sector both factors seem very likely to be unfavorable. That part of the informal sector that has some autonomous capacity to grow and is not simply dependent on the formal sector tends to consist of male rather than female activities (Scott MacEwan 1990).

Collective organization may in some cases be able to overcome some of the unfavorable characteristics of informal sector employment, the outstanding example being the Self-employed Women's Association (SEWA) in India (Bhatt 1989). Collective organization is the vital ingredient that may move female participation in paid labor from a survival strategy to a transformation strategy. Rosa (1989) provides an interesting discussion of this in the context of the Sri Lankan Free Trade Zone.

Collective organization in the community for self-help is another survival strategy, much commended as an ingredient in "adjustment with a human face" (Cornia, Jolly, and Stewart 1987:96, 98–98, 103). Most of these self-help schemes seem to be women helping one another to meet their practical gender needs. They formalize the informal female support networks that women everywhere construct, but they perpetuate the idea that unpaid labor for the benefit of others is "women's work" and they construct women's role in community organizing as an extension of their domestic role (Moser 1989). Men's role in collective organization in the community is typically different: Moser reports a consistent trend in the Third World community organizations she surveyed for local political organizations to be run by men, with mainly male members, while women organized collective consumption groups. Thus, for instance, in Lima, Peru, the Junta Communal is most frequently led and controlled by men while women run community kitchens (Moser 1987). These community kitchens are celebrated by UNICEF as an innovative survival strategy, but they enable not just survival but the perpetuation of existing gender relations.

A more community-based approach to the delivery of social services is also recommended by UNICEF (Cornia, Jolly, and Stewart 1987). This may sound fine, but what it means in practice is more mobilization of the unpaid labor of women as volunteers in the provision of health care and social infrastructure. The UNICEF urban basic-services program in India actually pays the men involved in the program, as officials, but requires unpaid work of women for its implementation (Moser 1989). Such schemes, while appearing to reduce the cost of services, simply add to the burdens of women.

Some household survival strategies clearly lead to a deterioration in the position of women: One is the disintegration of households with men leaving (perhaps to seek work elsewhere). The growth of female-headed households is no sign of emancipation from male power; in a society in which women as a gender are subordinate the absence of a husband leaves most women worse off. The core of gender subordination lies in the fact that most women are unable to mobilize adequate resources (both material and in terms of social identity) except through dependence on a man. Male migration reduces the expenses of the household— but all too frequently reduces household resources by an even greater extent. The number of women-headed households relying on insufficient and unstable remittances is reported to have grown (Cornia, Jolly, and Stewart 1987). Migration, in a growing number of cases, appears to be a polite word for desertion. It is a male survival strategy rather than a female survival strategy.

FROM SURVIVAL STRATEGIES TO
TRANSFORMATION STRATEGIES:
THE POLITICS OF CONSUMPTION

As Cornia, Jolly, and Stewart (1987) note, the existence of survival strategies may be used as an excuse for policy inaction. Our aim needs to be enabling women to move from survival strategies to transformation strategies—strategies that help to transform gender relations by meeting both women's practical needs and their strategic gender needs.

The final section of this chapter tentatively explores some possibilities for transforming consumption relations within the household and for transforming the organization of the public sector so as to put more resources at women's disposal and enhance women's dignity, autonomy, and bargaining power. The key ingredient is collective action in a politics of consumption directed toward the empowerment of women (Moser 1989).

The community self-help groups that women construct as survival strategies might provide a springboard to transformation if they were redirected toward women's strategic gender needs as well as toward their practical gender needs. They might do this by combining the organization of collective consumption with discussion that raises questions about the undervaluing of the contribution of women's unpaid labor and the highly unequal distribution of resources within the family. Why should men have the right to spend on personal desires for drink, tobacco, and entertainment, while women struggle to make do? Women all around the world tend to complain in private to their women friends and neighbors about the extent of men's personal expenditure. A vivid account of this is given by Hoodfar (1988) for a lower-income Cairo neighborhood. "Whenever women congregated, whether in the street or in someone's home, it was usual to hear complaints about their financial problems with their husbands." These husbands were typically better dressed than their wives, in jeans or western-style shirts, regularly went out to cafes and films, and spent little time in the home; and if they did buy consumer durables, they preferred televisions and cassette recorders to washing machines and cookers. Purely private discussion of such consumption patterns tends, however, to end in resignation. As Hoodfar reports: "However, once the talks—and at times tears—were over, they said, 'Alhadoullelah (praise be to God), at least I have my children,' or 'he is not as bad as (someone with a worse reputation),' and they tried to count the positive things they possessed, such as children or health" (Hoodfar 1988:126). Transformation of the situation requires the development of a politics of gendered consumption.

One kind of consumption politics that has had an intimate connection with women's movements in many countries is the politics of alcohol consumption. Men's alcohol consumption in most countries seems to be much greater than that of women. Such consumption not only diverts income away from the needs of the household as a unit; it is also strongly associated with domestic violence against women and children. Women have frequently been prominent in campaigns for temperance and prohibition.

The absence of beer halls in resettlement areas in Zimbabwe is suggested as one significant reason for an improvement of women's position in Resettlement Areas as compared to Communal Areas (areas created as labor reserves by the colonial state) (Pankhurst and Jacobs 1988). In the Resettlement Areas men tended to redirect more of their resources into the household than they do in the Communal Areas, and part of the explanation seemed to be lack of opportunity to consume alcohol, together with social monitoring by the Resettlement Officer.

Prohibition is, of course, notoriously difficult to enforce because of the large profits to be made by breaking the law, which provides ample resources for bribing officials. Poor women in India, which officially has prohibition, have been notably active in mass mobilizations against male use of alcohol. An article in *Manushi,* an Indian feminist magazine, reported:

> On 20 November 1971, more than 10,000 women of India's most poverty stricken district, Tehri Rarhwal (annual per capita income Rs 129), staged a massive demonstration against drunkenness. Fifty-six women were arrested and jailed for picketing outside a liquor shop. The agitation continued until drunkenness was well under control in the area.(Kishwar and Vanita 1984:129)

Women in one village in Tehri Rarhwal surrounded the house of the liquor distiller, caught hold of him, and tied him to a buffalo pole. They then walked ten miles to call the police to arrest him and traveled fifty miles to give evidence against him when the court case came up.

In another campaign, in 1972 in Maharashtra state, groups of rural women from the tribal communities went around all the liquor dens in an area of 150 villages in Dhulia district and broke all the liquor pots in a protest against husbands' drinking and wife beating. Wife beating and alcoholism were apparently considerably reduced, though they did not completely disappear (Kishwar and Vanita 1984). As one woman activist put it: "Persuasion will never stop liquor drinking. Only the organized action of women can stop it."

In the early 1980s landless women in Bodhgaya carried on a campaign against drunkenness and wife beating. An activist woman reported:

> When discussions were held about the drinking problem, women said that the worst consequence was wife-beating. . . . Women had other reasons for considering men's drinking oppressive. When the men spent their earnings on liquor, the whole financial responsibility for running the household fell on the women. The men would often beat up the women to demand money for drink. (Kishwar and Vanita 1984:159)

In this campaign the strategy was to hold a village meeting to discuss why men should stop drinking and why liquor brewing should cease. Generally, direct action was only taken once a consensus was reached that liquor brewing should be stopped, when liquor pots would be broken or confiscated. As a result, in some villages liquor brewing nearly stopped, but in others it started up again because of the lucrative nature of the trade, and a fresh campaign had to be mounted. These public campaigns not only served women's practical gender needs, they also served women's strategic gender needs through the experience they provided of political mobilization and organizing, enhancing women's self-respect and capacity for autonomy.

A less dramatic form of campaign might be for increases in taxation on alcohol, cigarettes, and places of public entertainment, the proceeds to be used to improve public sector services of particular importance to women and children. As Cornia, Jolly, and Stewart note, "increases in taxes on beer and cigarettes would also allow many countries in Africa to finance a good part of the local cost of primary health care" (1987:168). In some parts of Australia, state governments have indeed imposed an additional levy on cigarettes, which is used for health and other socially beneficial programs, some specifically targeted at women (Commonwealth Secretariat 1989:100). Hart (1989) reports that in the UK in the 1940s taxes on alcohol and tobacco, consumed mainly by men, were used to finance food subsidies and public services, redistributing income from husbands to wives. There are, however, several problems in relying on the fiscal system for such distribution. For instance, there is no guarantee that extra taxes on alcohol and cigarettes will be used to finance public expenditures beneficial to women. Moreover, men may simply reduce the amount of money they transfer to their wives so as to be able to maintain their preexisting level of alcohol and tobacco consumption. There will only be a net redistribution to women if reductions in intrahousehold transfers from men to women are more than matched by increases in transfers via the public sector to women. An additional consideration is that taxes on alcohol and tobacco tend to be regressive in many countries, bearing more heavily on poor men than rich men. If class as well as gender is taken into account then increases in income and property taxes might be argued to be better ways of financing expenditure of benefit to poor women. Finally, the use of the fiscal system tends to bureaucratize the issue, making it harder to construct a politics of consumption directed to women's strategic as well as practical gender needs.

The politics of consumption is also relevant to transforming the provision of public sector services. Some of the strategies explored in the UK in defense of the public sector from the late 1970s onward might be applicable. In the late 1970s women were in the forefront of local struggles about state provision of housing, schools, nurseries, transport, social security, and hospitals. Such campaigns included both women users of the services and women employed by the state to provide such services, with perhaps the most active campaigns directed against the closure of hospitals (Fryer 1979). In the late 1980s the socialist Greater London Council pioneered experiments in popular planning aimed at giving users a say in the provision of services provided by the council. It recommended the setting up of user committees, including representations from all relevant user groups and from those providing the service; such committees, it was suggested, should canvass opinion of a broad range of consumers through techniques like sample surveys and questionnaires in libraries and community centers. Resources were provided through a "popular planning" unit to facilitate the development of a politics of consumption of public sector services (Mackintosh and Wainwright 1987).

In the Third World, it might also be fruitful to consider the possibility of jointly organized action by women consumers of public sector services and women producers of public sector services. Structural adjustment under the auspices of IMF/World Bank programs entails a reduction in public sector employment and generally a worsening of pay and conditions for public sector employees. Greater "efficiency" of the public sector is obtained by devalorization of the labor of some employees and intensification of the labor of others. The public sector has hitherto provided one of the major sources of professional employment for women, albeit largely in the teaching and caring professions, which have been considered especially suitable for women. No comprehensive study is yet available of the impact of structural adjustment on women working in the public sector, but anecdotal evidence speaks of attempts to make women rather than men redundant because "women do not need jobs as much as men" and of women professionals (teachers, health workers, administrators) moonlighting in the informal sector because their frozen salaries no longer cover increased food costs.

A defense of the public sector against those who believe in the "magic of the market" is important for women both as users and providers of public sector services. But the public sector cannot be effectively defended in its present form: It is too vulnerable to many of the criticisms made by advocates of the market and privatization, largely because it has operated to serve the needs of public sector employees more than to serve the needs of the public. An effective defense of the public sector requires public sector employees to become more responsive to the needs of users. It is not enough to call for restructuring of public expenditure so as to direct it more effectively to those most in need. This is unlikely to get very far unless there is also a change in the way the public sector is organized and relates to consumers.

THE CONTEXT FOR SURVIVAL AND TRANSFORMATION STRATEGIES

In conclusion, I should like to stress that the degree to which survival and transformation strategies can be successful depends heavily on how the overall political process functions within each country and on what happens to the international financial system. The room for maneuver open to women in need is highly constrained. Focusing on strategies at the level of the household and community is important but not at the expense of ignoring national strategies for democratizing the state and international strategies for restructuring the international finan- cial system. The write-off of the debt of developing countries, in con- junction with the thorough-going democratization of the state in devel- oping countries, is likely to do more to enhance the survival of poor people than any number of self-help schemes, schemes to provide train- ing and credit for informal sector activities or supplementary feeding programs.

NOTES

I thank the participants in the Workshop on Economic Crises, Household Survival Strategies and Women's Work, Cornell University, September 1988, for their comments on the first draft of this chapter.

1. For an extensive development of this point see MacEwan and Tabb 1989.

2. I use "he" because most macroeconomists are, in fact, men. It would be an interesting exercise in the sociology of knowledge to compare the gender composition of the economists working on structural adjustment with that of anthropologists and sociologists researching the household.

3. The idea of decomposition of forms of subordination is developed at greater length in Elson and Pearson 1981.

REFERENCES

Addison, T., and L. Demery. 1986. *Poverty Alleviation Under Structural Adjust-*
    ment. London: Overseas Development Institute.
African Training and Research Centre for Women. 1988. *The Impact of the*
    Economic Crisis on the Vulnerable Groups in African Societies: Women.
    Economic Commission for Africa/International Conference on Human Devel-
    opment/88/47. Addis Ababa: United Nations Commission for Africa.

Agarwal, Bina (ed.). 1988. *Structures of Patriarchy—State, Community and Household in Modernizing Asia.* London: Zed Books; New Delhi: Kali for Women.

Benería, L., and M. Roldán. 1987. *The Crossroads of Class and Gender.* Chicago: University of Chicago Press.

Bhatt, E. 1989. "Toward Empowerment." *World Development* 17:7.

Bienefeld, M. 1988. "Structural Adjustment and Its Impact on Women in the Developing Countries." Canadian International Development Agency Discussion Paper.

Child Hill, R. 1989. "Division of Labor in Global Manufacturing: The Case of the Automobile Industry." In A. MacEwan and W. Tabb (eds.), *Instability and Change in the World Economy.* New York: Monthly Review Press.

Commonwealth Secretariat. 1989. *Engendering Adjustment for the 1990s.* London: Commonwealth Secretariat.

Cornia, Giovanni A., Richard Jolly, and Francis Stewart (eds.). 1987. *Adjustment with a Human Face,* Vol. 1. New York: UNICEF/Clarendon Press.

Dwyer, Daisy, and Judith Bruce (eds.). 1988. *A Home Divided: Women and Income in the Third World.* Stanford: Stanford University Press.

ECA (Economic Commission for Africa). 1989a. *Statistics and Policies.* Addis Ababa: United Nations.

———. 1989b. *Adjustment with Transformation.* EECA/CM.15/6/Rev. 3. Addis Ababa: United Nations.

Elson, D. 1988. "Review (1987)." *Journal of Development Studies* 25 (1).

———. 1989. "Bound by One Thread: The Restructuring of UK Clothing and Textile Multinationals." In A. MacEwan and W. Tabb (eds.), *Instability and Change in the World Economy.* New York: Monthly Review Press.

———. 1990. "Male Bias in Macroeconomics: The Case of Structural Adjustment." In D. Elson (ed.), *Male Bias in the Development Process.* Manchester: Manchester University Press.

Elson, Diane, and Ruth Pearson. 1981. "The Subordination of Women and the Internationalization of Factory Production." In K. Young, C. Wolkowitz, and R. McCullagh (eds.), *Of Marriage and the Market.* London: RKP.

Epstein, G. 1989. "Financial Instability and the Structure of the International Monetary System." In A. MacEwan and W. Tabb (eds.), *Instability and Change in the World Economy.* New York: Monthly Review Press.

Fernández-Kelly, M. P. 1989. "International Development and Industrial Restructuring: The Case of Garment and Electronics Industries in Southern California." In A. MacEwan and W. Tabb (eds.), *Instability and Change in the World Economy.* New York: Monthly Review Press.

Fryer, R. H. 1979. "British Trade Unions and the Cuts." *Capital and Class,* No. 8:94–111.

Hall, S., and M. Jacques (eds.). 1989. *New Times: The Changing Face of Politics in the 1990s.* London: Lawrence and Wishart.

Harrigan, J., and P. Mosley. 1989. "World Bank Policy-Based Lending, 1980–87: An Evaluation." Discussion Paper 18, Institute for Development Policy and Management, University of Manchester.

Hart, N. 1989."Gender and the Rise and Fall of Class Politics." *New Left Review*, No. 175:19–47.

Hoodfar, H. 1988. "Household Budgeting and Financial Management in a Lower-Income Cairo Neighborhood." In Daisy Dwyer and Judith Bruce (eds.), *A Home Divided: Women and Income in the Third World*. Stanford: Stanford University Press.

Joekes, S. 1987. *Women in the World Economy: An INSTRAW Study*. Oxford: Oxford University Press.

Kaplinsky, R. 1989. "Industrial Restructuring in the Global Economy." *Institute of Development Studies Bulletin* 20 (4):1–6.

Kishwar, M., and R. Vanita (eds.). 1984. *In Search of Answers: Indian Women's Voices from Manushi*. London: Zed Books.

MacEwan A., and W. Tabb (eds.). 1989. *Instability and Change in the World Economy*. New York: Monthly Review Press.

Mackintosh, M., and H. Wainwright. 1987. *A Taste of Power: The Politics of Local Economies*. London: Verso.

Mainardi, P. 1970. "The Politics of Housework." In Robin Morgan (ed.), *Sisterhood Is Powerful*. New York: Vintage Books.

Moser, C. 1987. "Are There Few Women Leaders or Is It that the Majority Are Invisible?" Paper presented at Conference on Local Leaders and Community Development and Participation, University of Cambridge.

————. 1989. "Gender Planning in the Third World: Meeting Practical and Strategic Gender Needs." *World Development* 17 (11):1799–1825.

ODI (Overseas Development Institute). 1988. "Commodity Prices: Investing in Decline?" Briefing Paper, London.

Pankhurst, D., and S. Jacobs. 1988. "Land Tenure, Gender Relations and Agricultural Production: The Case of Zimbabwe's Peasantry." In J. Davison (ed.), *Agriculture, Women and Land*. Boulder, Colo.: Westview Pres.

Rosa, K. 1989. "Women Workers' Strategies of Organizing and Resistance in the Sri Lankan Free Trade Zone." IDS Discussion Paper No. 266, Institute of Development Studies, University of Sussex.

Scott MacEwan, A. 1990. "Informal Sector or Female Sector? Gender Bias in Urban Labor Market Models." In Diane Elson (ed.), *Male Bias in the Development Process*. Manchester, U.K.: Manchester University Press.

Standing, G. 1989. "Global Feminisation Through Flexible Labor." *World Development* 17 (7):1077–1095.

Thomas, C. 1989. "Restructuring of the World Economy and Its Political Implications for the Third World." In Arthur MacEwan and William K. Tabb (eds.), *Instability and Change in the World Economy*. New York: Monthly Review Press.

World Bank. 1987. "Protecting the Poor During Periods of Adjustment." Development Committee Pamphlet No. 13.

World Bank and the United Nations Development Programme. 1989. *Africa's Adjustment and Growth in the 1980s*. Washington, D.C.: The International Bank for Reconstruction and Development/The World Bank.

3

Women & the Economic Crisis in the Caribbean

HELEN I. SAFA
PEGGY ANTROBUS

The magnitude of the economic crisis now reaches most of Latin America and the Caribbean, and in 1987 the total foreign debt of the region rose to approximately US$410 billion (ECLAC 1988). Though the severity varies from one country to another, the effect for the region as a whole has been a sharp decline in gross national product (GNP), with per capita national income 14 percent lower in 1986 than in 1980; increased unemployment, which grew 48 percent between 1980–1985; and a decline in real wages between 12 and 18 percent in the same period. The overall increase in income inequality has resulted in a growing proportion of the population living in poverty (ECLAC 1988). In desperation, several countries were forced to implement structural adjustment programs designed by the International Monetary Fund (IMF) to cut government expenditure, improve the balance of trade, and reduce the foreign debt. These policies, however, often resulted in greater hardship for the poor because they included: devaluation of the currency; the elimination of government subsidies for basic foods and subsidized credits to farmers; cuts in government expenditure, particularly for social services; and the freezing of real wages (Cornia 1987).

Poor women, especially those with families, have had to bear the major brunt of the economic crisis and structural adjustment policies. The economic crisis has made it even more difficult for families to survive

An abridged version of this chapter originally appeared as Chapter 3 in Carmen Diana Deere, Peggy Antrobus, Lynn Bolles, Edwin Melendez, Peter Phillips, Marcia Rivera, and Helen Safa, *In the Shadows of the Sun: Caribbean Development Alternatives and U.S. Policy* (Boulder: Westview Press, 1990).

TABLE 3.1   Jamaica and the Dominican Republic: Selected Economic and
Social Indicators

	Jamaica	Dominican Republic
GDP per capita 1989[a]		
(1988 U.S. dollars)	1,396	777
Exports of goods and services 1989[a]	1,793	1,799
(millions of 1988 U.S. dollars)		
Urban population (%) 1989[a]	51.4	62.3
Life expectancy (years) 1987[b]	73.9	66
Infant mortality (deaths per		
thousand) 1987[b]	18.0	65
School enrollment ratio 1986[b]		
Primary	105	133
Secondary	65	47

Sources: [a]Interamerican Development Bank, *Economic and Social Progress in Latin
America—1990 Report.* Baltimore: The Johns Hopkins University Press, 1990. [b]World
Bank, *World Tables 1989–90 Edition.* Baltimore: The Johns Hopkins University Press,
1990.

on a single wage, forcing additional women into the labor force to meet
the rising cost of living and the decreased wage-earning opportunities
for men due to unemployment and wage cuts or due to men's absence as
a result of migration. At the same time, structural adjustment policies are
forcing families to absorb a greater share of the cost of survival as a result
of cutbacks in social services, such as health and education, and the
elimination or reduction of subsidies on food, transportation, and utilities. By shifting more responsibility for survival from the state to the
household, structural adjustment policies are increasing the burden on
women, who have always assumed a primary role in household survival
strategies, securing and allocating usually meager cash and other resources to enable their families to make ends meet.

This chapter will examine the negative effects of the economic crisis
and structural adjustment policies on poor women in the Caribbean,
focusing on Jamaica and the Dominican Republic, two countries most
severely affected by the economic crisis.[1] Although the size of the debt
was not as great in the Caribbean in comparison to Latin America, its
effect was magnified by the small size of these economies and their
dependence on external trade and investment for economic growth. Their
current economic problems can be traced not only to adverse international terms of trade, which started in the mid-1970s, but also to patterns
of export-led economic growth that have long characterized both countries. As can be seen in Table 3.1, trade dependence is considerably
higher in Jamaica than in the Dominican Republic, but both countries
rely heavily on primary products for the bulk of export earnings: alumi-

num and bauxite in Jamaica; and sugar, ferronickel, and coffee in the Dominican Republic. In the 1960s, both countries tried to diversify their economies through a process of import substitution industrialization, which was later replaced by an emphasis on foreign investment in light manufacturing and tourism. These policies led to substantial growth rates in gross domestic product (GDP) initially, but they also contributed to agricultural stagnation, increased rural-urban migration, and growing dependence on imports, not only for the industrialization process, but also for basic food items. Despite high rates of economic growth and out-migration in both countries in this early period, unemployment remained above 20 percent.

This pattern of dependent development and increased integration into the global economy made these countries all the more vulnerable to international economic changes such as the rise in oil prices and the subsequent recession in the United States and Western Europe, which contributed to a reduction in demand for traditional exports such as bauxite in Jamaica or sugar in the Dominican Republic. As a result, Jamaican export earnings were reduced from US$992 million in 1980 to $569 million in 1985, while external debt in the same period grew from US$1,734 million to $3,400 million (Davies and Anderson 1987). In the Dominican Republic, external debt grew from US$855 million in 1975 to US$3.7 billion in 1985, which represents a per capita debt of US$560 or half of the GDP (Ceara 1987). As a result, both countries registered a negative balance of payments, which was generally much higher in Jamaica as a percentage of GDP than in the Dominican Republic (Nelson 1990: Table 5). Both countries suffered from worsening terms of trade and rising interest on the foreign debt.

In order to deal with the balance-of-payments crisis, the governments applied to the IMF—Jamaica in 1977 and the Dominican Republic in 1983. Similar structural adjustment policies were instituted in both countries, including increased concentration on export-oriented production in manufacturing and agribusiness; cutbacks in social services; continuing devaluation of the national currency; liberalization of imports; and removal of food subsidies and price controls on consumer goods. As a result, GDP per capita declined in both countries, but more precipitously in Jamaica than in the Dominican Republic because in the former country the crisis has been more severe and of longer duration. Jamaica's GDP per capita in 1960 was more than twice that of the Dominican Republic, but by 1980, differences had been substantially reduced (Table 3.1). However, health and education indices were markedly superior in Jamaica, particularly in regard to infant mortality. This appears to indicate a higher commitment to redistribution and social welfare in Jamaica and is reflected as well in the cuts in government expenditure resulting from the crisis, as we shall see in the following pages.

THE IMPACT OF THE ECONOMIC CRISIS
AND STRUCTURAL ADJUSTMENT ON THE POOR

The impact of the crisis and structural adjustment policies has been devastating for poor women due primarily to three factors: (1) a sharp fall in real wages combined with rising unemployment, (2) the unequal burden that the rising cost of living imposes on women, and (3) the reductions in public spending for services on which women rely. The crisis dramatically highlights existing structures of female subordination and exploitation that have long characterized both countries. There are important differences in the economic role of women in the English-speaking and Hispanic Caribbean, which are reflected in differences in labor force participation rates, economic autonomy, and dependence on a male breadwinner. Although female labor-force participation rates have increased dramatically in the Dominican Republic since 1960, the rates are still far below those of Jamaica, which have always been very high. It could be argued that Jamaican women, particularly in the working class, long ago ceased to be dependent on a primary male wage earner, and today Dominican women appear to be moving in that direction. However, economic autonomy has not ensured labor market equality for women in Jamaica or the rest of the English-speaking Caribbean.

Wages and Employment

Jamaican women are at a distinct disadvantage in the labor market, despite the fact that they have slightly higher educational levels and outnumber men in white collar occupations such as professionals and clerical and sales workers (Davies and Anderson 1987). In 1985, average weekly earnings for men stood at J$86.9 compared to J$68.3 for women (Table 3.2). Female unemployment in 1985 reached 36.6 percent, over twice that of men, reflecting the continued absorption of men in smallholder agriculture. Among the young aged 14 to 19, unemployment rates in 1985 approached 80 percent, and many of these young women have never been employed. The Jamaican census definition of the unemployed, which includes those not actively looking for work as well as those never employed, substantially raises labor force participation rates, especially for women.[2]

High unemployment rates for women are even more critical in Jamaica because of the high percentage of female-headed households. In 1985, 39 percent of all Jamaican households were headed by women, reaching

TABLE 3.2 Average Weekly Earnings of Males and Females, Jamaica, 1983–1985 (in Jamaican dollars)

	1983	1984	1985
Male			
Current dollars	72.3	86.9	86.9
Constant dollars	100.0	94.1	74.9
(1983 = 100)			
Female			
Current dollars	49.2	65.4	68.3
Constant dollars	100.0	103.9	86.6
(1983 = 100)			

Source: Adapted from Davies and Anderson 1987 (Table 14).

45 percent in the Kingston Metropolitan Area. In many cases, these women may be the sole source of income in the family. Labor force participation rates for female household heads are very high, standing at 81.9 percent for the Kingston Metropolitan Area, only slightly above that of wives (81 percent) and not far below the level of 91.9 percent for male household heads, who in most societies are traditionally viewed as the primary breadwinners (Davies and Anderson 1987). Nevertheless, poverty is particularly severe among female heads of households, among whom 72.6 percent had a 1984 monthly income in the Kingston Metropolitan Area under J$400, or the equivalent of US$18 a week, compared to 39.3 percent of male household heads (see Table 3.3). This finding is confirmed by another study showing that female-headed households in urban Jamaica had an average monthly income 22 percent less than that of households headed by a coresident couple (Miller and Stone 1985).

TABLE 3.3 Distribution of Monthly Income Among Household Heads in the Kingston (Jamaica) Metropolitan Area, March 1984

Jamaican Dollars	Male Household Heads (percent)	Female Household Heads (percent)
Under $200	14.6	40.8
$200–399	24.7	31.8
$400–599	23.2	11.3
$600–799	14.6	7.0
$800 or more	23.0	9.2
Total	100.0	100.0

N = 562, N = 444

Source: Davies and Anderson 1987:33.

TABLE 3.4   Female Economic Participation Rate and Proportion of Women in the Economically Active Population (EAP) by Year, Dominican Republic, 1960, 1970, and 1980

	1960	1970	1980
Female economic participation rate (percent)	11.0	27.8	37.5
Proportion of women in EAP	10.8	25.3	37.2

Source: Báez 1984 (Table 3.3).

Lower incomes among female heads reflect not only lower wages but a reduced number of wage earners per household (Bolles 1983).

Unemployment rates in the Dominican Republic are among the highest in all Latin America, reaching 27.2 percent in 1985. As in Jamaica, unemployment is higher for women than men, especially in rural areas, where in the 1981 census the rate was 20.9 percent for men and 29 percent for women (Santana 1985).[3] Underemployment is estimated at about 40 percent and is thought to be higher for women than men because of the high percentage of women in domestic service and other sectors of the informal economy. Average wages in the informal sector are estimated to be 56 percent lower than in the formal sector, though both have declined since 1980 (Santana 1985). Despite several increases in the minimum wage, the real wage in the Dominican Republic in July 1987 was estimated to be only 70 percent of that earned in January 1980 (Ceara 1987).

There have also been changes in the sex composition of the Dominican labor force since 1960. Male participation rates for men over 15 declined 10 percent since 1960 to 81.2 percent in 1980 (Báez 1984), probably due to the prolonged schooling for younger men starting in this period.[4] At the same time, female labor-force participation rates have increased dramatically in the Dominican Republic, from 11 percent in 1960 to 37.5 percent in 1980 (see Table 3.4). The rapid increase in women's labor-force participation rates in the Dominican Republic can be seen both as an attempt by business owners to take advantage of these cheap female wages as well as an effort by women to add to declining real income and to cope with rises in the cost of living.

As in Jamaica, major salary differentials continue to exist between women and men, especially in urban areas where the average monthly wage for women in 1980 was 150 pesos compared to 234 pesos for men (Báez 1984). At that time nearly 60 percent of urban women and 88 percent of rural women earned less than the monthly minimum wage of 125 pesos. This has a particular effect on female heads of households, who in 1980 represented about one-fifth of all Dominican households

TABLE 3.5   Average Monthly Income of Male and Female Household Heads, Dominican Republic, 1980 (in Dominican pesos)

Zone	Household Head		Male/Female Income Ratio
	Male	*Female*	
Urban	266	138	1.9
Rural	73	67	1.1

Source: Báez 1984 (Table 3.11).

(Báez 1984). This percentage is still lower than Jamaica, but it is increasing, especially in urban areas where the average monthly income of urban female heads of households is 138 pesos—nearly half that of male heads of household (see Table 3.5).

In short, the economic crisis has had a particularly devastating effect on women because in both countries they represent a more vulnerable segment of the labor force. They earn less than men and experience higher levels of unemployment. The economic crisis has also resulted in higher income inequality. In 1984, 20 percent of the poorest Dominican households absorbed 9.6 percent of total income, while the richest 20 percent absorbed 42.4 percent (Ceara 1987). The percentage of families under the poverty line increased from 23.3 percent in 1976–1977 to 27.4 percent in 1984 (Ramirez, Duarte, and Gomez 1986).

The Cost of Living

Though legal minimum wages have been increased in both Jamaica and the Dominican Republic several times, they have been unable to keep up with continuous increases in the cost of living. Consumer price increases from 1982 to 1985 rose 73.9 percent in the Dominican Republic in comparison to 99.5 percent in Jamaica (Vega 1988). In Jamaica, the weekly cost of a basic set of meals for a family of five virtually doubled in less than two years between September 1983 and July 1985, reaching far higher than the weekly minimum wage (see Table 3.6). In the Dominican Republic, the cost of a *canasta familiar agropecuaria* or family food basket also more than doubled between 1980 and 1986 (see Table 3.7).

Cost of living increases have resulted primarily from devaluation and inflation, which have an especially severe impact on small economies that are import-dependent. The monthly minimum wage in the Dominican Republic, for example, declined from a value of US$98.43 in January 1980 to US$67.20 in July 1987 (Ceara 1987). However, not even fully employed persons necessarily receive the minimum salary, especially women. In 1980 in the urban area, more than a third of the people working full time on fixed wages received less than the minimum wage

TABLE 3.6   Changes in Minimum Food Costs for a Family of Five and in the Minimum Wage, Jamaica, 1979–1985

	Cost of Basic Set of Meals (J$)	Weekly Minimum Wage (J$)	Cost as Percentage of Minimum Wage
June 1979	24.27	26.4	91.9
September 1983	65.31	30.4	217.7
December 1983	77.00	30.0	256.7
August 1984	101.46	40.0	276.2
July 1985	128.43	52.0	247.0

Source: Davies and Anderson 1987 (Table 10).

(Ramirez et al. 1988). The decline of the Jamaican dollar has been even more precipitous, falling 207 percent between January 1983 and February 1986 (Boyd 1988). As a result, the increase in the cost of living in the Kingston Metropolitan Area between January 1983 and December 1985 was 68 percent, almost twice the average for the previous three-year period (Davies and Anderson 1987). Price increases affected not only food, fuel, and clothing, but public utilities, which have been financed by external loans. Because of high debt-servicing charges, there was a 116-percent increase in electricity charges within the space of five months in 1983, and water rates in Kingston and St. Andrew increased 218 percent between September 1984 and October 1985 (Davies and Anderson 1987).

Increases in food prices fall particularly hard on the poor, as evidenced by the fact that food expenditure is assigned a weight of 53 percent in the Jamaican consumer price index (Davies and Anderson 1987). Price increases are due both to increased dependence on imports and to removal of subsidies and controls on the prices of food. In 1981 there was a 40-percent increase in food imports, due to the government's decision to remove existing import restrictions on a range of foodstuffs

TABLE 3.7   Indicators of the Rising Cost of Living, Dominican Republic, 1980–1986 (in Dominican pesos)

	Cost of Family Food Basket	Price Index	Purchasing Power of Pesos
1980	162.00	1.3652	1.00
1981	156.94	4.4681	0.93
1982	167.44	1.5802	0.86
1983	173.48	1.6897	0.80
1984	212.81	2.1027	0.65
1985	291.75	2.8918	0.47
1986	334.24	3.1735	0.43

Source: Ceara 1987 (Table 18).

that could be produced in Jamaica. This resulted in a 12-percent decline in domestic agriculture the following year, due to competition from cheaper imports (Davies and Anderson 1987). In 1986, locally produced foods represented only 13.7 percent of total foods consumed annually (French 1987). Because of growing malnutrition, the government instituted a Food Aid Program for primary school children, nursing mothers, and the indigent. Though this includes half the total Jamaican population, or one million people, in the first six months of 1984 when the program was instituted, it reached less than 20 percent of the targeted population (Boyd 1988).

Food production for domestic use has always been accorded lower priority than export-oriented agricultural production. Women are particularly affected by this decline, not only as consumers but as producers. In Jamaica, they produce 60 to 75 percent of the food for the local market and are responsible for over 80 percent of its distribution. At the same time, the drive to increase nontraditional exports in such areas as winter vegetables has fallen far short of its stated goal, and the level of export earnings in this sector is almost the same in 1985 as in 1983 (Davies and Anderson 1987).

Domestic food production has also declined in the Dominican Republic, starting with the drive to industrialization in the 1970s, but has been aggravated by the emphasis on export production in structural adjustment policies. Production of root crops such as batata, yucca, and potatoes, a staple of the Dominican diet, has fallen. Cheaper imports of soybean and vegetable oil have substituted peanut oil for cooking, and their value in imports doubled between 1973 and 1981 (Ramirez et al. 1988). At the same time, nontraditional exports such as melon, tomatoes, and pineapples have grown from 15 percent of total commodity export earnings in 1978–1980 to 19 percent in 1982 (World Bank 1985). In fact, the Dominican Republic has replaced Jamaica as the country with the greatest potential growth in agroindustry under the Caribbean Basin Initiative (CBI). These new exports are grown on the basis of either production contracts with small farmers or on large-scale, wage-based agroindustries, which often employ a high percentage of women (Mones and Grant 1987).

The decline in domestic production also contributed to an increasing reliance on food imports, which rose from 63 million pesos in 1973 to 151 million pesos by 1980 (Ramirez, Duarte, and Gomez 1986). Imports combined with a reduction of state price controls have contributed to a sharp increase in food prices on staples such as rice and beans, the cost of which almost doubled between April and September 1988.

Per capita food consumption in the Dominican Republic actually declined 10 percent from 1964 to 1980. Despite a significant increase in the consumption of meat and milk products, particularly among higher income groups, per capita calories and protein consumption have consistently remained below recommended nutritional levels (Ramirez et al. 1988:69–70). In both countries there were further declines in per capita consumption due to the crisis, but despite the severity of the crisis, per capita consumption is consistently higher in Jamaica than in the Dominican Republic. For example, in 1980 at the height of the crisis in Jamaica, per capita consumption in 1982 U.S. dollars was $1,580, compared to $1,026 in the Dominican Republic (Musgrove 1987:418). This comparison, like the GDP figures given earlier, appears to reflect a higher standard of living in Jamaica than in the Dominican Republic, although these per capita figures conceal sharp income inequalities.

Reductions in Public Expenditure

The poor in Jamaica and the Dominican Republic have suffered not only from increases in the cost of living, lower wages, and higher unemployment, but from reductions in public expenditures providing essential social services that the poor cannot afford to buy. According to UNICEF, real expenditure in Jamaica on services such as education, health, and social security fell from J$662 million in 1981–1982 to J$372 million in 1985–1986, a reduction of 44 percent over the last five years (Boyd 1988:145). Health clinics and hospital wards were closed without warning and even the most basic supplies were unavailable in schools and hospitals. Health services and drugs at public hospitals and health centers that were previously free now had to be paid for, making them inaccessible to those who could not afford them. We have already mentioned the cut in government subsidies on basic food items, though some of these were restored in early 1986 after growing protest.

Services related to economic infrastructure were also cut, such as transport and communications, roads, and agricultural and industrial services. In real terms the 1985–1986 expenditure for this category was 57 percent lower than the 1981–1982 level (Boyd 1988). As part of this reduction, the government divested itself of certain operations formerly run by the state, such as street cleaning, maintenance of markets, and urban public transportation, which have led to further unemployment and other hardships. For example, the decision to close the Jamaica Omnibus Service and allocate routes to individual minibus owners has resulted in wholesale congestion at certain transit points, overloading, and delays (Anderson 1987).

In the Dominican Republic, the Popular Democratic Party (PRD), which came into power in 1978, allocated a significant increase in public expenditure for health, education, and welfare, which reached 32 percent of the total budget in 1982 (Ramirez et al. 1988). However, structural adjustment measures brought about a systematic reduction in these expenditures starting in 1982, with a per capita reduction in public expenditure for education, from 17.67 pesos in 1982 to 13.30 pesos in 1986, and in health care the figures were reduced from 16.41 pesos to 12.99 pesos over the same period (Ceara 1987). There has been a serious deterioration in the health care system during this period. Hospitals cannot supply medicines, sheets, or even surgical supplies; patients are forced to buy their own. Over half of the vital equipment in hospitals and clinics is out of order, including such critical items as incubators, x-ray machines, sterilizers, and lab equipment. Hospitals are estimated to be operating at 50-percent capacity, with a severe shortage of nurses, and all medical personnel are underpaid. In 1983, one-fourth of all children admitted to a major children's hospital in Santo Domingo died, not of incurable diseases but of the combined effects of poverty and ill health (Whiteford, 1988) and, we would add, poor health care.

Not only has the quality of public health care in the Dominican Republic declined, but it does not reach much of the population it was designed to serve. The Ministry of Public Health is responsible for 80 percent of the population, but its coverage in 1986 was estimated at 40 percent (Ramirez, Duarte, and Gomez 1986). The major social security system (Instituto Dominicano de Segura Social or IDSS) is designed to cover wage earners through a combined contribution from employees, employers, and the state, but in 1981 it covered only 22.3 percent of salaried wage earners (Ramirez, Duarte, and Gomez 1986).

Significant educational improvements in the Dominican Republic since 1950 have resulted in a lowering of illiteracy rates (from 57 percent in 1950 to 25.8 percent in 1981) and increasing enrollments at the secondary and university levels. The 1970s was a decade of educational expansion, with a median annual increase of 7 percent, so that by 1980, one-fourth of the population aged 15 through 29 had more than nine years of schooling, with women showing greater gains than men. Nevertheless, serious inequities remain, in terms of both class and rural-urban differences. In 1981, more than one-third of the youth aged 6 through 19 did not attend school, and among children 6 to 9 the figure reached one-half. The focus on secondary and university education has been of greater benefit to students from the highest income groups, who received a third of educational subsidies in 1980 compared to 10 percent among the lowest income group (Ramirez et al. 1988).

The reduction in the rate of growth of public expenditures has also resulted in lower salaries and the laying off of government employees. In the Dominican Republic, for example, the average real monthly salary paid by the state sector has declined 51.3 percent from 1970 to 1984

TABLE 3.8   Jamaica: The Distribution of Female Employment by Industry in 1981 and 1985

Industry	October 1981 (percent)	October 1985 (percent)	Change in Numbers of Employed Females
Agriculture	21.1	22.2	+8,100
Mining, quarrying, and refining	0.2	0.2	0
Manufacture	7.0	8.7	+6,800
Construction and installation	0.1	0.2	+100
Transport, communications, and public utilities	2.7	1.7	−2,200
Commerce	23.4	25.1	+10,700
Public administration	19.3	13.4	−14,100
Other services	25.8	28.2	+13,100
Not stated	0.4	0.3	−200
Total	100.0	100.0	+22,300

N = 285,400, N = 307,700

Source: Davies and Anderson 1987 (Table 12, based on 1985 STATIN [Statistical Index] Labour Force Survey).

(Listin Diario 7/9/87 in Whiteford 1988). In Jamaica, employees of local government departments were the hardest hit as this part of the state sector was the prime target for budget cuts. Many are women receiving the lowest wages, such as cleaners at hospitals and schools. There has been a decline of 14,100 women employed by the public sector in Jamaica between 1981 and 1985, a loss higher than any other sector. Whereas public administration accounted for 19.3 percent of female employment in 1981, in 1985 this figure was reduced to 13.4 percent (see Table 3.8).

A major reason for cutbacks in public expenditure for social services and state employees is the increasing expenditure allocated to debt servicing. By the most conservative estimates, in 1986 debt-servicing commitments consumed 30 percent of Jamaica's export earnings and 16 percent of those of the Dominican Republic (World Bank 1988–1989).

Despite severe cuts in social services in both countries, Jamaica would appear to have a higher commitment to public health than the Dominican Republic. Even before the crisis, per capita government health expenditure (excluding social security) has always been much higher in Jamaica than in the Dominican Republic, and in 1984 stood (in 1982 U.S. dollars) at $52.70 and $12.87, respectively (Musgrove 1987). Cuts in health expenditure due to the crisis have also been more severe in the Dominican Republic, where they amounted to more than 40 percent compared to about 20 percent in Jamaica (Musgrove 1987). This is all the more difficult to understand when it appears, as we noted earlier, that the crisis has been more severe and of longer duration in Jamaica.[5]

SURVIVAL STRATEGIES

Caribbean women are not simply victims of the crisis but are developing innovative strategies for dealing with it. Four main strategies can be detected: (1) an increased number of women in the labor force, particularly in export processing; (2) an increase in the informal sector activities; (3) an intensification of household survival strategies, including changes in consumer and dietary patterns; and (4) international migration, now predominantly female, especially to the United States. Remittances are an increasingly important source of income for families left behind.

Increased Number of Women in the Labor Force

At first glance, the growing number of women in the labor force may appear contradictory in view of increased unemployment and underemployment in Latin America and the Caribbean generally. However, women are forced into the labor force precisely because of increased unemployment among men and because real wages of employed household members are decreasing, signifying an overall reduction in the household income. Women are able to find jobs even when men cannot because they work for cheaper wages, because the labor market in Latin America and the Caribbean (as in the United States) is highly segregated by gender, and because a high percentage of women work in the informal sector.

Several factors in the development process in the Dominican Republic favored the dramatic increase of women in the labor force: from 11 percent in 1960 to 37.5 percent in 1980. The factors include urbanization, the growth of the tertiary sector, and the growth of export processing. At the same time, changes were taking place in the female population that made them more employable, including a rise in educational levels and a marked decline in fertility (Duarte 1988). Although many of these same factors help explain the incorporation of Jamaican women into the labor force, in the past two decades there has been a relatively small increase in their participation rates, which have been traditionally high. In fact, female unemployment rates increased much faster than participation rates, reflecting the inability of the Jamaican economy to absorb the increased number of women in the labor force (Henry 1988).

Export manufacturing increased the demand for female labor in both countries. Export manufacturers have shown a preference for women workers, because they are cheaper to employ, less likely to unionize, and have greater patience for the tedious, monotonous work involved in assembly operations. Although Jamaica was chosen as the showpiece of the CBI at its initiation, export manufacturing never took off on the scale anticipated. The bulk of employment creation in export manufacturing in Jamaica in recent years has occurred not through the CBI, but through the preferences created by U.S. Tariff Code 807 for apparel assembled overseas from U.S. components.[6] Between 1981 and 1985, an additional 6,800 women found employment in the manufacturing sector, so that the proportion of women employed in manufacturing rose from 7 percent to 8.7 percent of the female labor force (Table 3.8).

Export manufacturing has had less appeal to U.S. firms in Jamaica than in Haiti or the Dominican Republic, and total employment is much lower, reaching only 8,500 in foreign firms in the Kingston Export Free Zone in 1987. However, much of the work is subcontracted to Jamaican manufacturers, perhaps because of fear of labor unrest. A U.S. Agency for International Development (USAID) study of the apparel industry in Jamaica revealed that U.S. firms see unions as a major obstacle to investment, although only one of the twenty-two factories in the Kingston Export Free Zone is unionized. There have been frequent public protests against work abuses such as low pay, excessive and forced overtime, occupational health hazards, arbitrary suspension and dismissal for protesting, and absence of trade union representation. Such complaints are common in export manufacturing and can also be found in the Dominican Republic. In addition, companies take advantage of government training programs to further reduce their labor costs, as trainees are paid about half the minimum wage (French 1987).

In the Dominican Republic, there has been a much greater growth in export manufacturing, so that now it can be considered the showplace of the CBI rather than Jamaica. The greatest increase has taken place after 1985, when the number of employees in the free trade zones quadrupled to an estimated 85,000 workers in 1988 (Table 3.9). The overwhelming majority of these workers in export manufacturing are women, who in 1983 represented 40.6 percent of the economically active population in manufacturing excluding sugar (Duarte 1988).

Wage reductions resulting from devaluation have increased the attractiveness of investment in export manufacturing in the Dominican Republic. Between 1981 and 1984 there was a 17-percent reduction in the actual average real wage in manufacturing, despite increases in the minimum wage (Joekes 1987). At the rate of exchange prevailing at the end of 1988, the average wage in free trade zones was approximately US$106

TABLE 3.9 Changes in the Number of Employees in the Free Trade Zones in the Dominican Republic, 1981–1988

	Number Employed
1981	19,456
1982	19,236
1983	21,387
1984	25,099
1985	22,720
1986	48,603
1987	72,735
1988	85,000[a]

[a] Preliminary.

Source: Abreu et al. 1989 (Table 6.3).

monthly. Average hourly wages in the Dominican Republic in 1988 were US$.60, and were cheaper only in Jamaica and Haiti (Abreu et al. 1989). In addition, under pressure from industrialists in the free trade zones, the Dominican government granted them access to the parallel market, which enabled them to buy local currency at a far more favorable rate. This new exchange rate policy lowered operating costs by approximately 30 percent and is another major factor behind the rapid growth in activity in the zones in the last few years (Joekes 1987).

In addition to low wages and other trade incentives, the weakness of the labor movement in the Dominican Republic attracts investors.[7] There are no unions in the free trade zones of the Dominican Republic, and workers are fired and blacklisted with other plants if any union activity is detected. Women who have tried to take complaints of mistreatment or unjust dismissal to the government labor office have generally been rejected in favor of management. Workers complain of the lack of public transportation, proper eating facilities, adequate medical services, or child care. Labor turnover is high because many workers cannot withstand the pressure of high production quotas, strict discipline, sexual harassment, and a work week of forty-four hours, in addition to overtime. In a study of the free trade zones conducted in 1981,[8] it was found that most of the workers are under thirty, but in a departure from the global pattern of young single women, over one-half are married and one-fourth are female heads of household. Their need to work is demonstrated by the fact that nearly three-fourths of the female heads of household and nearly half of the married women claim they are the principal breadwinner for the family (Ricourt 1986). In fact, employers in the Dominican Republic indicate a preference for women with children because they feel their need to work ensures greater job commitment (Joekes 1987).

Growth in demand for female labor has been greatest in manufacturing, but women have also been employed as wage laborers in the new agroindustries that have flourished recently in the Dominican Republic due to the CBI. A 1985 study of rural women revealed that wages in these agroindustries are even lower than in manufacturing, averaging 3 to 6 pesos daily in 1985, and the work is very unstable, concentrated in the harvest season (Mones and Grant 1987). Many women also work as unremunerated family labor on small farms, some of which produce for agribusiness on a contract basis.

In short, while export promotion has increased the demand for female labor, it has also taken advantage of women's inferior position in the labor market and reinforced their subordination through poorly paid, dead-end jobs. It is clear that women workers in the free trade zones of the Dominican Republic and Jamaica are exploited by management and receive little or no support from the government in their efforts to achieve better wages and working conditions. Both governments have attempted to control labor unrest in order to attract foreign investment. Under these circumstances it is understandable why workers have not organized or protested more vehemently, although in March 1988 there were widespread strikes among Jamaican garment workers in favor of higher wages and better working conditions. Thus, the failure to improve working conditions lies more with the lack of support women workers receive from government, political parties, and unions than with the women themselves. At present, these women workers have no adequate vehicles to express their grievances or to transform their sense of exploitation (which is very real) into greater worker solidarity.

Informal Sector

Despite its disadvantages, most women still regard jobs in export processing preferable to work in the informal sector, which generally provides no labor protection, minimum wages, social security, or other benefits (Anderson and Gordon 1987). The informal sector includes a high percentage of domestic servants, petty vendors, and other self-employed workers.

In Jamaica, the percentage of women in the informal sector is much higher than men; in 1984, 38 percent of women were in the informal sector compared to 11.8 percent of men (Anderson and Gordon 1987). The majority of both men and women are over 40. Undoubtedly this reflects the high percentage of Jamaican women who work as "higglers" or petty vendors, trading in foodstuffs and manufactured goods. Women's involvement in the marketing of food for the domestic market dates back to the days of slavery, providing them with the flexibility needed to manage their dual roles and a certain degree of independence. However, the higglering role itself has been transformed, as some women now travel internationally, buying clothing and other consumer goods in Miami to sell in Jamaica or selling Jamaican goods in Haiti and other areas (ECLAC 1988). In addition, as domestic food production has declined, higglers have moved to purchasing the surplus produce from large-scale farms (French 1987), and some are doing the same with manufacturing goods.

In the Dominican Republic, the economically active population in the informal sector grew from 38.6 percent in 1980 to 45 percent in 1983, with men outnumbering women (Duarte 1986). A study by PREALC (1983) concludes that unemployment following the crisis would have been much higher were it not for the growth of the informal sector, but that the jobs provided pay 60 percent less on the average than those in the modern sector. As usual, women are worse off, with 70 percent of those in the urban informal sector earning less than the poverty line (PREALC 1983). Many women are in domestic service, which still employs one-fourth of the female labor force (Báez 1984). Not only is this the largest occupational category for women, but it pays the lowest wages and in the Dominican Republic has practically no labor protection.

The growth of the informal sector may also reflect state policy, which with international support has encouraged the growth of microenterprises in Latin America and the Caribbean. Because of its capacity for labor absorption and cost advantage in a highly competitive international market, the informal sector is receiving increased support from both the public and private sectors in terms of credit, access to raw materials and foreign exchange, and other privileges formerly reserved exclusively for the formal sector (Safa 1987). A favorite mechanism of support is income-generation schemes such as the credit extension program of ADEMI (Association for the Development of Microenterprises, Inc.), founded in 1983 as a private voluntary organization by a group of influential Dominican business leaders with financial support from the Dominican government and USAID. The microenterprises are involved in a variety of manufacturing activities from making clothes, ceramics, and bread to the repair of refrigerators and mattresses. Research on the ADEMI credit program notes that the economic crisis in the Dominican Republic has led to modifications favoring larger, more stable firms. Loans were formerly given to both individuals and solidarity groups composed of several individuals, including a high percentage of poor women. With the eroding economy, loans were suspended to the solidarity groups, thereby eliminating 77 percent of the female beneficiaries (Blumberg 1985).

In Jamaica there is some evidence that garment manufacturers are turning to domestic homeworkers as a way of cutting their labor costs.

By contracting homeworkers, they avoid unionization, the payment of fringe benefits, and the costs of buildings, utilities, and machinery. However, the greatest advantage homeworkers offer is the flexibility of the labor force, which can be scaled up or down with market fluctuations. Wages for homework, which are paid by the piece, fall far below the minimum wage and clearly offer no stability of employment.

Both the informal sector and export manufacturing have been intensified in response to the economic crisis in Latin America and the Caribbean. They represent strategies by industries to reduce production costs at a time of intense international competition. They also represent strategies by the poor to augment their earnings to meet the increasing cost of living and reduction in real wages and high unemployment.

Intensification of Household Survival Strategies

Women in poor Latin American and Caribbean households have commonly sought to stretch family income by producing goods at home, rather than purchasing them in stores, or by adding wage earners to the family, or by making use of extended family and neighborhood networks. With the economic crisis, these patterns have been intensified to cope with declining household income, increased prices, and cuts in government services. Bolles (1983) has documented the way in which Jamaican women industrial workers attempt to cope with the effects of structural adjustment and the economic crisis. All households, for example, engaged in domestic exchange networks in which goods, services, and occasionally cash flowed between relatives, friends, and neighbors. Many women took advantage of commissaries at their place of work to purchase scarce items such as dairy goods or baby-care products in order to exchange them for food, child care, or other services. Rural kin were also incorporated, as higglers provided their urban kin with fresh vegetables in return for manufactured goods like flashlight batteries. A conscious attempt was made to avoid market transactions because of the increasing scarcity of cash.

Bolles also demonstrates how strategies vary with household composition. Among households headed by women, who constituted a majority of her sample, there was a greater tendency to incorporate additional kin into the household than among those headed by a stable co-residential unit. These kin serve two functions: They free women from some domestic chores and child care so that they can be full-time workers, and they often try to earn additional income through the informal sector. Where possible, household members are expected to help with the payment of rent and utilities, and this is particularly true of men, whether they are stable partners or boyfriends in visiting unions, or fathers of one or more of the woman's children. However, because of the high rate of unemployment among men, particularly in the urban area, many men are unable to fulfill these traditional financial obligations. Less than a quarter of the women in visiting unions and none of the single women then living alone with their children received regular support from their boyfriends or the fathers of their children (Bolles 1983).

Hence, while a series of sexual partners may have been a traditional means by which Jamaican women sought financial support, it would seem that the devastating impact of the crisis on male earning capacity has made the women even more reliant on their own wages and other sources of income. In Bolles's study, over 80 percent of the women who headed households were directly responsible for the major household expenditures, and 63 percent of the women in the stable unions also assumed this responsibility (Bolles 1983).

In the Dominican Republic, the economic crisis has had a similar impact, but the role of the male breadwinner is still more intact. In the study of the free trade zones conducted by Centro de Investigación para la Acción Femenina (CIPAF) in 1981, husbands are still considered the principal economic providers in many households and are chiefly responsible for basic items like food and housing. However, the great majority of single and married women also maintain that their families could not survive without their wages, suggesting that their wages are not supplementary but are making an essential contribution to the family income (Catanzaro 1986).

Women's contribution to the household economy is greatest among female heads of household, and their proportion has been increasing since the 1970s. The 1981 Dominican census puts the figure at 20.6 percent, but other estimates reach as high as 33.5 percent.[9] Undoubtedly, economic changes such as the increased percentage of women in the labor force and the increased difficulties men are facing in fulfilling their role as economic provider are contributing to this increase. Though female heads of household have higher rates of labor force participation than married women, they are a particularly vulnerable group, with lower incomes (see Table 3.5) and higher rates of unemployment, and they are twice the percentage of occasional laborers as male heads (Gomez and Gaton 1987).

Duarte (1988) believes that the incorporation of additional members into the household as a survival strategy may be one explanation for the continued large size of households in the Dominican Republic, which has remained at about 5.3 persons since 1920. This is surprising, given the sharp decline in fertility levels since the 1960s. Large households are found predominantly among extended families, among whom 69 percent have five or more members. Extended families continue to account for approximately 30 percent of all households, and the percentage is higher in urban than in rural areas, which runs counter to most demographic predictions (Duarte 1988). The increasingly high cost of housing and land may be one factor that forces families to double up and results in severe overcrowding among the urban poor.

In its studies on the impact of the crisis, UNICEF (Cornia 1987) also reports changes in consumption and dietary patterns, with increasing concentration on cheap sources of calories, such as rice or yucca, and declining protein intakes, such as milk or meat. Women and young girls are the family members most likely to be affected by declining food consumption because preference is given to male wage earners. In Jamaica, decline in the nutritional status of children under the age of four years, from 38 percent in 1978 to 41 percent in 1985, sums up the effects of these policies (Cornia and Stewart 1987). This trend was also confirmed by hospital admissions, which show that the proportion of children under five admitted to the Bustamante Children's Hospital for malnutrition and malnutrition/gastroenteritis rose from 2.7 percent of all admissions in 1980 to 8.4 percent in 1985 (French 1987). In addition, the percentage of pregnant women screened at antenatal clinics who were deemed anemic rose from 23 percent in 1981 to 43 percent in 1985 (French 1987). Moreover, the infant mortality rate has increased from 16 per thousand in 1980 to 18 per thousand in 1987 (World Bank 1982, 1989).

In the Dominican Republic, despite dramatic improvements in mortality and life expectancy rates starting in the 1950s, infant mortality still stood at 68 per thousand in 1980, much higher than Jamaica (Table 3.1). Other studies indicate that the rate of infant mortality is grossly underreported and is considerably higher in rural areas and among the lowest income groups (Ceara 1987). Maternal mortality, which also differs in urban and rural areas and by income group, stood at 56 per 100,000 in 1980 (World Bank 1989). In one major maternity hospital in the capital of Santo Domingo, where health services are superior to those in rural areas, maternal mortality increased from 15 to 22 per 100,000 from 1981 to 1985 (Ceara 1987). In a study conducted in the summer of 1988, Whiteford (1988) reports that women recovering from childbirth were well aware of the importance of a good diet, but because of cost, most had eaten only *suspua,* a weak soup made with plantains, yucca, sweet potatoes, and pigeon peas. It is estimated that one-fourth of all babies born in the Dominican Republic are children of malnourished mothers.

According to a study conducted by the Central Bank in 1976–1977, 90 percent of the Dominican population are below the recommended minimum of 2,300 calories and 60 grams of protein per day, with the poorest families significantly below this minimum standard. Among children aged one to four, the level of malnutrition in 1984 reached 40.8 percent (Ramirez, Duarte, and Gomez 1986:12). A USAID study in 1987 found the highest prevalence of malnutrition among infants aged five to eight months. This is attributed to a variety of causes: the abrupt cessation of breast-feeding as mothers are forced by economic circumstances to return to work, dilution of formulas, and lack of potable water used in infant feeding (quoted in Whiteford, forthcoming). However, the negative effects of women's employment on breast-feeding needs to be balanced against the income they add to the family (Leslie, Lycette, and Buvinic 1986).

International Migration

International migration has long represented a survival strategy for most of the Caribbean, with the volume per capita exceeding that of any other world area (Chaney 1985). However, several changes have taken place since 1960 that have particular significance for women. In the first place, the rate of female migration has increased rapidly, surpassing that of men. Second, more middle-class migrants are leaving for the United States. And third, the volume of migration has increased due to the economic crisis that hit the Caribbean in full force in the early 1980s.

Over a million migrants entered the United States legally from the Caribbean during the decade from 1976 to 1986, which represents about half the total since 1960. Migration began to pick up significantly after 1976 when the crisis began in the region and shows little sign of abating. As a result, about 10 percent of Caribbean people now reside in the United States, including a substantial number of illegal migrants (see Table 3.10). The total number of persons who migrated from Jamaica and the Dominican Republic is very similar, but as the total population of Jamaica is smaller this represents a much higher percentage of Jamaicans than Dominicans. In fact, Jamaica and the Dominican Republic ranked first and third, respectively, in the world in terms of per capita legal immigration to the United States in 1981 (Grasmuck and Pessar 1991).

International migration in Jamaica and the rest of the English-speaking Caribbean has a long history, dating back to the nineteenth century when Jamaicans migrated to Panama to build the canal or to Cuba to cut sugarcane. In the immediate postwar period, most of Jamaican migration was to the United Kingdom, but this was sharply curtailed by British immigration controls in 1962. From 1943 to 1960 there was a net migration loss of 195,000, or nearly a third of the natural increase. This net outflow increased during the 1960s, reaching a level of 280,000, or 53 percent of the natural increase in population. From 1976 to 1985, net out-migration

TABLE 3.10   Caribbean Migration to the United States: The Reciprocal Impact

Country	Population	Total Immigration 1950–1983	Est. Illegal Population in the U.S.	Migrants to the U.S. as % of Home Population
Cuba	9,771,000	910,967	0	9.3
Dominican Republic	5,762,000	318,664	225,000	9.4
Haiti	6,000,000	132,610	400,000	8.9
Commonwealth Caribbean				
Barbados	252,000	38,183	25,000	25.1
Guyana	795,000	80,462	0	10.1
Jamaica	2,225,000	288,464	250,000	21.4
Trinidad & Tobago	1,176,000	100,305	60,000	13.6
Total Caribbean	28,329,484	1,869,535	960,000	10.0

Source: Pastor 1985:12.

continued to represent close to half the natural increase for that period (Anderson 1988). Most of the migration since 1962 has been to the United States and Canada.

Migration before 1950 was dominated by men and is one of the factors accounting for the high percentage of female-headed households in Jamaica and other areas of the English-speaking Caribbean. Since 1960, however, the percentage of women emigrating from Jamaica is much higher than that of men (see Table 3.11). This partly reflects the U.S. Immigration Act of 1965, which gave higher preference to better educated, more skilled immigrants, which in the case of Jamaica included large numbers of female teachers and nurses. Domestic workers were given special labor certification in Canada as well. The law also gave preference to family reunification so that wives, mothers, and other female relatives joined earlier male migrants. Family reunification is the primary reason for female migration from the Dominican Republic, which also started as predominantly male. However, according to the 1980 U.S. census, women constitute 55 percent of the Dominican population of the United States (Del Castillo and Mitchell 1987), and other studies also indicate their predominance in the recent migration flow.

The preference given to the more skilled labor force suggests that it is not only the unemployed and very poor who migrate, as many once assumed. In fact, legal migration from Jamaica since the 1970s was notable both for its volume and for its high proportion of skilled and educated migrants. These Jamaicans were propelled by the blocking of avenues of domestic mobility brought on by the crisis as well as by the social upheaval and political violence of the last years of Michael Manley's first

TABLE 3.11   Distribution of Migrants to the United States by Sex:
Comparison of Three Decades

Sending Country	1950s	1960s	1970s	Total
Jamaica				
Male	59.6	41.3	45.6	49.3
Female	40.4	58.7	54.4	51.7
Santo Domingo				
Male	59.2	51.5	0	54.7
Female	40.8	48.5	0	45.3
Grenada				
Male	55.9	48.2	49.0	50.6
Female	44.1	51.8	51.0	49.4
St. Lucia				
Male	59.8	54.4	0	56.7
Female	40.2	45.6	0	43.3
Trinidad-Tobago				
Male	0	53.8	44.4	49.6
Female	0	46.2	55.6	50.4
Barbados				
Male	65.5	47.0	50.2	53.2
Female	35.5	53.0	49.8	46.8

Source: Chaney 1985:21.

administration. Between 1976 and 1985, professionals and managers accounted for 9.7 percent of all Jamaican migrants to the United States and Canada; craftspeople and operatives represented 12 percent. These two categories alone accounted for 22.2 percent and 27.6 percent, respectively, of the experienced migrant labor force in these occupations, which represents a serious loss of educated and skilled manpower (Anderson 1988). In the health sector, for example, over the 1978 to 1985 period, the number of doctors and nurses who migrated represented 78 percent and 95 percent, respectively, of those trained in these professions during this period (Anderson 1988). Clearly this loss of labor power reduces the adequacy of health care in Jamaica and reflects the country's incapacity to retain and effectively utilize its skilled labor at adequate levels of compensation.

Recent studies of migration from the Dominican Republic also confirm the growing importance of middle-class migrants (Grasmuck 1985; Gurak and Kritz 1985; Bray 1984), challenging earlier studies that emphasized their rural poor origins. One fundamental reason is the cost of migration, even for the undocumented, who must purchase false papers like social security cards and visas. Here again, political factors appear to play a role because the years following elections all show major surges in the number of Dominicans migrating (Bray 1984). Bray attributes middle-class migration to the failure of the dependent development model,

TABLE 3.12   Remittances of Emigrant Workers for Selected Caribbean Countries, 1985

	Total U.S. Millions	Merchandise Trade Exports	Percent of Merchandise Exports
Dominican Republic	205	735	28
Haiti	98	455	22
Jamaica	26	538	5

Source: World Bank 1987:220, 230.

which first created and then restricted the expansion of the Dominican middle class. This restriction became greater with the economic crisis when many lost their jobs, particularly in the public sector, and when the standard of living in the Dominican Republic was drastically reduced.

Women constituted 55.8 percent of Dominican migrants to New York City in 1980, and the data available suggest that most are not drawn from the poorest segments of the population (Gurak and Kritz 1985). A large 1981 survey of Dominican migrants between 20 and 45 years of age in New York City shows that women originate mainly from urban areas and have an average of nine years of schooling, which is much higher than the national average. Labor force participation rates show a remarkable increase from 31 percent in the Dominican Republic prior to migration to 49 percent in New York City, primarily in the garment industry (Gurak and Kritz 1982). This demonstrates that although family reunification is the primary reason for migration, paid employment is also an important motivation to go to New York and to remain there, as Pessar (1986) has shown.

Those who migrate are usually in their most productive ages (20 to 39) and often leave behind the very young and old. This results in much higher dependency ratios in the Caribbean than in the United States. The large number of dependents left behind explains the high level of remittances. Some of the smaller eastern Caribbean islands such as St. Kitts/Nevis are known as remittance societies because so many people have left and the population remaining is almost entirely dependent on remittances.

The level of remittances is much higher in the Dominican Republic than in Jamaica, reaching US$205 million in 1985 compared to US$26 million for the latter (see Table 3.12). In addition to serving as an important source of household income, remittances have a significant impact on these countries' balance of payments. In 1985 remittances amounted to 5 percent of the value of merchandise trade of Jamaica and 28 percent of that of the Dominican Republic. Data from the Bank of Jamaica suggest that the value of remittances in foreign exchange has shown a marked decline since 1975, which was only partially offset by the increased value of farmworkers' remittances (Anderson 1985). These are seasonal farmworkers temporarily admitted into the United States under the H2 contract workers' program.

In contrast, a study by the Central Bank in the Dominican Republic shows that the level of remittances has been increasing steadily since 1970, when it stood at only US$8.5 million (Del Castillo and Mitchell 1987). The 1981 study of Dominican migrants found that 59 percent of male heads of households send remittances compared to 44 percent of female heads of households, and that the average annual amount is nearly double for the former at US$1,124 in contrast to US$687 for the latter (Gurak and Kritz 1987). Undoubtedly, this reflects the lower income level of female heads, over half of whom were receiving some form of public assistance (Gurak and Kritz 1982). A more recent 1985 study found that the average monthly remittance had increased to US$183, which was nearly double the annual amount reported in 1981 (Del Castillo and Mitchell 1987).

Remittances appear to be most often spent on household expenses, consumer goods, and, when current needs are met, on improved housing. Therefore, they do not appear to contribute to productive investment in the Caribbean (Chaney 1985). There is also little effort to pool remittances, creating funds for community projects, as is common in some Mexican rural communities.[10] Remittances may in some cases reduce the need to seek local sources of employment. A 1980 study of migrants from Santiago, the second largest city in the Dominican Republic, reports a much higher percentage of unemployment among heads of households where a member has migrated compared to heads of nonmigrant families. The mean amount remitted per household was nearly equal to the 1979 median monthly wage in the city (Grasmuck 1985).

The increasing level of remittances to the Dominican Republic has had a particular impact on the housing industry, especially after the economic crisis. The number of housing construction permits issued was reduced more than 50 percent from 1981 to 1984. At the same time, 60 percent of housing loans issued in 1984 were given to Dominican migrants. Because their houses may be rented in their absence, this housing constitutes an important source of moderate-income housing, which the state has failed to provide. Migrants also constitute 22 percent of the tourists to the Dominican Republic in recent years, and the money they spent constituted nearly 29 percent of total tourist income (Del Castillo and Mitchell 1987).

The economic crisis is making it more difficult for migrants to return to live in the Dominican Republic. In 1980, return migrants already reported a high rate of unemployment, especially among female heads of household, nearly four-fifths of whom were unemployed (Grasmuck 1985). Unemployment induces many to think of leaving again and confirms the inability of the economy to absorb even these experienced workers, about a third of whom are in professional and managerial categories. In a parallel study of two agrarian communities, migration had led to the reduction of farming activities in one community, but in the community with better soil, roads, and marketing facilities, there had been considerable return migration and productive capital investment, notably in egg-producing firms. However, most of the firms went bankrupt due to the pricing strategies of monopoly firms. This points to the need for a state policy to protect the small migrant investor against monopoly enterprises (Grasmuck 1985).

With the increasing integration of Caribbean economies into the United States, there has been a rise in circular migration, with short-term and frequent movements to and fro, including the business class (Anderson 1988). However, the possibilities of permanent return are dimmed by the economic crisis, so that it could be argued that the better educated, more skilled migrants constitute another subsidy that poorer countries are supplying to richer, more industrialized countries like the United States. In addition, while remittances reduce the deficit in the balance of payments, they may also increase demand for imported goods, ultimately having a negative effect on the balance of payments (Grasmuck 1985). Therefore, migration and the remittances it generates may simultaneously alleviate the crisis and reinforce the pattern of dependent development in these Caribbean countries.

CONCLUSION

The data demonstrate that the economic crisis and structural adjustment have had a devastating impact on women and their families in Jamaica and the Dominican Republic. Women suffer higher rates of unemployment and lower wage levels and have been the most affected by cuts in government services and increases in the cost of living. In response, they are working even harder, eating and spending less, and migrating more. The toll this is taking in terms of increased malnutrition and other indices of poor health and the loss of skilled labor power will be paid by these households and by their countries for decades to come.

UNICEF studies have shown that health care and nutrition programs can effectively combat some of the worst consequences of the crisis, so that there is little connection between the severity of the crisis and health indices such as malnutrition, infectious disease, and mortality (Musgrove 1987). The data presented here on the Dominican Republic and Jamaica reinforce these findings. It would appear that the Jamaican government has maintained a higher commitment to health services than the Dominican Republic, although the indices of the crisis appear to be more severe and prolonged in the former. The gross differences in infant mortality rates in the two countries would appear to be one result of this contrast, although the rate is now increasing in Jamaica as well. Educational expansion in the Dominican Republic has also tended to favor higher income groups because of the emphasis on secondary and university students, who are commonly the most politically volatile.

Given the severity of the crisis, it is surprising that families in both Jamaica and the Dominican Republic have not organized collectively to meet their consumer needs, as was done in the communal kitchens in Peru, Chile, and some other Latin American countries. There are government programs attempting to deal with these problems, such as the Food Assistance Program in Jamaica, but they fall far short of need. Riots involving large numbers of women to protest the rising cost of living and IMF austerity measures have taken place in both countries: in 1979 and 1985 in Kingston and other towns in Jamaica, and in 1984, 1985, and 1987 in Santo Domingo and other cities in the Dominican Republic (Walton 1989). The 1984 riot in the Dominican Republic brought on by price increases left more than sixty people dead, hundreds injured, and one thousand arrested in just three days. Though initiated as a strike by local popular organizations in the poor neighborhoods of Santo Domingo, it spread quickly and went out of control. The government, political parties, and labor unions were caught completely by surprise, underlining their lack of awareness of the depth of public anger. The inability of labor or political parties to channel this anger, combined with government repression, led in both countries to eventual containment. Following the 1984 riot, the Dominican government did moderate some price increases, but new price increases were announced three months later, following further arrests. The riots did, however, split the ruling Dominican Democratic Revolutionary Party, contributing to its defeat in the 1986 election, just as the IMF austerity measures were an important factor in the 1980 defeat of Michael Manley in Jamaica. Riots and general strikes, which continued in the Dominican Republic in 1988 and 1989, reveal not only the depth of public anger, but the lack of institutionalized channels for airing grievances and for supporting collective solutions.

Mintz (1971) long ago attributed the individualization and the absence of corporate groups with an institutional or kin basis in the Caribbean to the divisive effects of a plantation economy upon community life. It is possible that differences in cultural heritage between the Caribbean and Latin America contribute to different levels of collective action, but they are not the sole explanation. As in the rest of Latin America (Jelin 1987), women's organizations have been largely ignored by male-dominated political parties and labor unions, who constitute the normal vehicle for channeling grievances to the state. Nevertheless, consciousness of gender subordination is growing, and in the past two decades the number of national and regional women's organizations in the Caribbean has grown significantly, helping to build alliances focused on issues of poverty and social change, and transcending some of the boundaries of language, culture, class, race, and political affiliation in the region. They have been aided by a proliferation of nongovernmental organizations designed to promote women and development programs through popular education, job skills and training, income-generation projects, production and marketing cooperatives, and health and nutrition campaigns. Progressive religious groups have also been active in supporting the poor, as illustrated by the establishment of Catholic base communities in Haiti and the Dominican Republic, and by the activities of the Caribbean Conference of Churches, which has promoted issues such as peace and regional economic development in the English-speaking Caribbean. As yet, however, these organizations have not been very successful in urging governments to provide a more equitable distribution of resources or to become more responsive to the needs of vulnerable groups such as women and children. On the contrary, governments and international agencies appear to take advantage of women's ability to draw on traditional networks of support to introduce policies that have been particularly devastating to their needs. Until women's demands are recognized, it is difficult to see how structural change will take place in the Caribbean and how the region can emerge from its current crisis.

NOTES

1. Peggy Antrobus wrote the first draft of this chapter, based on Jamaican material only. A revised version of her draft has been published as "Gender Implications of the Debt Crisis" (Antrobus 1989). We also made extensive use of the studies commissioned by UNICEF in Jamaica by Davies and Anderson (1987) and in the Dominican Republic by Ceara (1987), as well as unpublished papers by Isis Duarte (1988) and Linda Whiteford (forthcoming).

2. According to Patricia Anderson (personal communication), in the Jamaican Labor Force Surveys the category of unemployed includes persons who did not actively look for work during the reference week of the survey but who wanted work and were able to accept it. This group, usually referred to as "nonseekers," is larger for women than for men. However, even when nonseekers are excluded from the unemployed and from the labor force, the differential between levels of male and female unemployment remains. In October 1985, using this narrower definition of the labor force, the "job-seeking rate" stood at 13.3 percent, with the male rate being 8.5 percent and the rate for women at 17.9 percent.

3. According to a survey conducted in 1980, rural unemployment among Dominican women actually reached 53 percent (Santana 1985). As in Jamaica, this includes in the labor force all those who indicated a willingness to look for work if they had some chance of being employed, even if they were not currently looking. Santana argues that the survey is a more accurate portrayal of Dominican reality.

4. Standing (1989) notes a more general trend toward a decline in male participation rates in developing as well as advanced industrial countries and suggests that it may be due to the pursuit of lower wages by business and the substitution of women for men.

5. Higher per capita expenditures on health and education in Jamaica as compared to the Dominican Republic may be at least partially explained by differences in historical background. British colonial policy in Jamaica and other areas of the English-speaking Caribbean instituted social welfare policies that date back to the worker riots of the 1930s and were promoted by the Moyne Commission and the British Labour Party. In contrast, in the Dominican Republic, the social security and labor legislation still in existence was designed by the Trujillo regime primarily to legitimize his dictatorship and to contain labor struggles before they become too vocal. The contradictions between this system of "protective paternalism" and working class demands only became evident after the fall of Trujillo in 1960, but much of the working class remains unorganized (Duarte 1986; Espinal 1988).

6. The Super 807 program, or 807A, announced by President Reagan in 1986, guarantees CBI country access to the U.S. market outside established quotas for apparel assembled from fabric formed and cut in the United States. Although this is an added inducement to export expansion, it also reduces the level of investment and labor in the CBI country.

7. Espinal (1988) attributes the weakness of the Dominican labor movement to a series of factors including low levels of unionization and splinter politics, limited support from the PRD (Partido Revolucionario Dominicano) in power from 1978 to 1986, an intransigent business community, and the economic crisis.

8. The 1981 study of women in the free trade zones of the Dominican Republic was conducted by CIPAF (Centro de Investigación para la Acción Femenina), a feminist research center directed by Magaly Pineda. With the permission of CIPAF, Quintina Reyes (1987) and Milagros Ricourt (1986), two members of the CIPAF research team, as well as Lorraine Catanzaro (1986) subsequently wrote their M.A. theses at the University of Florida using these data. We thank CIPAF and these researchers for their data and analysis.

9. Báez (1984) argues that the percentage of female-headed households is underestimated because it relies on the opinion of the informant surveyed. The higher figure is obtained utilizing a method suggested by the United Nations, which measures the percentage of households where there are women with younger children and no adult men. If we assume that headship denotes family authority and responsibility, it could be argued that many households with a resident male are also headed by women, or that women and men are sharing this responsibility, as many women maintain in our survey of Dominican and

Puerto Rican factory workers (Safa, forthcoming). However, census data do not capture these changing patterns of family authority and responsibility, and we have followed the conventional term of "male head of household" used in most of the studies we consulted.

10. Pastor (1989) has proposed the creation of national and regional remittance banks to provide incentives for Caribbean migrants to invest their remittances in their home countries. These investments could, in turn, be used as government counterpart funding for international development projects.

REFERENCES

Abreu, Alfonso, Manuel Cocco, Carlos Despradel, Eduardo García Michel, and Arturo Peguero. 1989. *Las Zonas Francas Industriales en la República Dominicana: El Exito de Una Política Económica.* Santo Domingo, Dominican Republic: Centro Internacional para el Desarollo Económico.

Anderson, Patricia. 1985. *Migration and Development in Jamaica.* Kingston: University of the West Indies, Institute of Social and Economic Research, Paper No. 2.

————. 1987. *Minibus Ride: A Journey Through the Informal Sector of Kingston's Mass Transport System.* Kingston: University of the West Indies, Institute of Social and Economic Research.

————. 1988. "Manpower Losses and Employment Adequacy Among Skilled Workers in Jamaica, 1976–1985." In Patricia Pessar (ed.), *When Borders Don't Divide: Labor Migration and Refugee Movements in the Americas.* New York: Center for Migration Studies.

Anderson, Patricia, and Derek Gordon. 1987. "Economic Change and Labour Market Mobility in Jamaica, 1979–84." Paper presented to First Conference of Caribbean Economists, Kingston, Jamaica.

Antrobus, Peggy. 1989. "Gender Implications of the Debt Crisis." In George Beckford and Norman Girvan (eds.), *Development in Suspense: Selected Papers and Proceedings of the First Conference of Caribbean Economists.* Kingston: University of the West Indies.

Báez, Clara. 1984. *La Subordinación de la Mujer Dominicana en Cifras.* Santa Domingo: Dirección General de Promoción de la Mujer and International Research and Training Institute for the Advancement of Women (INSTRAW).

Blumberg, Rae L. 1985. *A Walk on the "WID" Side: Summary of Field Research on Women in Development in the Dominican Republic and Guatemala.* Washington, D.C.: Agency for International Development.

Bolles, A. Lynn. 1983. "Kitchens Hit by Priorities: Employed Working-Class Jamaican Women Confront the IMF." In June Nash and M. Patricia Fernandez Kelly (eds.), *Women, Men and the International Division of Labor.* Albany: State University of New York Press.

Boyd, Derick. 1988. "The Impact of Adjustment Policies on Vulnerable Groups: The Case of Jamaica, 1973–1985." In Giovanni A. Cornia, Richard Jolly, and F. Stewart (eds.), *Adjustment with a Human Face.* Vol. II. New York: UNICEF; Oxford: Clarendon Press.

Bray, David. 1984. "Economic Development, the Middle Class and International Migration in the Dominican Republic." *International Migration Review* 18 (2):217–236.

Catanzaro, Lorraine. 1986. "Women, Work and Consciousness: Export Processing in the Dominican Republic." M.A. thesis, Center for Latin American Studies, University of Florida.

Ceara, Miguel. 1987. *Situación Socioeconómica Actual y Su Repercusión en la Situación de la Madre y el Niño.* Santo Domingo: Instituto Techológico de Santo Domingo (INTEC) and UNICEF.

Chaney, Elsa. 1985. *Migration from the Caribbean Region: Determinants and Effects of Current Movements.* Washington, D.C.: Center for Immigration Policy and Refugee Assistance.

Cornia, Giovanni A. 1987. "Economic Decline and Human Welfare in the First Half of the 1980s." Pp. 11–47 in Giovanni A. Cornia, Richard Jolly, and F. Stewart (eds.), *Adjustment with a Human Face.* Vol. I. New York: UNICEF; Oxford: Clarendon Press.

———. 1987. "Adjustment at the Household Level: Potentials and Limitations of Survival Strategies." Pp. 90–104 in Giovanni A. Cornia, Richard Jolly, and F. Stewart (eds.), *Adjustment with a Human Face.* Vol. I. New York: UNICEF; Oxford: Clarendon Press.

Cornia, Giovanni A., and Francis Stewart. 1987. "Country Experience with Adjustment." Pp. 105–130 in Giovanni A. Cornia, Richard Jolly, and F. Stewart (eds.), *Adjustment with a Human Face.* Vol. I. New York: UNICEF; Oxford: Clarendon Press.

Davies, Omar, and Patricia Anderson. 1987. "The Impact of the Recession and Adjustment Policies on Poor Urban Women in Jamaica." Paper prepared for UNICEF. Kingston: Institute of Social and Economic Research, University of the West Indies.

Del Castillo, José, and Christopher Mitchell (eds.). 1987. *La Inmigración Dominicana en los Estados Unidos.* Santo Domingo: Universidad APEC (Asociación Pro Educación y Cultura).

Duarte, Isis. 1986. *Trabajadores Urbanos.* Santo Domingo: Editora Universitaria, UASD.

———. 1988. "Crisis, Familia y Participación Laboral de la Mujer en la República Dominicana." Paper presented at the Center for Latin American Studies Annual Conference, University of Florida.

ECLAC (Economic Commission for Latin America and the Caribbean) 1988. *Women in the Inter-Island Trade in Agricultural Produce in the Eastern Caribbean.* L. 465 (CRM 4/9). Trinidad: ECLAC.

Espinal, Rosario. 1988. *Torn Between Authoritarianism and Crisis-prone Democracy: The Dominican Labor Movement.* Notre Dame, Ind.: University of Notre Dame, Kellogg Institute, Working Paper #116.

French, Joan. 1987. "The CBI and Jamaica: Objectives and Impact." Report prepared for the Development Group for Alternative Policies. Washington, D.C.

Gomez, Carmen Julia, and Maria Gaton. 1987. "La Mujer Jefe de Hogar y la Vivienda." *Población y Desarrollo,* Ano VI, Número 19:3–22.

Grasmuck, Sherri. 1985. "The Consequences of Dominican Urban Outmigration for National Development: The Case of Santiago." In Steven E. Sanderson (ed.), *The Americas in the New International Division of Labor.* New York: Holmes and Meier.

Grasmuck, Sherri, and Patricia Pessar. 1991.*Between Two Islands: Dominican International Migration.* Berkeley: University of California Press.

Gurak, Douglas, and Mary Kritz. 1982. "Dominican and Colombian Women in New York City." *Migration Today* 10 (3/4):15–21.

———. 1985. "The Caribbean Communities in the United States." *Migration Today* 13 (2):6–12.

———. 1987. "Los Dominicanos en los Estados Unidos." Pp. 151–184 in José Del Castillo and Christopher Mitchell (eds.), *La Inmigración Dominicana en los Estados Unidos.* Santo Domingo: Universidad APEC.

Henry, Ralph. 1988. "Jobs, Gender and Development Strategy in the Commonwealth Caribbean." In Patricia Mohammed and Catherine Shepherd (eds.), *Gender in Caribbean Development.* Kingston: University of the West Indies, Women and Development Studies Project.

Jelin, Elizabeth (ed.). 1987. *Ciudadanía e Indentidad: Las Mujeres en los Movimientos Sociales Latino-Americanos.* Geneva: United Nations Research Institute for Social Development (UNRISD).

Joekes, Susan. 1987. Employment in Industrial Free Zones in the Dominican Republic: A Report with Recommendations for Improved Worker Services. Washington, D.C.: International Center for Research on Women. Prepared for U.S. Agency for International Development (USAID)/Dominican Republic.

Leslie, Joanne, Margaret Lycette, and Mayra Buvinic. 1986. "Weathering Economic Crises: The Crucial Role of Women in Health." Washington, D.C.: International Center for Research on Women.

Miller, Barbara, and Carl Stone. 1985. "The Low-Income Household Expenditure Survey: Description and Analysis." Syracuse, N.Y.: Syracuse University, Metropolitan Studies Program, Jamaica Tax Structure Examination Project, Staff Paper No. 25.

Mintz, Sidney. 1971. "The Caribbean as a Socio-Cultural Area." Pp. 17–46 in Michael Horowitz (ed.), *Peoples and Cultures of the Caribbean.* New York: The Natural History Press.

Mones, Belkis, and Lydia Grant. 1987. "Agricultural Development, the Economic Crisis, and Rural Women in the Dominican Republic." Pp. 35–50 in Carmen D. Deere and Magdalena Leon (eds.), *Rural Women and State Policy: Feminist Perspectives on Latin American Agricultural Development.* Boulder, Colo.: Westview Press.

Musgrove, Philip. 1987. "The Economic Crisis and Its Impact on Health and Health Care in Latin America and the Caribbean." *International Journal of Health Services* 17 (3):411–441.

Nelson, Joan. 1990. "The Politics of Adjustment in Small Democracies: Costa Rica, Jamaica and the Dominican Republic." In J. Nelson (ed.), *Economic Crisis and Policy Choice.* Princeton: Princeton University Press.

Pastor, Robert. 1989. "Migration and Development in the Caribbean Basin: Implications and Recommendations for Policy." Washington, D.C.: Commission for the Study of International Migration and Cooperative Economic Development, Working Paper No. 7.

Pastor, Robert (ed.). 1985. *Migration and Development in the Caribbean: The Unexplored Connection.* Boulder, Colo.: Westview Press.

Pessar, Patricia. 1986. "The Role of Gender in Dominican Settlement in the United States." In J. Nash and H. Safa (eds.), *Women and Change in Latin America.* South Hadley, Mass.: Bergin and Garvey Publishers.

PREALC (Programa Regional de Empleo para América Latina y el Caribe). 1983. "Empleo y Política Económica de Corto Plazo." Santo Domingo: Memorandum preparado para ONAPLAN (Oficina Nacional de Planificación). Working draft.

Ramirez, Nelson, Isis Duarte, and Carmen Gomez. 1986. *Población y Salud en República Dominicana.* Boletin del Instituto de Estudios de la Población, No. 16.

Ramirez, Nelson, Isidoro Santana, Francisco de Moya, and Pablo Tactuk. 1988. *República Dominicana: Población y Desarrollo 1950–1985.* San José, Costa Rica: Centro Latinoamericano de Demografía (CELADE).

Reyes, Quintina. 1987. "Comparative Study of Dominican Women Workers in Domestic and Free Trade Zone Industries." M.A. thesis, Center for Latin American Studies, University of Florida.

Ricourt, Milagros. 1986. "Free Trade Zones, Development and Female Labor in the Dominican Republic." M.A. thesis, Center for Latin American Studies, University of Florida.

Safa, Helen. 1987. "Urbanization, The Informal Economy and State Policy in Latin America." In Michael P. Smith and J. R. Feagin (eds.), *The Capitalist City: Global Restructuring and Community Politics.* New York: Basil Blackwell.

———. "Women and Industrialization in the Caribbean." In J. Parpart and S. Stichter (eds.), *Women, Employment and the Family in the International Division of Labor.* London: Macmillan (forthcoming).

Santana, Isidoro (with Antonio Tapies). 1985. *Tendencias Recientes y Perspectivas de la Situación Ocupacional en República Dominicana.* Boletin del Instituto de Estudios de Población, Jan.-Mar.

Standing, Guy. 1989. "Global Feminization Through Flexible Labor." *World Development* 17 (7):1077–1096.

Vega, Bernardo. 1988. *El Ajuste de la Economía Dominicana (1982–1986) dentro de la Crisis Financiera Latinoamericana.* Santo Domingo: Fundación Cultural Dominicana.

Walton, John. 1989. "Debt, Protest, and the State in Latin America." In Susan Eckstein (ed.), *Power and Popular Protest.* Berkeley: University of California Press.

Whiteford, Linda. Forthcoming. "Child and Maternal Health and International Economic Policies." *Social Science and Medicine.*

World Bank. 1982. *The World Development Report 1982.* Washington, D.C.: World Bank.

———. 1985. Dominican Republic: Economic Prospects and Policies to Renew Growth. Washington, D.C.: World Bank.

———. 1987. *The World Development Report 1987.* Washington, D.C.: World Bank.

———. 1988–1989. *World Debt Tables.* Vol. 2. Washington, D.C.: World Bank.

———. 1989. *The World Development Report 1989.* Washington, D.C.: World Bank.

4

The Mexican Debt Crisis: Restructuring the Economy & the Household

LOURDES BENERÍA

In your countries those who own the banks are getting richer with our debt while we are getting poorer and poorer.

—Doña A, owner of a small vegetable shop in
Mexico City, and mother of three children

The 1980s will be remembered as the decade in which the foreign debt crisis and the policies that were followed to deal with it had devastating effects on the lives of millions of people in the Third World. In many countries, after some decades of economic growth, the 1970s already represented a turning point in what had been taken to be a gradual, even if slow, path to development. The 1980s saw instead a desolated picture of negative growth and rapidly declining living conditions, raising questions about the ability of many social groups, and not exclusively the poorest, to survive under minimal subsistence standards. The structural adjustment that has accompanied the crisis has intensified the chronic problems of labor absorption by the modern sector, which cannot generate the employment necessary to provide an adequate standard of living for a large proportion of the population.

Focusing on the case of Mexico, this chapter examines the set of structural adjustment policies (SAP) that have been implemented since 1982 to deal with the debt crisis, their impact on the process of economic restructuring as well as on income distribution and living standards, and on the dynamics generated at the level of the household in order to deal with these changes.

One of the questions often posed, in Mexico and elsewhere, is how the poor survive the crisis. Given the already precarious conditions under which the poorest sectors of the population lived before the crisis erupted, how have they managed to cope with the new situation? What are their "survival strategies," or do the poor have any real choice between those strategies?[1] Have collective strategies to deal with daily survival emerged? How is the crisis lived within a specific household, and how does it affect different household members? Does it have a differentiated impact by gender and age? How has it affected women? What implications for action and policy do the answers to these questions suggest? These were the initial concerns behind the research done for this chapter during the summer of 1988.

The chapter has two parts. The first briefly summarizes the main aspects of Mexico's adjustment policies designed to deal with the debt crisis, with particular emphasis given to policies that have had an impact on the distribution of resources and living standards. The second part deals more specifically with the coping mechanisms that have been followed at the household level. The empirical data used for this analysis provide the basis for my main argument, namely, that the profound restructuring of the Mexican economy has been accompanied by a parallel reorganization of daily life in the area of reproductive as well as productive activities, with specific gender dimensions that make the distribution of the burden of survival among household members unequal.

DEBT AND "*MODERNIZACIÓN*"

The most salient facts about the Mexican debt crisis are well known: an outstanding debt of $108 billion in 1989, seven years after its severity surfaced in the summer of 1982 when the IMF and the U.S. government "rescued" Mexico from international insolvency with loans of $3.5 and $1.8 billion, respectively; the second largest debt in Latin America after Brazil; one of the heaviest long-term debt-service ratios taken as a percentage of exports; a burden of debt payments for foreign and domestic debt that, on the average, has represented close to 60 percent of the federal budget; and a declining economic performance that saw a decrease of 3.1 percent in real GNP during the 1982–1988 period and a debt/GNP ratio of over 95.

Yet Mexico is viewed by the U.S. government and the international financial community as a showcase of debt management and restructuring. It is for these reasons that it was the first country to benefit from debt reduction and renegotiation through an agreement announced in July 1989 as a result of the Brady initiative. To back up this program of debt reduction, Mexico received new loans of $3.6 and $1.5 billion from the IMF and the World Bank, respectively, during the spring of 1989. By the time the final results of negotiations were announced in February 1990, the debt had been reduced to $80 billion, the first to be completed under the Brady Plan.

This expression of support on the part of the international financial community represents the seal of approval for the very orthodox adjustment policies initiated with the August 1982 "rescue" and that continue up to the present time. These IMF-type adjustment policies also launched Mexico into a process of economic restructuring that has had a profound effect on Mexico's economic landscape. The key features in this process, typical of most SAP, can be summarized as follows:[2]

1. A process of devaluation of the peso throughout the period, which resulted in its depreciation from 23 pesos to $1.00 in the summer of 1982 to 2,500 pesos in the summer of 1989. The price increases that followed resulted in a rapid deterioration of real wages; during the 1981–1988 period, the urban real minimum wage decreased by 46.4 percent, the largest decrease (together with Ecuador) in Latin America during that period (CEPAL 1990).

2. An austerity program that began with drastic cuts in government spending and subsidies and that decreased the amount and quality of government services to severe limits. These cuts in basic areas such as health, education, and social security resulted in unemployment among previously well-paid government employees, with its corresponding impact on other sectors. For those employed, real wages over the period fell to unprecedented low levels. Such was the case for teachers, over half a million of whom joined a wildcat strike in April of 1989 while asking for a 100-percent wage increase.

3. A process of economic restructuring that includes privatization of state-controlled firms, reduction of public investment, trade liberalization, the promotion of foreign investment, and an aggressive policy of export promotion as a means of financing the debt. This is what is often referred to in Mexico as *modernización,* a process very much supported by Salinas de Gortari, as current president of Mexico and as secretary of the Department of Planning and Budget (SPP) under the previous presidency of Miguel de la Madrid. Privatization has been intended to increase productivity and competitiveness through the economy as a result of the new emphasis on "rationalization" and reorganization of the public sector, the introduction and update of modern technologies in the public and private sectors, and the high priority given to the rationality of the market—all of it very much along the orthodox IMF model of SAP.

This process initiated a new period for the Mexican economy following a neoliberal model that is similar to that followed by other countries. Debt-related adjustment policies have been used to shift Mexican capitalism to a new stage of higher integration with the global economy, including the opening of doors to international trade and finance and setting the stage for Mexico's participation in the proposed North American Free Trade Association. As Rendón and Salas (1988) have argued, these changes amount to a shift from a model of accumulation based on the domestic market and import substitution to one oriented toward the international market. They also amount to a major shift in Mexico's orientation toward the United States, with a profound impact on Mexico's foreign policy.

Given that exports have increased and that Mexico has faithfully kept up with debt interest payments, together with the orthodoxy with which the IMF-style adjustment policies have been followed, Mexico is viewed as the model that other countries should follow to deal with their own debt crisis. As Martin Feldstein (1987) put it at a conference on world economic restructuring held in Mexico City in 1987, "current changes in Mexico are part of a process of economic restructuring that will modify and wake up the entire world."

THE SOCIAL COSTS OF ADJUSTMENT

As observed in other countries as well, these policies have been implemented at high costs and devastating consequences for a large proportion of the Mexican population. Rising unemployment, price increases, the reduction of services, and the reorientation of the economy away from the domestic market have resulted in a persistent deterioration of living standards, particularly for those whose living depends on wages and salaries and on casual earnings. This is what some authors have referred to as the "crushing of labor" as the relative share of GNP going to labor fell drastically over the decade.[3] The disparity between price and salary increases had an impact on most social classes, as we will see below, although it is obvious that the poor have been the most affected, given that their very subsistence was threatened.

To illustrate, according to a study released in August 1988, a standardized basket of twenty-eight products considered absolutely indispensable for survival (*Canasta Obrera Indispensable* or COI) was estimated to cost 12,924 pesos per person daily, almost 5,000 pesos above the daily minimum wage.[4] Many poor households, of course, did not even have anybody earning a minimum wage—their survival depending upon the pooling of income among different household members.

To be sure, severe problems of poverty existed in Mexico before the debt crisis erupted. The poor have traditionally included peasant and agricultural workers as well as urban households outside of the formal economy (Lustig 1987; Benería and Roldán 1987). It is well known that, despite its relatively good economic performance during the post–World War II decades, Mexico maintained a very skewed distribution of income and resources, which often resulted in welfare indicators below those of other countries with a similar per capita income. This has been the case for health, nutrition, and education as well as housing (Lustig 1987).

All indications seem to suggest that the redistribution of resources generated by the debt crisis and the implementation of SAP intensified these inequalities. In particular, the diminishing proportion of income going to labor and the drastic cuts in government expenditures contributed to this trend.[5] As the modernization process and cost reduction policies to meet international competition continued, the pressure to reduce real wages and weaken labor organizations intensified. This affected precisely a sector of the working population that previously had enjoyed relatively high wages and stable employment, namely, the stable working class and middle class, whose relative position deteriorated over the decade.

Income distribution seems to have deteriorated overall. Rudiger Dornbusch (1988), for example, has stated that "there is little doubt that distribution has worsened over the 1980s." Official statistics for 1977 show that the richest 20 percent of the population controlled 54.4 percent of the income, whereas the poorest 20 percent received only 2.9 percent; more recent private surveys suggest that the tendency has been toward higher inequality (Quick 1989). At the same time, some sectors of the business class benefited considerably from the economic changes associated with the restructuring of the economy, particularly those connected with the export sector, the internationalization of the Mexican economy, and the deregulation of economic activity. The financial sector has been one of these sectors. Thus the Mexican stock exchange, like others in many countries during the period, had been booming previous to the Wall Street crisis of October 19, 1987. Brokerage houses (*casas de bolsa*) reported net profits as high as 88.4 percent of capital in 1987 and an average of 53.1 percent for the 1986–1988 period (Lissakers and Zamora 1989).

For some sectors of the population, drastic reductions in living standards have been quite well documented. However, the details of this reduction are still a matter of controversy. Lustig (1987:245), for example, had argued that, regarding basic food consumption, "it is possible to say that the crisis has not resulted in problems of food availability, nor has it resulted in a clear deterioration of the average daily diet." Yet, as Lustig herself also points out, average aggregate figures can be very misleading. All indications suggest that, at least for the poor, the decrease in food consumption during the decade was drastic.

Social indicators also point toward diminishing health and educational standards as well as toward a deterioration of the quality of life—as suggested by an increase in the crime rate and by the dramatic deterioration of public transportation problems and pollution standards (Lustig 1987; Rohter 1989). In addition, some negative consequences of economic restructuring have been felt with particular intensity in specific areas and sectors, as illustrated by the retrenchment in steel towns affected by government divestiture and the pressure of "modernization."[6]

It is no wonder, therefore, that many of these changes resulted in a progressively more open public discontent and generated also drastic political changes. The appearance of Cardenismo as a serious threat to the governing party in the 1988 elections is an illustration. Cardenismo responded to that discontent and to the class recomposition taking place in Mexican society and that was parallel to similar changes in other countries (Cypher 1988). The political significance of these changes as a potential shift to the left was not underestimated at the time and explains the continuous and strong U.S. interest in Mexico as an economic and political partner and as a model for handling the debt. In the next section, I illustrate in more detail the effects of SAP and their corresponding social costs at the level of the household.

A SAMPLE OF MEXICO CITY HOUSEHOLDS

The research on which the following analysis is based was carried out in Mexico City in the summer of 1988. In addition to posing the questions listed earlier in this chapter, the study responded to a concrete interest: How had some of the households that we had visited during a study of industrial homework in 1981–1982 (Benería and Roldán 1987) survived under the severe burden of the crisis? Fieldwork began at the time when many Mexicans were still questioning the results of the presidential election in which Carlos Salinas de Gortari had been declared the winner. The political truce between government, business, and workers created by the pre-1988 election wage-and-price freeze (*Pacto de Solidaridad*) was starting to wear thin, and Mexicans seemed to be caught between the massive demonstrations in which Cuautémoc Cárdenas became the central figure/symbol of the opposition and the expectations created by the new presidential term.

The empirical analysis in the chapter is based on interviews with members of a nonrandom sample of 55 households scattered in different areas of Mexico City.[7] Generalizations from this sample should be viewed

TABLE 4.1   1988 Income Categories (in Mexican pesos)

Category	Mean Income	Percent of Households	Average Household Size	Average Rent/Mean Income
1. Extreme poverty	114,475[a]	38.2	6.0	.31
2. Subsistence	210,750	14.6	6.3	.12
3. Poor	299,000	27.3	5.8	.19
4. Lower middle class	626,600	9.1	4.6	.29
5. Middle class	1,116,666	10.9	5.0	.12
Sample	338,712	100.0	5.7	.22

The breakdown in income categories was established as follows:

	Income range
1. Extreme poverty: below COI[b]	< 193,999
2. Subsistence: COI-COB estimate[c]	194,000–224,999
3. Poor but adequate income	225,000–499,999
5. Middle class	> 1,000,000

[a]2,300 pesos to US$1 (summer 1988).
[b]COI—*Canasta Obrera Indispensable* (minimum living basket of goods).
[c]COB—*Canasta Obrera Básica* (basic basket of goods).

with caution. However, the case study is illustrative of the type of responses generated by the crisis among urban households, and its findings are quite similar to those reported by other researchers in Latin America (Moser 1989; González de la Rocha 1986). The interviews, which took place, with only two exceptions, within the homes of those interviewed, were carried out in a variety of *colonias* or neighborhoods.[8] In most cases, the questions were answered by women—usually by the housewife/mother but also by others such as a grandmother, sisters, and daughters—although, in the few cases in which the husband/father was present, he often took an active role in the exchange.

The average household size in the sample was 5.72, slightly lower than that reported by studies carried out in the early 1980s (Benería and Roldán 1987). Variations by income category are reported in Table 4.1 and suggest a negative correlation between household size and income. Nuclear family households represented the large majority in the sample, with only 12.7 classified as extended families, and 14.5 percent headed by women. Average biweekly income was 338,712 Mexican pesos or about US$147. As expected, practically all households had more than one income earner—the average being 2.3—and 50.3 percent of those working for an income did so in some form or other in the informal sector.

Table 4.1 includes a breakdown of households according to income categories that were estimated to represent: (1) extreme poverty, (2)

TABLE 4.2   1988 Consumption Indicators by Income Category (percent of households)

Income Category	Car	TV	Radio	Refrig.	Stove[a]	Sewing Machine	Washing Machine	Type-writer	Phone
1.	15	85	90	55	65	45	40	50	10
2.	25	75	100	37	75	50	25	37	12
3.	20	100	80	67	80	53	46	60	27
4.	80	100	100	100	100	60	60	80	80
5.	100	100	100	100	100	67	50	100	67
Total	33.3	90.7	90.7	64.8	77.7	51.8	42.5	59.2	27.7

[a]Refers to large stove with oven.

subsistence, (3) poor but with basic needs covered, (4) lower middle-class range, and (5) middle-class standards. The majority of households in the sample were poor, with the largest proportion classified within the ranges of extreme poverty or bare subsistence levels. A similar picture emerges from data on housing: The great majority of the households were living in very poor housing, with the largest proportion (46.3 percent) living in dwellings with tin roofs and tenements under very precarious conditions, 24.1 percent in "poor but adequate" dwellings, and the rest (close to 30 percent) in apartments and residential homes.

Similarly, Table 4.2 presents a breakdown of consumption indicators by income categories, which shows that the possession of telephone and car was the most visible sign of a middle-class standard. On the other hand, a high proportion of poor households owned radio and TV sets, even though, as will be seen below, the crisis had made many of them useless for lack of repair.

HOW HOUSEHOLDS COPE

The effects of the crisis were felt strongly by all households included in the sample, although there were differences across income levels. "Great difficulties" in making ends meet were reported by the great majority (over 80 percent) of the poor and lower middle class and by almost 50 percent of the middle-class households, with drastic adjustments made in their budgets and consumption habits. Even those that did not fall in this category reported that they had "some difficulties" and had made "important adjustments" in their daily expenses. Unemployment, housing, and debt were also among the problems causing great difficulties, even though the proportion of households mentioning them were significantly lower. On the other hand, unemployment and debt were reported by households in all income categories as having caused "some difficulties"—the proportion ranging between 17 and 20 percent for unemployment and between 33 and 62 percent for debt. Belt-tightening, therefore, has been felt deeply across households in different socioeconomic categories.

Interestingly enough, very few households complained about the availability of food or other basic goods. Only in a few cases there was mention of occasional difficulties finding some products in the market. During the time of fieldwork, long and tense lines developed in some *colonias* in front of shops that distributed government-subsidized food (*Canasta Básica*) at lower prices.[9] However, the same products for which women stood in line were readily available, often in the same shop, although at higher prices. The "great difficulties" mentioned in many households therefore were not caused by food scarcity or deficiency in distribution but by insufficient income to buy it. The problems implied were clearly summarized by a 23-year-old energetic mother: "When our income can't pay for what I need to buy every day, I feel desperate and I ask myself whether we can survive this situation." As the mother of four children and housewife of a household classified under "extreme poverty," the situation she was referring to actually meant that there were no chairs in the house for the interviewers to sit, the children did not wear shoes, the roof leaked, the floor was not paved, the inside walls were extremely dirty by any standard, the house had only three small rooms (kitchen, dining room, and a bedroom) while some extra space, with very poor conditions, was rented to another large family for very little money. Job insecurity for the father and only occasional paid work for the mother were a constant source of anxiety and even despair. Yet, despair was not exclusive to extremely poor households. Tension and anguish about making ends meet was found among better-off households as well. In all cases, the depth of the crisis was felt in a way that escaped statistics and analytical quantification.

What kind of adjustments have been made to deal with this situation? One of the overwhelming impressions during fieldwork came from the observation that, in the absence of a welfare state and of collective efforts in daily survival at the neighborhood and community level,[10] it was at the level of the household where the fierce struggle was centered. The majority of households *were* surviving, even if at a very high cost. In our sample there were, in fact, two types of families. A small proportion (just over 5 percent of the total) were practically disintegrating under what seemed to be insurmountable problems: unemployment, inability to generate the income necessary for bare survival, domestic violence, housing deficiencies, absence of any community support, abandonment, and so on. These were cases often associated with a drunken husband, prostitution, drugs, or some other forms of criminal behavior; the economic crisis is likely to have intensified rather than created these problems.

The large majority of households, however, had reorganized their lives to cope with the problems brought about by the crisis and were succeeding in various degrees. In what follows, the different coping mechanisms observed are classified under three basic categories: labor market adjustments, budget changes, and restructuring of daily life.

Labor Market Adjustments

A common response to the crisis was the increase in the number of household members participating in the labor market in order to contribute to family income. Two groups in our sample were the most affected by this response. One was the population of teenagers who had to discontinue their education in order to earn an income, particularly by not moving to higher levels of schooling or by reducing it to evening classes. This was found to be common among teenagers finishing secondary education in public schools. Given the duration of the crisis, interruptions in schooling are likely to be permanent, therefore leaving a lasting negative impact on the educational and skill levels of the population.

Women constitute the second group affected; their initially lower involvement in the labor force makes them part of the labor pool on which the household can rely at a time of crisis. Although increased participation in paid activities was typically observed among women without children, mothers with male partners were the last family members to engage in paid work and have remained at home to a relatively high degree (34 percent in our sample).[11] Still, the large majority, that is, 66 percent of the mothers with a male partner in the sample, earned some income, two-thirds of them working in the informal sector either continuously or sporadically and under the poor working conditions associated with this sector. The other third had jobs in the formal sector, but this was confined particularly to middle-class women.

The importance of the informal sector for women's earnings was therefore obvious and due to at least two reasons. First, it was difficult for poor women to find employment with any degree of job security. Second, women tended to prefer work that can be done either in the home (as in the case of industrial homework) or in the surrounding community in order to better integrate it with reproductive activities. This preference, however, was highly determined by the lack of alternatives to deal with child care and domestic work because it confined their ability to earn an income to these activities.

The increase in women's participation in paid work as a result of the crisis in Mexico and elsewhere has also been pointed out by other studies, which have also underlined the corresponding reduction of time dedicated to domestic activities and leisure and the intensification of their work (Oliveira 1988; Moser 1989; Safa and Antrobus, this volume; Pérez-Alemán, this volume; and Tripp, this volume). That this increase was found to be smaller, at least in the Mexican case, among mothers with a husband or a male partner is not surprising. There seemed to be three main reasons for this. One was the prevalent division of labor that assigned to the mother the primary task of child care and domestic work, that is, the main responsibility for reproductive activities. This division of labor, with the notion that the mother should stay at home, particularly if children are small, is still deeply ingrained in the Mexican family and reinforced by the lack of day-care facilities. Related to this was the still rather prevalent opposition of the husband or male companion to the mother's paid work. This explains, for example, the case of some women who, despite serious financial difficulties and their desire to earn an income, were not in the paid labor force because the husband "would be humiliated" or "would not let her work outside of the home." Finally, women tend to be the least schooled family members, a fact that makes them less able to find formal employment requiring even a minimum of literacy skills.

A different labor-market strategy was found among those who worked overtime or had more than one job. This normally involved the more "established" workers in the formal sector as, for example, nurses and carpenters and other construction workers. For unskilled workers, the precariousness of employment conditions made it difficult to find extra work in the formal market. On the other hand, some skilled workers had become self-employed; given the possibility to increase prices for their services, they were among those who could cope best with the crisis.

A clear conclusion to be drawn from this information is that, despite the effort at increasing the participation of diverse family members in paid production, there remained a good proportion of untapped labor that was underemployed or working at the margins, including men and women of all ages that could not find a full-time job and others looking for better job opportunities and working conditions. One of the consequences of the crisis has been that the absorption by the informal sector of this labor reserve has taken place under increasingly deteriorating conditions (Roberts, forthcoming). In addition, the debt crisis intensified the problem of labor absorption, thereby further facilitating the process of labor flexibilization, a very important component in Mexico's modern-. ization.

Budget Changes

It is probably no exaggeration to say that the austerity programs altered the budgets of practically all Mexican households. Budget adjustments gradually turned drastic for a large proportion of the population. In our sample, 69.4 percent of the households regularly bought less food, clothing, shoes, and other daily expenses such as transportation, drinks, and snacks than during the pre-1982 period. What exactly had been cut, however, varied according to household income and class background. Thus, although practically all households had curtailed meat consumption, poor families had eliminated it altogether from their diet. Similarly, the poor had completely eliminated other products, such as canned foods and a rather large number of fruits and basic foods, such as milk, unless they were subsidized.[12] Most poor households were no longer buying *new* clothes and shoes nor could they afford to replace any household equipment that, in some cases, had been sold for cash.

Middle-class families had a thicker cushion to start with. Their budget cuts concentrated primarily on nonessential goods such as olives and wines, photography-related expenses, gifts, domestic service, clothing, trips, particularly trips abroad, and parties. For many, this appeared as a shift down the social ladder that for some households was a source of great anxiety.

For households under extreme poverty or at subsistence levels, the pressure to concentrate on the most urgent needs implied a continuous neglect of other expenses such as home upkeep. Unpainted walls, unpaved floors, leaking roofs, and broken tables and chairs were a common sight not just in the poorest homes but in others that had regularly taken care of these tasks. We found several homes with a variety of broken household items (refrigerators, TV sets, washing machines, radios, mixers) that could not be used because repairs were not affordable. As one mother with five school-age children put it, "our priority is to buy the minimum of school supplies that we can afford and to postpone repairs." This implies that the infrastructure of households was deteriorating, leading to an underestimation of the negative impact of the crisis. Likewise, some households had sold their consumer durables and had recurred to indebtedness as the only means to obtain urgently needed cash.

Our data also suggest that the crisis has had an effect on fertility rates; 46.7 percent of the families in the sample had decided either to stop or to postpone having children during the 1982–1988 period. Perhaps as a result, and in comparison with the fieldwork carried out in 1981–1982, women were much more open to talk about birth control and family planning. Although it is difficult to sort out the effects of the crisis in this respect from those resulting from longer-term fertility trends, its connection with the economic crisis was often pointed out. Among poor women, the most common form of birth control was the *operación* or tying of the tubes, often performed under stress after a birth and, in some cases, without consultation with the husband or male companion.

The Restructuring of Daily Life

Budget adjustments had generated many changes in the way households organized themselves and lived their daily lives. The following changes were typical among these readjustments.

Changes in Purchasing Habits. Close to 73 percent of the households in our sample stated that they were shopping in cheaper markets, most of them regularly. For poor families, this often meant buying daily supplies from street vendors whose products tend to be of lower quality than those in regular shops. The tightness of budgets and the difficulties of storing food—such as with cases of unrepaired refrigerators—also reinforced this tendency; in such cases only small quantities can be bought at a time, therefore making shopping a daily chore, with the corresponding intensification of time spent on this aspect of domestic work. Among households that could afford weekly shopping, trips to the large central market were common in order to obtain better food at lower prices. Given the size of Mexico City, these trips could be done only with a car or by organizing several family members to help with the shopping, usually on Saturdays; the latter required a planning effort that only a few households could manage.

For middle-class families, the search for lower prices often meant shopping in markets away from their neighborhoods. In some cases, it also meant the coordination of shopping with other family members, including the use of extended family networks. A young middle-class woman who had married in 1985 explained, "my aunts know where the bargains are; I see them and my mother more than I ever did." In any case, the greater availability of private transportation, and also of cash, for middle-class families made it more possible for them to benefit from shopping in large quantities and in the less expensive markets outside of their communities.

Intensification of Domestic Work. The crisis had resulted in an increase in the number and often length of activities that make up domestic work—from daily shopping due to more restrictive budgets, to the need for increased cleaning and tidying when spaces are reduced, to more cooking, fixing, mending, and sewing at home. Although all family members participate in these tasks, a large proportion of this work fell upon women, regardless of whether they were also working in the labor market or not. Thus, in 68.8 percent of the households in which the crisis had generated changes in domestic work, it was perceived that women's work had increased. For some middle-class housewives, this was accompanied by a reduction in domestic help, with the subsequent perception of isolation, loss of social status, and downward social mobility. The intensification of work for women was therefore a significant factor in their daily life, an aspect still in need of quantification.

For working daughters, the pressure to participate in domestic work had contributed to what seemed to be a rising consciousness regarding a gender-based asymmetry in the division of labor, thus creating new tensions between them and, in particular, their brothers. Thus, in 53.1 percent of the households in which the crisis had generated changes in domestic work, it was felt that daughters had to help more.[13] Older daughters in particular felt this burden most intensely; even when they held a full-time job, they were expected to take a great deal of responsibility in the home—responsibility not expected from their older brothers or fathers. In comparison with their mothers, the daughters' higher level of skill made them more likely candidates for the labor market and raised expectations regarding their contribution to household income ("they expect that I can solve all their problems"). This "oldest daughter syndrome" resulted in a few bitter complaints by some daughters, leading to "defensive" strategies on their part, such as an early marriage or threats of migration.

In the case of households headed by women, the burden on the mother (or grandmother) depended on the age and composition of other family members: Although the burden could be heavy if children were small, it was alleviated when they, and particularly daughters, were old enough to contribute some income and share responsibilities. The absence of an adult male income in any case explains why all women who headed a household in our sample were engaged in paid work; the choice between work at home and work in the market was even less possible in their case.

Changes in Social Life. A different type of adjustment resulted from the need to save on transportation and other daily expenses. Thus, almost 51 percent of the households in our sample had decreased or eliminated trips to visit relatives and friends and attendance at family parties and religious holidays. This applied to intracity visits as well as to traditional annual or semiannual trips to other parts of Mexico, such as for those associated with Christmas and other religious holidays, vacations, and other family gatherings. Recent immigrants to Mexico City complained bitterly of their inability to return to their hometowns "as they were used to before the crisis." Others pointed out that, as new immigrants to Mexico City, they had not been able to fulfill the promises of remittances to their aging parents and other family members. For some sectors of the middle class, the curtailment of travel abroad as an important reduction in their expenses represented a drastic change in their living standards and also a source of bitter complaints.

Social life had also been affected by the reduction or elimination of expenses associated with parties and other social activities. The traditional and important "fiesta" organized for the fifteenth birthday of daughters in Mexico could no longer be afforded by many families. In one neighborhood, at least one of the churches had begun to organize parties to honor several 15-year-olds at the same time. This was, in fact, one of the few coping mechanisms encountered that represented a semicollective form of dealing with the crisis. Finally, the need to reduce expenses had changed the way different household members organized leisure time. For example, some parents of teenagers pointed out that, on Sundays, they no longer went anywhere outside of their neighborhood ("weekend movies have been cut to a minimum") and preferred to let their children go out.

THE PRIVATIZATION OF SURVIVAL
AND THE FAMILY

During the time of our fieldwork, the Mexico City daily *El Excelsior* published an article emphasizing the role of the Mexican family as the main pillar in the effort dealing with the crisis. Our study confirms this thesis. The "culture of ingenuity" around which daily life was being organized for daily survival was indeed centered in the family. There had been a major gathering of forces at the household level together with a *privatization* of the struggle; in the absence of a welfare state and in the face of decreasing governmental services and subsidies, the family had become the only source of support and of alternatives for survival. Its role in this respect is best understood as being facilitated by the traditionally close Mexican family ties; although it may have parallels in other Latin American countries, it should not be generalized to other culturally specific contexts.

An initial question in our research was to investigate the extent to which some collective efforts had been developed, as had been the case with Peru's *comedores populares,* or soup kitchen, and with the *olla común,* or common pot, in Bolivia and Chile (Sara-Lafosse 1986; Cornia, Jolly, and Stewart 1987). Despite the fact that much collective organizing at other levels had developed in Mexico City and elsewhere,[14] the virtual absence of such efforts *at the level of daily life* provided a sharp contrast. The private household, therefore, had been left facing the crisis alone, with some help received only from the extended family. However, given the nuclear character of the urban household in Mexico City, this help was found to be minimal—the most common in our sample being the grandmother's help in domestic work and child care so as to allow the mother to participate in paid work.

To be sure, this predominantly private struggle for survival was dev-astating for the households that were disintegrating. However, for the large majority, the gathering of forces and pooling of resources repre-sented a heroic effort, described by some of our interviewees as resulting from greater family unity ("we are more united now because we can't risk fighting among ourselves") and ability to plan ("we have to plan everything and our level of communication has increased"). No family member could evade this effort, particularly in poor households. This is not to say that tensions did not develop within the family but that a conscious effort was made to avoid them in order to deal with the most pressing issues.

Tensions in fact *did* develop because this unity and resourcefulness came at a cost and the burden of survival was distributed unequally. First, the continuous struggle of each household seemed to be accom-panied by mistrust and hostility toward outsiders. Thus, interviewees often complained about the behavior of their neighbors and community members ("They stole chickens from our backyard" or "we cannot rely on them for help"). A question inquiring about the extent to which the neighborhood organized around common needs often was met with a smile and a sarcastic comment about the absence of such an effort. Likewise, feelings of frustration were often expressed as aggression toward outsiders ("when I am upset, I don't want to take it out on my sister, so I push people when I get on the bus").

Second, tensions resulted from the unequal distribution of the burden of survival among family members. Although all household members had to mobilize their effort as a result of the crisis, women had been partic-ularly affected due to their increased participation in the labor market and the intensification of domestic work. As shown above, this had affected women of all ages and had made gender asymmetries within the household more visible.

In addition, the crisis did not visibly change previous inequalities in income pooling and intrahousehold distribution of resources; although this was not the focus of our research, we found no clear change in previous patterns by which women's income is totally used for household expenses while men's is pooled only partially (Benería and Roldán 1987). As in the earlier study, many women received an allowance from their husbands or male companions, often without knowing the men's total earnings. When the allowance was viewed as very small, or when it was sporadic and uncertain, it tended to be a source of bitterness and complaints. In households at the verge of collapse, the burden on the mother tended to be overwhelming; the usual problems of survival in these cases were intensified by the tensions generated by domestic violence, inability to meet the family's needs, and the awareness of sinking into a world of despair.

In sum, the crisis intensified the contradictory forces within the family. On the one hand, it was the only source of protection for all members; there was nowhere else to turn. The family was essential for survival, even for fun and social activity, for warmth, love, and protection. The degree to which these functions have been exercised in the midst of such difficulties is indeed moving. The household represents the locus of this survival—realized through the interdependency of its members. On the other hand, this should not be perceived as a romanticization of the family; the effort takes place within the context of a "forced" unity, a patriarchal family structure and other existing tensions, which are intensified by the sheer weight of the struggle as well as from its unequal distribution among family members. As the young married woman who reported seeing her mother and aunts more often as a result of the crisis put it, this family unity resulted out of need rather than out of choice (*por necesidad más que por gusto*). Likewise, this should not be understood as an "inevitable mechanical solidarity between members of poor families" (Wolf 1990). Our sample suggests that, first, family ties are being used by households across income categories and, second, *solidarity* is different from the *mutual dependency* among household members; it is the latter that gets intensified at a time of crisis. This dependency might best be represented by a model that includes ties of love and solidarity as well as bargaining, tensions, and conflicts among family members. The fact that the family might turn inward and behave aggressively toward outsiders underlines the negative aspects of the family, as emphasized by Barrett and McIntosh (1982) in *The Anti-Social Family*. However, the picture emerging from this family dynamics is best captured by a view of the family as contradictory and paradoxical.[15]

Some family tensions generated by the crisis might be at the root of future changes. For example, the pooling of work and income and, in particular, the responsibilities taken on by women might undermine some patriarchal privileges. As expressed by a man whose relative contribution to household income had been declining while that of his daughters and son increased, these changes might result in his loss of authority ("they no longer pay attention to me") and be at the root of bitter and unsuccessful complaints. The outcome of these tensions will depend on a variety of factors, including the length of the crisis.

CONCLUDING COMMENTS:
ADJUSTMENT, POLICIES, AND
TRANSFORMATIVE STRATEGIES

This chapter shows that the profound restructuring of the Mexican economy resulting from the debt crisis and subsequent SAP also forced the restructuring of daily life. The privatization of the economy has a parallel in the privatization of survival, which in Mexico City centered around the (mostly nuclear) household. Although the cycle of social (and class) reproduction was indeed shattered, most families have survived the crisis through a heroic effort in which all members have participated through new combinations of work for self-consumption and work for income. This increased the involvement of different household members in market work, but it also intensified work in reproductive activities, often resulting in an unequal distribution of the burden within the household. The irony of these "strategies" is that they made possible the continuation of adjustment policies imposed at enormous social costs.

Perhaps the most painful legacy of the past decade is that no alternatives to the IMF-type policies of adjustment have emerged. The Brady Plan of debt forgiveness and renegotiation might alleviate the debt burden of a handful of countries but is unlikely to change it significantly and to shift their development prospects. Even if Mexico can overcome the most severe consequences of SAP and embark on a new path of economic growth, the deterioration of living standards of the 1980s will not disappear easily while new SAP packages are being adopted in other countries. To be sure, a series of alternative proposals have emerged that suggest other adjustment paths aimed at overcoming the shortcomings of the orthodox model (ECA 1989; ECLA 1990). Some of them include a gender dimension as an integral part of the policies suggested (Commonwealth Secretariat 1990). How these general recommendations will be translated into concrete policies and changes signaling the beginning of a truly democratic and equitable development model remains the big challenge of the 1990s.

In the meantime, what actions can be recommended at the level of daily survival? What kind of "transformative strategies" (Elson, this volume) are likely to help in the fierce struggle under way for a large proportion of the population? A variety of actions have emerged from different countries and others could be recommended for the *short run*. The following are given as illustrations:

1. The implementation of national policies to counterbalance some of the most urgent problems generated by SAP. The Ecuadorian government, for example, has initiated a program to set up open markets, collective kitchens, and neighborhood stores that would provide goods at relatively lower prices, thereby alleviating problems created by inflation (Lind 1990). Such a program could build on the various efforts that have already been initiated at the local level.

2. The setting up of policies to redistribute productive resources, such as expansion of credit programs of medium and small firms, creation

of cooperatives, and self-help programs for peasants and small farms. Many of these policies can easily include a gender dimension specifically dealing with women.

3. A new set of tax policies to redistribute the burden of adjustment as part of a progressive tax reform.

4. An intensification of actions taken by political parties, unions, and other appropriate institutions that will exercise pressure toward establishing mechanisms to provide social services, such as child care, nutrition programs, health clinics, and training programs for different groups of workers.

5. The fostering of traditional self-help institutions and support mechanisms that, particularly in urban areas, might have been weakened by modernization, such as extended family networks and relations of *compadrazgo* (parent-godparent ties) that extend beyond the nuclear family.

6. The fostering of women's networks, many of which have begun or intensified their efforts to deal with crisis-related programs at the local and national levels.

Measures such as these will tend to alleviate the symptoms rather than deal with the roots of the debt problem. In the *long run,* they will only succeed if current trends in the flow of resources from the debtor to the creditor countries are reversed.

NOTES

This chapter has benefited from the work of a variety of people. I thank M. A. Díaz González for her research assistance and A. Bottum, E. Harber, and A. Lind for their help with computer work. My special thanks for W. Goldsmith, O. Hernández, and P. Olpadwala for their comments on the original draft.

1. As has been pointed out by other authors, the word "strategy" implies the possibility of choosing among alternatives. Yet, choices are very much reduced by the extreme scarcity of resources and precarious living conditions. In such cases, the expression "survival strategies" is therefore not very appropriate.

2. For more detail on these policies, see Benería 1991.

3. By 1982, this share represented 36 percent of GNP, down from 40 percent in 1987, and it declined further throughout the decade (Edel and Edel 1989).

4. The basket of 28 products was selected from a larger basket of 118 products or *Canasta Obrera Básica* (COB) considered to be basic for an adequate working-class standard of living (Uno Más Uno, August 8, 1988).

5. The proportion of total income going to wages and salaries diminished from 42 percent in 1982 to less than 30 percent in 1987 (Lustig 1988).

6. Such is the case with the cities of Monterrey and Moncloa in the northeast, which were rapidly affected negatively by the government's policies toward the steel industry, resulting in the loss of thousands of jobs, with their corresponding negative impact on the cities' economy.

7. Close to 50 percent of households were derived from an original list of 140 on which the 1981–1982 study had been based. This nonrandom sample included the first 27 households that were found living in the same address as in the first study. The rest were arrived at through a snowballing technique that included middle-class households for comparative purposes.

8. They concentrated in the following *colonias:* Palmitas, San Rafael, San Andrés de Atoto, Lázaro Cárdenas, El Molinito, Moctezuma, Oriente, Cándido Aguilar, Narvarte, Coyoacán, and Portales.

9. The tension was due to the fact that shops often run out of the subsidized product and those in line (overwhelmingly women) were fighting to be as close as possible to the head of the line.

10. By collective efforts I refer to community- and neighborhood-based strategies of dealing with the crisis, such as collective kitchens, which require an important organizing effort beyond the nuclear household.

11. This is a conclusion arrived at also by other observers (conversation with J. A. Alonso).

12. Some families survived literally with a few basic staples, namely, rice and beans, oil, tortillas, chiles, milk, and some inexpensive fruits. During fieldwork, we encountered anxious housewives worrying about how they would pay for the beans and rice that they needed for the day.

13. In her study of the effect of the crisis on households in Guayaquil, Ecuador, Moser makes a similar point and adds that this has a specific negative effect on the education of girls, given that they have less time to do homework than their brothers "causing them to fail in school and this in turn may affect their future educational potential" (Moser 1989:15).

14. One example is provided by the many groups that over the decade organized around housing and tenants' rights at the city level (symbolized by the popular figure of Superbarrio, who by 1988 had become a national figure). Similarly, other forms of organizing developed around food distribution and urban services issues at the community and neighborhood level (Ramírez 1986). Political mobilization intensified around issues connected with the crisis. Municipal election campaigns, for example, have been used to organize around basic needs and democratic rights. However, most of these efforts have been carried out at the *political* level, such as through political parties and numerous women's organizations, not at the level of daily life around the household, as has often been the case in other collective efforts in Latin America. During the past few years, however, many efforts have emerged, particularly among women's organizations, to organize collective projects around basic needs issues.

15. Feminist analyses have criticized the concept of the household as a harmonious unit and have emphasized the need to focus on unequal gender relations and asymmetries within it (Benería and Roldán 1987; Folbre 1988; Wolf 1990). However, much remains to be done to conceptualize the complexities of

the contradictory nature of the family that is emphasized here. Amartya Sen's theoretical insights into "cooperative conflicts" provide one of the most appropriate and useful models for capturing bargaining processes within the household (Sen 1990).

REFERENCES

Barrett, Michèle, and Marg McIntosh. 1982. *The Anti-Social Family.* London: Verso Editions.

Benería, Lourdes. 1991. "Structural Adjustment, the Labor Market and the Household: The Case of Mexico." In G. Standing and V. Tockman (eds.), *Towards Social Adjustment: Labor Market Concerns in Structural Adjustment.* Geneva: International Labour Organization.

Benería, Lourdes, and Martha Roldán. 1987. *The Crossroads of Class and Gender: Industrial Homework, Subcontracting and Household Dynamics in Mexico City.* Chicago: The University of Chicago Press.

CEPAL (Comisión Económica Para América Latina). 1990.

Commonwealth Secretariat. 1990. *Engendering Development for the 1990s.* London: Commonwealth Secretariat.

Cornia, Giovanni A., Richard Jolly, and Frances Stewart (eds.). 1987. *Adjustment with a Human Face.* Oxford: Clarendon Press.

Cypher, James M. 1988. "The Crisis and the Restructuring of Capitalism in the Periphery." *Research in Political Economy* 11:45–82.

Dornbusch, Rudiger. 1988. "Mexico: Stabilization, Debt and Growth." Massachusetts Institute of Technology, unpublished paper.

ECA (Economic Commission for Africa). 1989. *African Alternative Framework to Structural Adjustment Programmes for Socio-Economic Transformation.* New York: United Nations.

ECLA (Economic Commission for Latin America). 1990. *Transformación Productiva con Equidad.* Santiago de Chile: ECLA.

Edel, Mathew, and Candace Kim Edel. 1989. "Analyzing Mexico's Accumulation Crisis." Paper presented at the Social Sciences Research Workshop on "Issues in Mexico's Security," Mexico City, February 22–24.

Feldstein, Martin. 1987. "El Curso Probable de la Economía en los Proximos Años." In Miguel de la Madrid et al. (eds.), *Cambio Estructural en Mexico y en el Mundo.* Mexico City: Fondo de Cultural Económica/Secretaria de Programación y Presupuesto.

Folbre, Nancy. 1988. "The Black Four of Hearts: Toward a New Paradigm of Household Economics." Pp. 248–264 in D. Dwyer and J. Bruce (eds.), *A Home Divided: Women and Income in the Third World.* Stanford, Calif.: Stanford University Press.

González de la Rocha. 1986. *Los Recursos de la Pobreza. Familias de Bajos Ingresos en Guadalajara.* Guadalajara: El Colegio de Mexico/Centro de Investigaciones y Estudios Superiores en Antropologia Social/Secretaria de Planificación y Presupuesto.

Lind, Amy. 1990. "Economic Crisis, Women's Work and the Reproduction of Gender Ideology: Popular Women's Organizations in Quito, Ecuador." M.S. thesis, Cornell University.

Lissakers, Karin, and Julio Zamora. 1989. "The Financial Sector in Mexico's Economic Reform." Presented at the conference on Mexico, "Contrasting Visions," New York City, April.

Lustig, Nora. 1987. "Crisis Económica y Niveles de Vida en Mexico: 1982–1985." *Estudios Económicos* 2 (2) (July–December):227–249.

———. 1988. "La Desigualdad Económica." *Nexos* (August):8–12.

Moser, Caroline. 1989. "The Impact of Recession and Adjustment at the Micro-level: Low Income Women and Their Households in Guayaquil, Ecuador." *The Invisible Adjustment: Poor Women and the Economic Crisis.* New York: UNICEF.

Oliveira, Orlandina de. 1988. "Empleo Femenino en Mexico en Tiempos de Recesión Económica: Tendencias Recientes." Unpublished manuscript.

Quick, Stephen A. 1989. "Mexico's Macroeconomic Gamble." U.S. Congress, Joint Economic Committee, Conference Paper No. 12. Washington, D.C.: GPO.

Ramírez Saiz, Juan Manuel. 1986. *El Movimiento Urbano Popular en Mexico.* Mexico City: Siglo Veintiuno Editores.

Rendón, Teresa, and Carlos Salas. 1988. "Wages and Employment in Mexico." Paper presented at the Union for Radical Political Economics (URPE)/American Social Science Association (ASSA) meeting, December.

Roberts, Bryant. 1991. "Urban Labor Services and Structural Adjustment." In G. Standing and V. Tockman (eds.), *Towards Social Adjustment: Labor Market Concerns in Structural Adjustment.* Geneva: International Labour Organisation.

Rohter, Larry. 1989. "Mexico City's Filthy Air, World's Worst, Worsens." *The New York Times* (April 12).

Sara-Lafosse, Violeta. 1986. "Communal Kitchens and the Low-income Neighborhoods in Lima." Pp. 90–204 in M. Schmink and J. Bruce (eds.), *Learning about Women and Urban Services in Latin America.* New York: The Population Council.

Sen, Amartya. 1990. "Gender and Cooperative Conflicts." In Irene Tinker (ed.), *Persistent Inequalities.* Oxford: Oxford University Press.

Wolf, Diane L. 1990. "Daughters, Decisions and Domination: An Empirical and Conceptual Critique of Household Strategies." *Development and Change* 21:43–74.

5

Crisis, Islam, & Gender in Bangladesh: The Social Construction of a Female Labor Force

✑ SHELLEY FELDMAN

This chapter describes the growth of the export sector in Bangladesh in the context of the 1980s global economic crisis. I will examine how national policy commitments have been reshaped in response to International Monetary Fund (IMF) and World Bank demands to meet structural adjustment requirements. With the shift from an import substitution to an export-led growth strategy, new policies initiating the establishment of export-processing enclaves have challenged the existing employment structure and helped reshape both the urban and rural labor markets. The result has been the creation of new opportunities for and demands on women workers. In addition, changing employment opportunities place new demands on Bangladeshi households that are forced to compete for work in either the agricultural or industrial sector. Segments of the rural and urban population have been differentially able to respond to these demands, but the general change for Bangladeshi people has been a redefinition of appropriate "women's work," a rethinking of appropriate female behavior, and a reconsideration of family status.

A specific concern of this chapter is how the reorganization of production has reshaped the gender division of labor in Bangladesh. I am particularly interested in the growth of export garment manufacture and the demand for female employment in a context previously characterized by the lack of female workers in both the public and private employment sectors. Women, until the early 1980s, had been relatively absent from the ranks of professional and technical workers and underrepresented among clerical, service, and sales workers, and were only slowly increasing their representation among field agricultural workers. Women, however, have always played essential roles in agricultural production, home-based enterprises, and in *bari*-based (courtyard) cottage industries. Yet their contribution in these predominantly nonwaged sectors has been largely underreported and invisible until the effects and efforts of the UN Decade for Women forced a rethinking of the ways in which data on women's work are collected and measured.

Although Bangladeshi women's participation is marked in export production, employment in this sector remains quite low relative to total employment. Estimates reveal that women comprise approximately 90 percent of the 200,000 to 300,000 export workers (Phelan 1986; Feldman, forthcoming). Most astounding about the magnitude of their representation in export production, though, is the rapidity with which women appeared on the streets of Dhaka and Chittagong, the country's two largest cities. Startling, too, is the class composition of the new industrial work force. Between 1982, following the government's New Industrial Policy (NIP), and 1984 there was a marked contrast in the number of young, educated women living and working in Dhaka, whereas prior to this period this city and all other towns and rural communities were notable for their absence of women either employed or unaccompanied on the street.[1]

I will argue that patterns of economic restructuring, especially those related to the reorganization of industrial production and the restructuring of the labor process, have been reshaped by the policy environment in Bangladesh. New labor processes have, in turn, created new wage-earning opportunities for a segment of the rural population heretofore either ignored or significantly underestimated in discussions of employment demand. These changes have occurred, however, in an environment where the growing presence of the conservative Islamic fundamentalist party, the Jamaati-i-Islam, may challenge the immediate mobility of young women and their long-run employment opportunities.

The chapter is divided into three parts. The first outlines a number of salient themes in the contemporary debate on economic crisis and the impact of this crisis and conditions of declining living standards on how households negotiate resources and skills in the creation of strategies to meet their daily subsistence needs. The second section examines the global economic crisis as it is shaped by relations of debt dependence in Bangladesh. Here, I focus on sectoral shifts in resource allocation and the structure of employment since the initiation of structural adjustment lending in the late 1970s. The third part highlights the contradictory policy environment that shapes Bangladeshi women's employment opportunities. The chapter draws on qualitative interviews with workers and entrepreneurs collected between 1977 and 1984, which focused on the changing rural economy and its relationship to urban migration and employment.[2]

I interviewed employees from a range of enterprises who had different labor histories and experience with other working people. What is important to note about the in-depth interviews carried out with factory employees in the export-processing enclave is that the interviews were not permitted by factory owners, and many employees were initially hesitant to be included among our sample, especially if they were likely to draw the attention of supervisors or owners. Thus, interviews were arranged when workers left the factory during their lunch break and were scheduled for the late evening hours, usually at the residence of the employee. As factory lists of employees could not be garnered from supervisors or owners, a referred sampling design was used. Hence, the study includes a concentration of respondents from selected regions of the country, selected factories, and a disproportionate number of male employees.

THE CONTEMPORARY DEBATE ON ECONOMIC CRISIS

The debt crisis, economic restructuring, and structural adjustment programs evoke an image of Latin American and African countries with high debt-dependence ratios, spiraling inflation, declining wages, increasing prices, and falling agricultural and industrial output. As of 1984, Latin American countries had the highest indebtedness among all Third World countries, with an average debt-service ratio of 44.6 percent, followed by Africa with an average of 24.9 percent, and Asia with 9.9 percent. Brazil, Mexico, and Argentina led the list of countries with debts ranging from 103 to 48 thousands of millions of dollars. One consequence of these differences is that little scholarly attention has been focused on the costs of the global economic crisis for countries in Asia and the Pacific Rim.[3]

During the 1980s, selected countries in Latin America and Asia faced new demands from the IMF and the World Bank under their structural adjustment lending agreements to renegotiate their debt. Debt rescheduling, however, is neither a new phenomenon nor one limited to Latin America. As early as 1956, Argentina rescheduled one of its debts, and this was followed by rescheduling agreements in other Latin American countries between 1956 and 1981. However, during the early 1960s and 1970s, a number of Asian countries also rescheduled their debts: Indonesia in 1966, 1967, 1968, and 1970; India in 1968 and each year between 1972–1976; Pakistan between 1972 and 1974; and Bangladesh in 1974 (Hardy 1982:2).

What makes debt rescheduling during the contemporary period an indicator of crisis? Why have the Asian costs of these changes not been a focus of attention for scholars and policymakers? Answers to these questions begin to appear when we examine the differences between debt renegotiation during the earlier period and today and the patterns of capital and finance markets and investment patterns that characterize each period. Present-day Latin American debt, for example, is primarily from private sources: Private debt for Brazil, Mexico, and Argentina is 79.4 percent, 87.4 percent, and 88.6 percent, respectively, of total long-term debt. For Bangladesh, India, Pakistan, and Sri Lanka, on the other hand, debt from private sources does not exceed 22.3 percent of total debt outstanding (World Bank 1988b:194). In fact, Bangladesh is not even noted in the *World Development Report,* where debt from private sources is shown to range from a low of 7 percent for Pakistan to a high of 100 percent for Venezuela.

Aggregate figures on debt service presume that the debt-service ratio of a specific country is an important indicator of the likely costs of the crisis for its constituent households and individuals. It thus underestimates the differential effects of the crisis on diverse and heterogeneous populations within specific countries. That is, if we disentangle the debt crisis from other forms of debt dependence, it is clear that a range of countries beyond Latin America face similar burdens in regard to the economic declines faced by various segments of the population—the most vulnerable as well as those dependent on fixed or declining incomes. For example, a comparison of the burden of indebtedness in countries with different levels of development indicates that South Korea with a per capita gross national product (GNP) of $1,528, a per capita debt of $461, and per capita disposal income estimated at $1,373 has a debt burden of 34 (expressed as a percentage of disposable income). Bangladesh, on the other hand, has a per capita GNP of only $126, a per capita debt of $41, and per capita disposal income estimated at $37 with debt (expressed as a percentage of disposable income) of 111—three times that of South Korea (Korner et al. 1986:11).[4]

Figures also reveal that export earnings in Bangladesh for 1988 financed only 41 percent of imports, and remittances financed a further 24 percent. External aid financed the remainder, maintaining a current debt-service ratio of 23.4 percent (World Bank 1988a:18). Thus, even in countries with relatively low private-capital investments and a small debt burden, the effects of debt dependence can be devastating. Hence, recognizing the differential effects of debt dependence within countries encourages an assessment of countries less privileged in current discussions of the debt crisis and recognizes as well the costs of structural adjustment lending on local clienteles.[5] Important to emphasize here is not the politics of the debt crisis discourse, which masks the burden of indebtedness in countries with different aid regimes and with different levels of development, but the diverse impact of this burden on the everyday lives of people. Said another way, instability and change are reshaping how the production and exchange of agricultural commodities, manufacturing goods, and services are creating new patterns of interdependence among countries and conditioning patterns of persistent poverty within countries. Yet, contemporary studies of the debt crisis generally underestimate the costs of the crisis for households, for individuals, and for social reproduction.[6] The general argument regarding the debt crisis also tends to underestimate how structural and institutional reforms made in response to the major disproportions in global production and consumption integrate countries via new production structures and labor exchanges into the global economy.

Aspects of the current crisis requiring further analysis include patterns of uneven development and declining employment stability that are not narrowly tied to private indebtedness but that nonetheless mediate national policy initiatives and shape new processes of capital accumulation. For example, with the shift from import substitution strategies to export-led growth strategies, which build upon and are shaped by the reorganization of the world economy, national labor processes and labor markets have been radically transformed. These changes were made under pressure to generate foreign currency and meet the financing obligations of the IMF and the World Bank. Of particular concern here is the globalization of production and the reconfiguration of the international labor market as it patterns the Bangladeshi response to structural adjustment demands and reorganizes employment opportunities for Bangladeshi women. I propose that the integration of Bangladesh into the world economy has reorganized sectoral employment, decentralized production units, increased the numbers of and reformulated small and cottage-based home-production units and subcontracting firms, and enabled the emergence of export-processing enclaves to facilitate both foreign and domestic private investment in export production. The latter has occurred in order to increase foreign currency earnings and meet debt service payments.

At this juncture it is worthwhile to identify the major themes shaping the debate about the economic crisis. First, a number of researchers argue that the economic crisis experienced by many countries since the mid-1970s and the specific debt crisis of the 1980s has been generated by the uneven development among nation states reflected in the international financial order. This understanding helps us to interpret IMF and World Bank efforts that respond to nations individually on an ad hoc and piecemeal basis and that focus primarily upon the containment of poverty through schemes to improve social welfare among the most vulnerable. As Elson notes, "International Monetary Fund and World Bank programs have assumed that what is required is a piecemeal, country-by-country adjustment of internal economic structures, focusing on the reallocation of real resources" (Elson, this volume).

Second, although multilateral assistance may represent a clear set of interests aimed at facilitating accumulation and securing hegemony, especially as it supports the restructuring of employment and trade and tariff reforms, multilateral agencies lack an overall strategy that is likely to address the logical constraints to global processes of capital accumulation. This lack suggests that loan rescheduling and the development of export promotion enclaves are merely temporary interventions that are unable to correct the structural limitations of long-term growth with equity. Again Elson's foresight is noteworthy: "Recovery to 'normal' conditions is believed to be just around the corner; and adjustment can proceed on a case-by-case basis, with ad hoc measures to protect the poor" (Elson, this volume).

THE BANGLADESH POLITICAL ECONOMY:
THE PRESENT CRISIS IN CONTEXT

The structural and institutional changes characterizing the political economy of Bangladesh act in concert with, and in response to, the restructuring of the global economy. For example, the shift from U.S. economic hegemony to new forms of competitive capitalism has generated new areas of competition and investment. In Bangladesh, as in other countries, recent attention has focused on its integration into the international redivision of manufacturing enterprises to draw on its competitive advantage regarding low wages and limited experience in union activity. At present, there is a layering of financial investment emerging between industrialized countries and the newly industrializing countries (NICs) of Korea, Taiwan, Singapore, and Hong Kong, whereby the NICs establish subcontracting arrangements with new producers located in the least developed capitalist economies. These investments have occurred despite the aggregate decline, since 1975, in foreign direct investments (FDIs) to dependent economies. That is, developing countries attracted over 30 percent of all direct investment, which reached a peak of 41.8 percent in 1975. Since then, there has been a decline of FDIs in developing countries, with a shift of relative shares to the developed countries. "By 1983 . . . the developing world captured under a quarter of net investment flows . . ." (IFC 1988:16).

The location and expansion of export manufacturing firms in Bangladesh is the result of strategic planning and policy reform following negotiation by the government and multilateral and bilateral lending institutions representing direct foreign investors and multinational corporations. In the early 1980s, countries like Bangladesh with low or no quota restrictions on exports to the United States and the European community, as well as limited tariff and trade restrictions, tax holidays, liberal repatriation policies, and low wages, encouraged investors from countries such as Singapore and South Korea to invest in joint ventures and partnerships with an emerging cadre of local industrialists. An examination of existing FDIs in Bangladesh reveals that over 40 percent of the companies are Asian, with Singapore, South Korea, and Hong Kong accounting for 75 percent of these firms (IFC 1988).

Seventy percent of these investments have been in textiles and garments, and one can presume that such investments were made because the import quotas in the United States from these countries were already exhausted. These quotas are important to acknowledge because the U.S. market accounts for a major proportion of the goods exported from Bangladesh. Despite the expansion of foreign direct investment by the NICs, and despite the fact that Bangladesh has among the lowest labor costs in the world, the country has been relatively unsuccessful in attracting FDIs and ranks lowest among eight countries with relatively similar economic and demographic characteristics. Indonesia, for example, has attracted an average annual investment of $825 million, Thailand $217 million, but in Bangladesh only $4 million was invested (IFC 1988:5). Lower than expected investments in Bangladesh reflect an ideology and a policy environment that characterize the country as the "basket case of the world" with limited natural, industrial, and infrastructural resources, and with a work force known to embody very low education levels, employment experience, and skills.

This view of economic conditions in Bangladesh suggests a set of infrastructural arrangements that would be unable to support the new conditions of production promoted in the country. Thus, there has been considerable pressure on the government to restructure its economy in anticipation of expanding FDIs. Responsibility for the conditions that presently characterize the country and that have limited the country's competitive advantage in the global economy is assumed to lie with the character of domestic development policy rather than with external demands on state capacities. Domestic policy formation is also assumed to be an autonomous process with no economic and planning relationship between the type of capitalist investment strategies within the country and trends in the world economy. In this view, domestic policy formation derives solely from the national interests of Bangladesh or, more negatively, from the inability of the Bangladesh bureaucracy and government to manage the economy and attract an increasing amount of foreign investment. As an International Finance Corporation report suggests (IFC 1988:16):

> The situation in Bangladesh . . . seems unlikely to have been strongly affected by global economic trends. The "debt crisis," which has been severest in those countries hardest hit by the decline in FDI, has had no impact on Bangladesh. Low commodity prices, mounting protectionism, or any array of other external factors have not exerted a significantly negative force on flows of FDI to Bangladesh. . . . Bangladesh is on its own, and its success or failure owes to its own efforts—not to change in the world economy or to the actions of neighboring countries.

This interpretation of why Bangladesh has been unsuccessful in attracting FDIs represents a "blaming the victim" ideology, which has had consequences for financial support allocated for industrial infrastructure. It also has had consequences for the view shared by investors about what the Bangladesh state should do to encourage future investments. The result has been to increase pressure on the Bangladesh state to make even greater concessions to international capital by putting increased financial resources into infrastructural support, providing greater incentives to investors, and tightening controls on labor.

Neither the lack of foreign investments nor the controls on labor resulting in the banning of trade unions have challenged the government's interest in the promotion of export-led growth leading to an increased demand for labor, especially women's labor. The demand for work corresponds to two broad changes in the rural economy that focus on new patterns of agricultural and nonfarm labor relations. The first is the transformation of agricultural labor relations, which is epitomized by the consolidation of land and capital in the hands of larger agricultural producers and the fragmentation and decline in landholdings among smaller producers. For large-scale agricultural producers the concentration of landholding indicates the expansion of both economic and political power in the consolidation of a class of rural elites. These elites have traditionally not invested solely in agriculture but have diversified their resource base through moneylending, trade, retail enterprises, and petty production. Land concentration and increasingly capitalized forms of agricultural production have resulted in an increased policy focus on income and investment diversification and on the expansion of rural employment, both in agriculture and in nonfarm enterprises. Rural investment and employment initiatives include increased credit availability to rural-based small and cottage enterprises, increased training and information available through the Bangladesh Small and Cottage Industries Corporation, and support for microenterprises, cooperative ventures, and independent home-based productive activities through nongovernmental credit schemes, most notably the Grameen Bank Project. These policy commitments have spurred the growth of rural manufacturing and trading enterprises and generated a small but growing demand for rural nonfarm wage labor.

From a policy perspective, the effort to limit rural unemployment and growing poverty represents a move away from agricultural production and agricultural employment to a focus on reconfiguring the urban labor market (World Bank 1983). Part of this reconfiguration indicates the commitment to employment generation for the rural unemployed, who have been the target of relief and development assistance efforts and whose work can be characterized by the daily labor contracts they receive for road construction and maintenance. These initiatives are exemplified by Food for Work programs where food and nominal wages are paid for temporary employment. In Food for Work schemes there is no long-term investment in skills development or sustained employment, although it is increasingly recognized that such programs can no longer be limited to seasonal temporary relief efforts (World Bank 1988a).

The commitment to employment generation also emphasizes the creation of an export-processing enclave to meet the employment needs of the semiskilled and skilled rural and urban underemployed and unemployed. As we will see below, this initiative does not build on the specific employment needs of the Bangladeshi work force but on parallel shifts in the international division of labor and economic restructuring. The point to emphasize here is that the political economy of Bangladesh has been restructured to better adapt to the state's need to maintain international credit, to generate foreign exchange, and to respond to the interests of multinational garment and textile firms and subcontractors in their search for cheap sources of labor. Both bilateral and multilateral lending institutions and national policy facilitate the interests of the private sector in their demand for economic restructuring through their support for the implementation of an export-led growth strategy.

The roots of this policy commitment are grounded in the regimes of both Zia Rahman and General Hossain Ershad, covering the period since 1975. The strategy emphasizes export-led growth, the denationalization of selected industries, and increased allocations to private sector development. Allocations to the private sector have increased from 11 percent in the First Five Year Plan to about 35 percent in the Third Plan. Support for private sector development represents 35.2 percent of the government's allocation (Bangladesh 1988:19).

Among the growing numbers of landless households and undersubsistence agricultural producers there has been an expanded dependence on male wage employment both in and outside of agriculture. The limited opportunities for secure, full-time agricultural employment have expanded the search for nonagricultural employment among those marginalized from the subsistence economy, generated a new cadre of entrants into the labor market, and increased the dependence of a growing number of households on the labor market. This has required a growing proportion of rural households to diversify their resource-producing strategies, thus placing increased demands on both the formal and unprotected labor markets.

Low wages and seasonal agricultural employment have meant that the shift from subsistence production to a dependence on the wage labor market has also come to increasingly require that each household member secures her or his own subsistence. The result is a growing demand for work among women and children. The Rural Industries Survey carried out in 1980 indicates that about 33 percent of rural industry workers are female, and the 1983/1984 Labour Force Survey indicates that personal services and manufacturing account for 28.2 percent and 24.6 percent, respectively, of the employed population over the age of five (Hossain 1987:27; Bangladesh 1984:33). Additionally, the Bangladesh Manpower Survey of 1980 indicates that 31.8 percent of rural women between the ages of 15 and 64 are engaged in the production and transport sector (Bangladesh 1982:36). Moreover, estimates of nonagricultural households for the year 2006 reveal an annual growth rate of 4.2 percent, with nonagricultural rural households expected to increase by 3.0 percent annually.

The individuation of social reproduction represents the erosion of both village and household resources and networks that once provided the arena or backup for daily maintenance (Feldman 1989). Those engaged in Food for Work schemes and as daily household laborers most clearly characterize the undermining of family subsistence during the contemporary period. But women who seek wage employment from middle-class rural families similarly represent a process of eroding family security as the family wage is no longer sufficient to meet subsistence costs. Yet, whether from poor or middle-class families, the opportunities and constraints that individuals face in seeking to ensure their own survival are located within a web of social processes imbedded in household and family patterns of negotiation and decisionmaking. These patterns are characterized by a household gender division of labor and intrahousehold resource distribution as well as cultural practices imposed by both religious ideology and village tradition.

The second change in the Bangladesh political economy was the NIP, which was formally initiated in 1982 and revised in 1986. The NIP, created with support from the World Bank, restructured import and export facilities, inaugurated trade and tariff reforms[7] to encourage increased investment in both domestic manufacturing enterprises and those in the export-processing enclaves, diversified credit opportunities to a broad range of entrepreneurs, and provided social and technical infrastructural support for the development of rural industrial estates and export-processing enclaves.[8] Private sector development includes as well the commitment to expand nontraditional agricultural and fish product exports through the increased capitalization and privatization of these sectors.

The government's receptivity to the IMF and World Bank privatization strategy is partly due to the country's dependence on external assistance to meet both development and revenue budget expenses. It is also due to the nature of aid agreements between the government and the multilateral and bilateral aid community, which tie particular aid commitments to selected policy reforms. International donor pressure has also required that state initiatives be taken to mobilize domestic resources, including efforts at tax reform to counter tax evasion, impose customs duty on selected imports, and increase excise tax on natural gas. This development strategy was an explicit shift away from the policies of the postcolonial regime of Sheik Mujibur Rahman, which had emphasized nationalization of industries, relatively large subsidies to agriculture, and an expressed, if less than coherent, socialist posture. Politically, the rhetoric associated with more recent export-led growth initiatives has focused on the expansion of off-farm employment opportunities to meet the growing demand for both urban and rural work.

Bangladeshi entrepreneurs quickly responded to support for export processing with the rapid expansion in garment and apparel manufacturing enterprises. They were assumed to benefit from the growing costs of production in the NICs, the seeking of cheaper labor sources by multinational textile and apparel manufacturers, and by entrepreneurs in the NICs seeking new subcontracting arrangements in response to increased quotas on U.S. imports from these countries.

The implementation of this export-led growth strategy, especially as it embraces the creation of a female-dominated textile and garment manufacturing work force, is particularly interesting in Bangladesh where women have been traditionally excluded from participation in the labor market. What consequences does the expansion of urban employment have for women? What are the contradictory consequences of this process for women whose position outside the labor market has been legitimated by the ideology of *purdah* or female seclusion? In addressing these questions I draw on Pearson's critique of contemporary analyses of the new international division of labor, which assumes that gender relations and gender ideologies are social constructions.

Rather than assume the conditions in which a labor force is created, Pearson focuses on the actual processes through which it is created:

> The analysis of the new international division of labor has ignored the complexities and contradictions of producing the desired social relations of production involved in creating a new sector of wage labour. . . . What has not been addressed is the availability or construction of cheap labour. It has not been acknowledged that either capital or the State might need to intervene to deliver the suitable labour required; it has been assumed that this was axiomatic on the existence of high levels of unemployment or underemployment in the Third World locations. . . . It was (also) assumed that the absence of industrial employment for women in the immediate economic history of the country meant that there would be no problem in making this labour available in the quantities and qualities required. (1988:450–451)

The questions that Pearson asks include: How is a labor force composed of a particular gender, age, and skill base created to correspond to structural economic changes that include a reconfigured labor market? How have the ideology of *purdah* and the set of normative proscriptions shaping women's behavior, including their participation in the labor market, changed in concert with the creation of an export-processing enclave seeking female workers?

Bangladesh provides an interesting opportunity to examine how state practice and development policy and planning have facilitated the incorporation of women into export manufacturing. In particular, this focus signals the importance of how institutional restructuring and ideological rearticulations of normative assessments are supported both by the government and through alliances forged between Islamic fundamentalist parties in Saudi Arabia, Pakistan, and Bangladesh. These alliances reflect a more explicit commitment to Islamic religious and ideological concerns than those characterizing the secular state under Sheik Mujibur Rahman and support new interpretations of *purdah* and Islamic proscriptions characterizing women's appropriate behavior. The Eighth Amendment to the Constitution passed in June 1988, which made Islam the state religion, highlights the salience of Islamic doctrine in state practice and epitomizes the policy environment created during the latter half of the 1980s.

OPEN COMPETITION: THE NIP
CONFRONTS ISLAMIC FUNDAMENTALISM

As recently as 1974, the female labor-force participation rate in Bangladesh was estimated at only 4 percent (ESCAP 1981). This low employment rate has been contested because it underestimates agricultural labor, domestic service, and other forms of informal labor expenditure. Nonetheless, Bangladesh does have one of the lowest female employment rates in the world. This low rate has been interpreted as a legacy of Islam, where women's productive contribution remained hidden in the household or *bari* (courtyard compound). These religious practices have been critical in establishing the conditions under which female and family status has been constructed.

A growing number of poor women sought agricultural and off-farm rural employment in the 1970s, and throughout the 1980s an increasing number of women have competed for government positions. Yet, during this period educated rural women still represented a minority of those who sought wage work. Prior to this period young, unmarried, educated daughters of the aspiring rural and urban middle classes were generally limited by the lack of employment opportunities or forbidden from participating in the work force by their families. For many rural families, having a working daughter often signified the lack of concern with *purdah* and appropriate female behavior and was interpreted by other villagers as representing the lack of family status and resources sufficient to enable the care and well-being of a daughter until marriage.

For the young woman who did seek and secure work, often in the public sector as extension agents and family planning workers, the process of negotiating personal and familial status tended to be a contentious one. Interviews with these female workers revealed the creative ways they managed to observe *purdah* and maintain their jobs: A few chose to work in their own village and live with their parents, while others wore a *burkha* (veil) as they walked from their village to their office and removed it once at work. This latter strategy minimized the harassment by other villagers and respected the propriety of the worker's family. In short, throughout the 1970s and early 1980s an increasing number of educated women joined the labor force, although there were no government policies or explicit encouragements from employers to do so.[9]

In an environment where women have been traditionally excluded from wage employment and where they have only limited experience with work in government service and public and private sector enterprises, it is surprising that the demand for educated women workers to fill the newly created positions in export manufacturing could be "constructed" in the brief period of less than two years. It is equally surprising that the demand for such workers would be met by a segment of the population that traditionally was the least likely to encourage or allow daughters to seek wage employment.

Implicit in the 1982 NIP and the Revised Industrial Policy of 1986, female workers were defined a priori as the preferred labor force, following the tradition and ideology established for garment and apparel manufacture in the export-processing zones (EPZs) around the world. However, in Bangladesh, tailoring has been a traditional male occupation located in public bazaars, and it is only in response to development programs of the 1970s and premised on a Western notion of sewing as women's work that women were encouraged to learn tailoring and work within their households. Not surprisingly, women were unable to compete with male tailors located in the marketplace (Feldman, Akhter, and Banu 1980). Hence, while implementation of the EPZ strategy generated new opportunities for a segment of the female population traditionally excluded from participation in the labor market, its success required the creation of a labor force skilled in sewing and production work. This was accomplished by drawing on women who had learned sewing at home or through nongovernmental programs with special training schemes for women. Alternatively, women were hired as apprentices at reduced salary rates while "learning the trade." Although there was general agreement that skills could be learned within a fairly brief period, apprenticeship status was often extended beyond a critical six-month period so as to continue paying exceedingly low wages, often at a rate of 6 takas (Tk6) or US$.30 per day. Even though the proportion of workers engaged in garment and other export-processing activities has been quite limited relative to national labor-force participation rates, apparel manufacture has required forms of women's engagement in the public arena that challenge traditional notions of female behavior and make women more visible in public places, forcing greater interaction between women and men. Broad areas of this interaction include new patterns of urban migration, collective living arrangements, the unaccompanied use of public transportation, increased market activity, new consumption patterns, and new forms of political expression.

The New Industrial Policy, with its commitment to private sector entrepreneurial expansion, also generated new relations of production in the industrial sector expressed in terms of both a new urban industrial elite and a growing working class. As indicated earlier, between 1983 and 1984 there emerged in Dhaka city a labor force of approximately 200,000 employees, 80 to 90 percent of whom were young, unmarried, educated girls between the ages of 12 and 21 years old. Supporting this expansion of female workers were programs supported by nongovernmental organizations (NGOs) offering skills training to women to improve their chances of securing employment in export production. Moreover, programs such as that offered by the Young Women's Christian Association (YWCA) also created small shops for handicraft production where women worked as pieceworkers. These training opportunities and the networks that developed with garment workers at these small shops provided a vehicle for young women to secure employment in export-processing firms.

The demand for housing female workers was met in part by organizations such as the YWCA, which established dormitories and hostels for them. Although dormitories were used primarily by single working women, this new living arrangement challenged the more traditional form of seclusion, which kept young unmarried women under the purview of the family. Ironically, only two or three years earlier, efforts to increase hostel facilities at Dhaka University met with only limited success, and single women living without a male partner or kin member found it almost impossible to rent rooms or an apartment in private dwellings. Working men were slowly able to find housing in small groups or what is referred to locally as living in a "mess" or house-share arrangement. Fewer women have sought similar arrangements but for those who have, these communal experiences have created opportunities for information sharing and friendship previously unavailable to unmarried women. These arrangements have also increased women's autonomy by making them responsible for organizing domestic life—either hiring a person to cook and shop for them or requiring them to meet these responsibilities on their own. How do these new employment opportunities fit within the cultural context of Bangladesh? How have patterns of Bengali family and kinship relations, a rigid gender division of labor, and a powerful ideology of female honor and propriety shaped by female seclusion facilitated as well as hindered the social relations of recruitment and production? To be sure, the articulation of *purdah* in Bangladesh has differed markedly from its expression in either Pakistan or the Middle Eastern countries, which tend to provide the stereotypic example of women under Islam. For instance, the integration of Islam into Bengali/Bangladeshi culture has traditionally been characterized by the separation of state and religion. In Pakistan, on the other hand, religion has been used as a legal sanction; people can be publicly flogged for committing adultery, and one's right arm can be cut off for robbery. In this sense, the enforcement of Bengali-Islamic practice is more fluid and flexible than it is in either Pakistan or the Middle East.

During the preindependence period, for example, Bangladeshis were known to be devout but relaxed about their religious beliefs. In fact, one of the themes of the Independence War in 1971 was the communal tension initiated by the West Pakistanis against Bengalis, who were seen to be improper Muslims. However, this more liberal interpretation of Islam did not mean that women were relatively more mobile in Bangladesh than in other Islamic countries. It only suggests that civil rather than state forms of control have governed the behavior of Bangladeshi women. For example, although daily prayers and Islamic practice infuse the culture, under Sheik Mujibur Rahman (1971–1975) Islam was neither employed as a state ideology nor manipulated as a dominant form of state control. Thus, while Islam has not been the central mechanism of generalized state control, it continues to reinforce forms of gender subordination and gender segregation through mechanisms of social control. This means that Islam has legitimated and reinforced the gender division of labor in agriculture and limited women's access to and control of landed property and technical inputs, including credit and extension services. As indicated earlier, Islam has also contributed to limiting women's access to the urban labor market and kept invisible their contribution to both rural and urban production.

Earlier I noted that the capitalization of agriculture, increasing rural under- and unemployment, and poverty have required that each household member secure her or his own subsistence and reproduction. Therefore, despite the normative expression of Bangladeshi *purdah,* which limits and keeps invisible women's participation in the labor process, poor and landless rural women have increasingly participated in the labor market, seeking employment in the homes of wealthier peasant households rather than in field-related activities so as to minimize contact with males and maintain *purdah* as best they could (McCarthy 1980; McCarthy and Feldman 1983). The post-Independence period, in fact, can be characterized by women's increasing participation in development programs, which take them outside the village, and in government-supported programs such as Food for Work. In areas where men are able to secure off-farm employment, poor and landless women are also increasingly represented in field production (McCarthy 1979; McCarthy and Feldman 1983). These jobs were sought and secured by women for whom poverty rather than personal choice and career frames their employment interests.

The individuation of social reproduction has been identified as a problem for middle-class rural families as well as for the very poor. For middle-class households, where daughters are more likely to have been educated and family income is secured from agricultural production as well as from trade, services, and professional employment, unmarried daughters have been increasingly visible among the professional cadres. Increasing numbers of educated women, for example, have sought and found employment in the growing rural health and family planning sector and as primary schoolteachers in the expanded educational sector. But for these women, the process of negotiating their personal and familial status is quite different. For instance, it has not been unusual to see middle-class rural women wearing a *burkha* to and from work. They use the *burkha,* however, as a cultural adaptation to facilitate mobility and access to new resources and opportunities, not as an expression of subordination and oppression (Feldman and McCarthy 1983). Rather than being "hidden in the household," rural women are emerging as working people who may move "under the seclusion" of the *burkha* to work outside the home, visit friends and family, and enjoy the cinema.

These changes, which reflect a new articulation of appropriate female behavior and deportment and new employment opportunities and labor force participation rates for women, suggest not a cataclysmic ideological challenge to traditional Islamic practices, but rather the slow erosion of economic security among families with educated daughters forced to seek nonagricultural rural employment and work in the new industrial sector. Begun slowly in the 1960s with increasing numbers of women who sought work as female household laborers, this trend continued so that by the late 1970s one study found that between 16 percent and 24 percent of all households included at least one female household laborer (McCarthy 1980). Additionally, the early 1980s saw an increase in the number of women seeking public sector employment following the government's passing of the 10-percent quota. The 1980s also witnessed the expansion of small and cottage industry production (which depended on female family labor), public and private support for women's training schemes, and the realization that women's projects were a growth industry. Women also drew attention as the target for rural credit schemes both in agriculture, the Integrated Rural Development Programme, and in petty commodity and food-processing schemes (the Grameen Bank Project). These changes, in concert with the persistence of rural and urban poverty, created an environment wherein the conditions and constraints faced by a heterogeneous female population are slowly being recognized.[10] Along with these increasing demands to secure waged and in-kind work, women have managed to create means by which they both manipulate definitions of appropriate female behavior and challenge their exclusion from paid employment.

The process whereby cultural practices change in concert with changing forms of economic security supports the contention that uneven development and economic crises nationally and in the world economy are not epiphenomenal events. Rather, they represent the articulation of general processes of capitalist development, which require the continual mediation of cultural practices. Moreover, although new employment opportunities challenge the range of choices that have previously defined women's work patterns, new work patterns are not simply knee-jerk reactions to new circumstances but represent how Bangladeshi women have fashioned creative responses to changing conditions that result from the slow erosion of everyday life. The changed forms of behavior and interaction that emerge among women and between women and men include more heterogeneous work relations on the factory floor and the breakdown of the extended family/household as the primary means of the social comfort of women. Exemplifying women's independence from male family members' control are the unaccompanied inter- and intracity travel previously unusual for young unmarried women and the varied dress that young women wear. Increasing numbers leave the *sari* and *burkha* behind and don *shalwar* (long shirt)and *comise* (loose trousers) to reflect their age and mobility.

The changing demands on women's behavior, required if they are to participate in the export manufacturing sector, have also come in response to the changing nature of state practice, which heretofore supported the exclusion of women from the labor force. With government support to establish EPZs has come the need to provide public transportation for women traveling alone and a relatively safe environment for women, at least during the hours to and from work, walking the streets of the city. These conditions represent changes in how the state legitimates new forms of female behavior. Hence, the articulation of new cultural expressions of appropriate female behavior may change the nature, expression, and experience of gender subordination and thus identify the contradiction between prior forms of female subordination, as expressed in the doctrine of female seclusion, and the demand for female workers initiated by the government's NIP.

The tension between traditional normative principles governing female behavior and the new demands by women for work and by employers for female workers illuminates how gender relations are socially constructed. The process of social construction is one that builds on normative values but does so in the context of new social relations. Moreover, gender construction must be viewed as a process that changes over time and is dependent on changing economic relations as well as the interests and needs of social actors. Accepting a social constructionist view helps to challenge the axiomatic principle identified by Pearson (1988) that there is always a ready and available labor force, a reserve army of labor, to correspond to the shifting mobility of capital. Such an argument asserts but does not explain how this reserve army is created and maintained so as to be available, in appropriate proportions and with appropriate skills, for hire by export manufacturers. Although there has indeed been a small segment of women that could be drawn upon to seek remunerative employment in garment manufacture, it is also true that employers and state agencies have recognized the normative proscriptions shaping gender relations and drawn upon traditional definitions of female propriety and seclusion within the family and patterns of village guardianship to construct recruitment strategies and legitimate new living arrangements in Dhaka city.

For instance, the largest proportion of those recruited in selected firms are women who work for an industrialist who comes from their home village. Export-processing entrepreneurs often return to their family village and recruit the daughters of their village kin, assuring them that they will be protected once they arrive in Dhaka. The opportunities for "appropriate" employment for educated daughters generally include assurances by employers to their parents that safe and proper housing will be available, that young women will live with women they know near the factory, and will work with other women on the factory floor. These employers are generally regarded as "village heroes" both because they have found success and have therefore constructed a reputation of good standing in their home areas and because they offer villagers opportunities otherwise denied them. Moreover, because many villagers have not had the opportunity to live in or even visit the capital, they accept the promises and knowledge of their more experienced kinsfolk. It is not surprising, therefore, that "word of mouth" or a direct connection to the garment manufacturer is the major form of recruitment of female export-processing workers. This pattern of recruitment represents a carryover of male guardianship, safety, and patriarchal control once limited to male immediate-family members (Feldman 1984).

As argued earlier (Maguire 1986; Feldman, forthcoming), this recruitment strategy has contradictory effects for women workers. On the one hand, such connections provide women with an opportunity for employment previously denied them. On the other hand, however, they tie women to forms of obligation and social control that establish new forms of subordination and domination, such as pressures placed on women workers not to join unions. It may also be exhibited by the deployment of selected village kin as informers who rat on workers engaged in worker actions in exchange for pay increases and promotion (Feldman 1984).

What is interesting about women export-processing workers is that they may have an M.A. or B.A. degree, but they often have no work experience or skills in garment manufacture or other forms of employment. The training offered by nongovernmental agencies, as noted earlier, may provide some skill training, but the assertion of a reserve army of labor "available in the quantities and qualities required" would lead one to expect that male tailors would have served as the appropriate labor force. What makes the selection of a female labor force especially salient in the early 1980s was the importance the Ershad regime gave to the use of Islam as a mechanism for maintaining forms of gender exploitation while "freeing" women to engage in modern sector activities. The contradiction posed by increasing the demand for women workers while simultaneously increasing the salience of Islam in public discourse highlights the malleability of cultural practice and the emergence of new definitions of female status and marriageability, new forms of mobility, and gendered patterns of class formation and class relations.

Afshar (1985:66) has argued that state-authorized Islam in contemporary Iran has enabled men to benefit from women's increased exploitation under capitalism by maintaining market control in the hands of men while employing women as a cheap source of labor. As she notes,

> In the Third World, the dynamics of capitalist relations of production are severely constrained . . . by the social and political control of men over women's lives. In this context there is a strong psychological and ideological dimension that enables men to exchange women and to control . . . women's productive . . . capacities. . . .

During the latter part of the regime of Zia Rahman (1975–1981) there was a growing trend toward integrating Islam into everyday discourse. In 1979, for example, a constitutional amendment removed the four state principles, including secularism, and inserted the words *"Bismillah-ar-rahman-ar-rahim"* (in the name of Allah, the beneficent, the merciful) in the preamble to the constitution. Similarly, in 1982, the army attempted to tar the midriffs of middle-class women wearing short sari blouses while shopping in one of the largest markets in Dhaka city. After an immediate and broad-based negative response by Dhakites, the action was quickly called a mistake by the government. Finally, in 1983, the regime attempted to replace English with Arabic as the second language of instruction. This, too, was immediately abandoned by the government after demonstrations erupted on the Dhaka University campus.

Between 1985 and 1988 there has been a resurgence of the fundamentalist Islamic party, the Jamaati-i-Islami, which encouraged selected elements of the urban middle classes to adopt more conservative Islamic practices. These practices included increasing women's observance of *purdah* as epitomized by the wearing of a *burkha* in public places and paying Dhaka women Tk700 per month (greater than an average monthly take-home salary of government employees and equivalent to US$21) to visit middle-class homes to convince other women to observe Islamic practice. Female university students were also paid to wear a *burkha* and to actively encourage others to do likewise. Rather than challenge these efforts, the government moved toward an increased rapprochement with the Islamic party in order to build its own political hegemony.

But by far the strongest and most institutionalized pro-Islamic action taken by the Ershad government was the June 7, 1988, passage of the Eighth Amendment to the Constitution, which made Islam the state religion. Numerous intellectuals and government officials interpreted this action simply as a mechanism used by Ershad to secure his own power. One explanation, for example, suggested that the passage of the Eighth Amendment simply represented the regime's effort to co-opt the growing strength of the Jamaati-i-Islami Party. Others suggested that it should be understood as an effort by the regime to diffuse the political impact of the opposition parties which, during the late 1980s, numbered more than twenty under the broad umbrella of the Bangladesh Nationalist Party (BNP) of ex-President Zia Rahman[11] and the Awami League, representing an eight-party alliance led by the daughter of Sheik Mujib, Sheik Hasina Wajed. Finally, still other observers interpreted the passage of the amendment as a weak effort by the Ershad regime to gain the support of the conservative, but not necessarily fundamentalist, elements in the society. As the prime minister made clear, "the bill would consolidate national unity and resist the growth of fundamentalism" (Kamaluddin 1988:14).

The interpretation of the Eighth Amendment as a symbolic political device to co-opt opposition forces was undoubtedly partially correct, but such an interpretation has underestimated, if not ignored, the possible consequences of this political strategy for women, especially in terms of their relatively recent access to public and private sector employment and in terms of the labor conditions in EPZs. Moreover, the interpretations of the new amendment do not identify the likely costs of Islamicization for working women who, in the context of their increasing demand for wage employment, and the increasing demand for their labor, are unlikely to be able to observe restrictive Islamic practices. To the extent that these practices include limits on women's mobility and employment, they also challenge the safety of women already employed in EPZs.[12]

An incident at Dhaka University in 1988, for instance, suggests the harassment and violence that women may face as they seek higher education at coeducational institutions or employment in the industrial sector. During a university examination, a woman was called from class, ostensibly to talk with a relative about an illness in the family. The woman left the classroom, however, only to be accosted by a man wearing a *burkha* who challenged her for not doing likewise. Similar incidents in Chittagong and Rajshahi universities, which were assumed to be the responsibility of the Jamaai-i-Islami Party, were ignored or only minimally challenged by university officials or the Ershad regime. As isolated incidents, one might not call into question the government's benign neglect of these happenings. However, in Bangladesh as in Pakistan, incidents such as these are not isolated but are likely to represent a trend that may portend difficult times for women.

The decline of the legitimacy of the Ershad regime throughout the late 1980s, despite efforts to co-opt elements of the opposition parties, resulted in his being ousted in late 1990. His ouster was partially the result of increasing violence, the breakdown of government bureaucratic functions, fragmentation of support among the military, growing campus unrest, and broad charges of corruption. The victory of the BNP under Begum Zia suggests the continued presence of factions within the army and more indirect support for Islam.[13]

Not surprising given the myriad of ways development programs and opportunities have provided women greater access to each other—a result of the rural cooperative movement, nongovernmental rural development programs, and group credit and training schemes—the passing of the Eighth Amendment brought forward a strong response from a number of female constituencies. There were two marches in Dhaka city immediately following the constitutional decision, one by the women's arm of the Communist Party (Mahila Samity) and the other organized by a coalition of women's groups including academic women and liberal and leftist elements of the NGO community. These responses followed more circumscribed responses of women to challenges to their control of resources and activities within development programs and would have been unthinkable two decades earlier. They represent a growing confidence and power garnered by the opportunity for women to come together and to politicize their personal claims to autonomy and struggle. Quite surprising, however, has been the limited response from the international donors to the fundamentalist turn of events and the possible effects of the amendment on their demands for an export-led development strategy. Sadly, the natural disasters of spring 1991 have drawn attention away from long-range planning initiatives, including the stability of export production in the country, and focused available resources and attention on meeting the needs of those struck by the recent typhoons, floods, and tornadoes.

CONCLUSIONS

I have argued that in both their ideologies and cultural practices people shape and respond to processes of global and domestic economic restructuring in organizing their daily lives. Through an examination of the changing policy environment in Bangladesh, I have drawn attention to how women's opportunities for employment have emerged as a process of negotiation between changing expressions of appropriate behavior under Islam and the demand for female workers by a small but growing number of export-processing firms. I have also drawn attention to the changing employment demands of women well before the institutionalization of export production, emphasizing the way in which the availability of a female labor force is constructed over time. I have also extended the analysis of the impact of the global economic crisis beyond those of Latin America and Africa to countries with limited private-bank credit, slower inflation rate increases, and fewer problems with meeting debt payments.

Lastly, the chapter has drawn particular attention to the contradictory consequences for women of ideologies that support gender segregation and a rigid gender division of labor and to the ways in which normative expectations of women's status have been used to construct strategies of recruitment and labor relations. On the one hand, parental and familial authority under Islam were assumed to protect women from conditions of exploitation and inequality in the marketplace. Similarly, recruitment dependent on the privilege of male entrepreneurs has been used under the guise of protecting young women joining a garment-manufacturing firm. On the other hand, however, such paternalism has limited women's access to and control of state and private resources that would enable their autonomous and independent activity. It has also placed women workers in vulnerable positions vis-à-vis their employers, who take advantage of their village connection to control the expression of women workers in various forms of labor activity and organization. I have also identified a popular interpretation of the resurgence of Islam in Bangladesh, which suggests that it simply represents political maneuvering of the regime in power but will have no impact on the country's ideological posture or on its development strategy. It is equally possible to propose that the incorporation of fundamentalist ideas into state doctrine will pressure the government to declare the country an Islamic state and to replace secular law with Islamic law. The example from Pakistan is noteworthy because the establishment of Islam as the state religion brought with it the replacement of the family code with Shariat law, significantly reducing women's rights to property, divorce, and decisionmaking.

NOTES

This chapter benefited from the critical reading of Florence McCarthy and Linda Shaw.

1. Middle-class urban women can be found in some markets, but men and young children continue to take much of the responsibility for most rural marketing. Moreover, although the numbers are indeed dramatic, the increasing visibility of women workers—in construction and food-for-work jobs—is indicative of a slow process of immiseration rather than a cataclysmic change in the economic stability of households.

2. The study of export production workers and the New Industrial Policy was carried out between March and November 1984, and was supported by Fulbright

Grant No. 83-006-IC (Feldman 1984). Valuable assistance was provided by Fazila Banu. Data coding and analysis were assisted by the College of Agriculture and Life Sciences, Cornell University. Data used here are drawn from an interregional comparative study of workers in domestic and export manufacturing firms.

3. Some attention has been focused on Indonesia, the Philippines, and Malaysia, especially since the debt crisis of 1982. However, given the extent to which the debt crisis, as a specific form of global instability and uneven development, has been used synonymously with other indicators of crisis, the research emphasis has been on its Latin American character.

4. These figures take into account the differences in population size and gross national product.

5. Bangladesh has not been faced by drastic inflation although given the small margins under which most households live, even modest changes have undermined daily survival for more than half the population.

6. A notable exception to this has been the pioneering work of UNICEF (Cornia, Jolly, and Stewart 1987) despite its focus on the most vulnerable. The term "social reproduction" means the maintenance and re-creation of the conditions of everyday life.

7. These reforms include tax holidays, easy credit terms, and easy repatriation terms for foreign investors.

8. The reason for the establishment of an export-processing enclave as opposed to an export-processing zone reflects the impoverishment of the Bangladesh economy to set aside land and create the infrastructural supports, including power, water, and road facilities, to enable the concentration of export production units. Throughout the chapter the terms "enclave" and "zone" will be used interchangeably.

9. The 10-percent quota for women required for all public sector jobs introduced with the Second Five Year Plan (1980–1985) was the first explicit consideration given to integrating women into the development process after nearly three decades of development planning in the region. Interestingly, the 10-percent quota actually served as a means of limiting women's equitable access to public sector jobs because the demand for such jobs exceeded the stated quota and resulted in limiting the hiring of women to 10 percent.

10. Recognizing the conditions of female poverty does not necessarily suggest an appreciation of women's needs, interests, or work commitments. It simply identifies the availability of a usually cheap female labor supply and the need to support women if households and children are to be maintained. One example of this is the growth of vulnerable group-feeding programs that identify women and children in need of food (and work) but do not build on the specific interests and concerns of women.

11. The BNP was composed of a seven-party alliance under the leadership of Begum Zia.

12. There is some evidence to suspect that a declining market for Bangladeshi exports and increased tariffs and restrictions on Bangladeshi goods could contract the market for Bangladeshi labor, generating a declining demand for female export-processing workers. One could argue that the effort to develop a rap-

prochement between Ershad and the Jamaati-i-Islami Party could provide the ideological justification for forcing women out of the labor market and limiting employment opportunities to men. There is insufficient evidence to elaborate this further here. See Feldman and McCarthy (forthcoming).

13. The coming to power of the Awami League might have led to more secular forms of state practice.

REFERENCES

Afshar, Haleh. 1985. "The Position of Women in an Iranian Village." Ch. 3, pp. 66–82, in Haleh Afshar (ed.), *Women, Work, and Ideology in the Third World*. London: Tavistock.

Bangladesh. 1982. "Manpower Situation in Contemporary Bangladesh: Findings of the Bangladesh Manpower Survey of 1980." Dhaka: Ministry of Planning, Bureau of Statistics.

———. 1984. "Preliminary Report on Labour Force Survey, 1983–1984." Dhaka: Ministry of Planning, Bureau of Statistics.

———. 1988. "Memorandum for the Bangladesh AID Group 1988–89." Dhaka: Ministry of Planning, Bangladesh AID Group (March 20).

Cornia, Giovanni A., Richard Jolly, and Francis Stewart (eds.). 1987. *Adjustment with a Human Face*. Oxford: Clarendon Press.

ESCAP (Economic and Social Commission for Asia and the Pacific). 1981. "Population of Bangladesh." New York: United Nations, Country Monograph Series No. 8.

Feldman, Shelley. 1984. Fulbright Islamic Civilization Research Program Field Notes. Grant No. 83-006-IC (10/4/83).

———. 1989. "The Changing Rural Landscape: Emerging Proto-Industrial Interests in Bangladesh." Paper presented at Association of Women in Development Conference, "The Global Empowerment of Women," Washington, D.C., November 17, 1989.

———. "Contradictions of Gender Inequality: Urban Class Formation in Contemporary Bangladesh." In Alice Clark (ed.), *Gender and Political Economy: Explorations of South Asian Systems*. Delhi: Oxford University Press (forthcoming).

Feldman, Shelley, Farida Akhter, and Fazila Banu. 1980. An Analysis and Evaluation of the IRDP Women's Programme in Population Planning and Rural Women's Cooperatives. Dacca: Bangladesh, Consultancy Report.

Feldman, Shelley, and Florence E. McCarthy. 1983. "Purdah and Changing Patterns of Social Control Among Rural Women in Bangladesh." *Journal of Marriage and the Family* (November):949–949.

———. *The Gender and Development Matrix: Development Policy in Bangladesh*. London: Macmillan (forthcoming).

Hardy, Chandra S. 1982. Rescheduling Developing-Country Debts, 1956–1982: Lessons and Reconnaissance. Overseas Development Council, Monograph 15.

Hossain, Mahabub. 1987. "Employment Generation Through Cottage Industries— Potentials and Constraints: The Case of Bangladesh." Pp. 19–57 in Rizwanul

Islam (ed.), *Rural Industrialisation and Employment in Asia.* New Delhi: International Labour Organisation, Asian Employment Programme.

IFC (International Finance Corporation). 1988. "Foreign Investment in Bangladesh." Washington, D.C.: IFC (January).

Kamaluddin, S. 1988. "The Islamic Way." *Far Eastern Economic Review* (June 23):14–17.

Korner, Peter, Gero Maass, Thomas Siebold, and Rainer Tetzlaff. 1984. *The IMF and the Debt Crisis.* London: Zed Books Ltd.

Maguire, Michael. 1986. "Recruitment as a Means of Control." Pp. 58–74 in Kate Purcell, Stephen Wood, Alan Waton, and Sheila Allen (eds.), *The Changing Experience of Employment.* London: Macmillan Press Ltd.

McCarthy, Florence E. 1980. "Patterns of Employment and Income Earning Among Female Household Labour." Dacca: Ministry of Agriculture.

McCarthy, Florence E., Roshan Akter, and Saleh Sabbah. 1979. "Rural Women Workers in Bangladesh: A Working Paper." Dacca: Ministry of Agriculture and Forests, Women's Section, Planning and Development Division, mimeo.

McCarthy, Florence, and Shelley Feldman. 1983. "Rural Women Discovered: New Sources of Capital and Labor in Bangladesh." *Development and Change* 14:211–236.

Pearson, Ruth. 1988. "Female Workers in the First and Third Worlds: The Greening of Women's Labour." Pp. 449–466 in R. E. Pahl (ed.), *On Work.* Oxford: Basil Blackwell.

Phelan, Brian (additions by Dan Jones). 1986. *Made in Bangladesh? Women, Garments and the Multi-Fibre Arrangement.* London: BIAG (Bangladesh International Action Group).

World Bank. 1983. *Bangladesh Selected Issues in Rural Employment.* Washington, D.C.: World Bank Report No. 4292-BD (March 11).

———. 1988a. *Bangladesh: Adjustment in the Eighties and Short-Term Prospects.* Vol. I. Washington, D.C.: The World Bank, Report No. 7105-BD.

———. 1988b. *World Development Report 1988.* Washington, D.C.: The World Bank.

6

The Politics of Bolivia's Economic Crisis: Survival Strategies of Displaced Tin-Mining Households

✒ WENDY McFARREN

Many observers point to Bolivia as a country that successfully implemented structural adjustment measures. The 1985 IMF-sponsored policy, Decree 21060, certainly had almost miraculous effects there. The inflation rate, for example, dropped from 20,000 percent in 1984 to 20 percent by 1988. Food could be found in the stores, general strikes were curtailed, and the banking system had an inflow of currency into its empty vaults. Yet, this recovery has been fragile, as growth is stagnant and the country continues to depend heavily on foreign aid. Furthermore, those who point to this apparent success fail to ask a number of fundamental questions about the effects of this adjustment: What were the social costs, and, more importantly, who paid the price?

This chapter is based on fieldwork I conducted in Bolivia during January and February 1988. I was concerned with understanding how Bolivian mining households were affected by and responded to Decree 21060. The central component of the decree was the restructuring of the nationalized tin industry and the closing of most of the Bolivian tin mines. By January 1987, over 27,000 of the 30,000 mining labor force had lost their jobs. As a result, the displaced workers, called the *relocalizados,* migrated with their families to urban and tropical colonization areas. Approximately 4,000 families moved to the capital city of La Paz, and most of them to El Alto, the peripheral city located on the 13,000-foot (4,000-meter) plateau bordering the La Paz canyon.

I conducted interviews with thirty women who migrated to newly created El Alto settlements. I wanted to learn how the economic crisis affected them and their families and how they responded to it. My findings highlight a number of important dimensions of the effects of economic adjustment. First, miners as a group paid a great part of the cost of Bolivia's adjustment, both in economic and political terms. Second, women of Bolivian mining households played a central role in compensating for rapidly declining resources at a household and a community level. Third, their ability to provide these resources was greatly affected by past organizing experience within the Mining Housewives Federation. This past participation empowered them to take action to obtain resources. And finally, gender and political ideology greatly influenced the nature and success of resource mobilization efforts.

The following is the story of one country's experience with economic adjustment and how it affected one particular social group. I begin with a macroeconomic analysis of the debt and tin crises, which brought on the adjustment measures and set the framework for household-level activities. I follow this overview of Bolivia's economic situation with a comparative microlevel account of the experiences of migrant mining families in two El Alto neighborhoods several years after the restructuring plans were announced.[1]

BOLIVIA'S ECONOMIC CRISIS

In 1984, Bolivia's economy was in a perilous condition. Although return to democratic rule after two decades of dictatorship initially brought hope to the country, the transition was marred by a severe economic crisis. A sense of hopelessness loomed in the air, in great contrast to the excitement after electoral democracy was reestablished in 1982. Escalating inflation was certainly creating much havoc. Market women refused to sell their wares, and even eggs had to be purchased under the table. Furthermore, inflation and speculation essentially made the formal banking system dysfunctional: The peso was worthless, and Bolivians purchased dollars on the black market instead of investing in the banks.

The new left-wing government of Hernan Siles Zuazo[2] tried to control the rise of inflation and the growing trade deficit. He attempted to implement six austerity measures, called *paquetes*. But in each case the militant Central Workers' Union (COB), disillusioned with his compromise with the IMF, called for a general strike when Siles did not meet its wage demands. These general strikes paralyzed the country to the extent that for over thirty days in 1984 most economic activity stopped. The cycle of economic deterioration was vicious: Inflation rose, Siles announced another measure, the wage value rapidly deteriorated, and in response the unions demanded wage increases. When their demands

were not met they called for another general strike. Production deteriorated, and as a result the balance of payments worsened. After two years
of office it became evident that Siles could not counter the power of the
labor unions and even less confront the country's crisis. As a result, he
was forced to call for early elections in 1984. When President Victor Paz
Estenssoro took office in 1985 he was therefore determined to stop the
COB from standing in the way of his neoliberal adjustment measures.

In this section I outline the causes of Bolivia's economic crisis that
both presidents tried to confront during their presidencies. I also examine
how the tin miners—the primary targets of adjustment—responded to
these measures. I believe that this economic and political context must
be examined to understand the household and community survival
strategies of the El Alto mining families.

THE DEBT CRISIS

Perhaps the most significant cause of Bolivia's economic crisis
was the large debt that its military government incurred in the early
1970s. During this period the government of General Hugo Banzer Suárez
took out large loans from eager international lenders who were greatly
oversupplied with petrodollars. Like many other Latin American dictators,
Banzer used these funds for political favors required to ensure support
for his military regime and also to finance speculative high-technology
industries such as agroindustries and natural gas production in the
lowland Santa Cruz region of Bolivia (Malloy 1987).

This economic strategy created a boom production period in the
1970s, but the damage it inflicted on Bolivia's economy became obvious
beginning in 1978. By 1985 Bolivia's external debt totaled $3.9 billion;
although it was small compared to other Latin American countries it was
significant for a country of 6.4 million people (see Figure 6.1). During
this same year, debt servicing represented 29.1 percent of exports,
compared to 11.3 percent in 1970. And as a percent of gross national
product (GNP), outstanding external public debt grew from 47.3 percent
in 1970 to 136.8 percent in 1985 (*World Development Report* 1987).

THE TIN CRISIS

The crisis of the Nationalized Tin Company (COMIBOL) is the
other fundamental cause of Bolivia's severe economic crisis. COMIBOL
experienced serious problems because the global economic recession
reduced the price and demand for natural resource commodities.[3] The
industry's crisis is similar to that of other primary, producing Third World
countries. Throughout the Third World, export receipts fell by approxi-

Figure 6.1   Official Bolivian Foreign Debt, 1972–1984: Multilateral and Bilateral Loans (in millions of U.S. dollars)

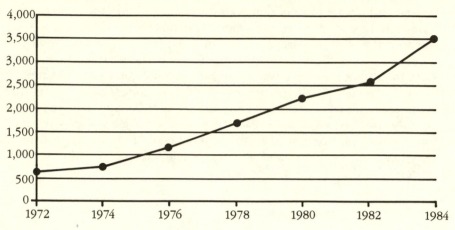

Source: Malloy and Gamarra 1988.

mately 3 percent from 1979 to 1983. In contrast, manufacturing receipts increased by 45 percent (Van de Hoeven and Richards 1987). The effect of these changes therefore struck Latin American and African countries the hardest because they could not compete for manufacturing with the Asian newly industrialized countries (NICs). Fluctuations in tin prices seriously destabilized Bolivia's tin-based economy. In 1985 the price of tin was only $6.00 per pound, falling to $2.50 in 1986 after the collapse of the tin market (Tin Statistics 1987). COMIBOL's losses grew from an estimated $30 million in 1980 to $165 million in 1985, and tin's contribution to legal export earnings dropped from 62.3 percent in 1980 to only 21.7 percent in 1986.

This price reduction also represented a serious blow because Bolivia, of all tin-producing countries, had the highest extraction cost of $6.47 per pound due to the nature of extractive mining (UNITAS 1987). To reach the ore, workers needed to drill through solid rock in difficult-to-reach mines located above 13,000 feet (4,000 meters). In contrast, producers in Malaysia, Indonesia, and Brazil use dredges to extract tin from alluvial deposits at much lower costs. Production levels in Bolivia were also low because previous governments did not reinvest in the mines; rather, they transferred mining revenues to other economic sectors such as lowland agroindustry. Because of the resulting lack of exploration, technology became obsolete, equipment deteriorated, and the veins were depleted. Tin production, as a result, dropped dramatically in the 1980s, in contrast to the 1970s when tin prices were high and COMIBOL experienced a production boom.

Figure 6.2   Bolivia's Exports, 1980–1986 (in millions of U.S. dollars)

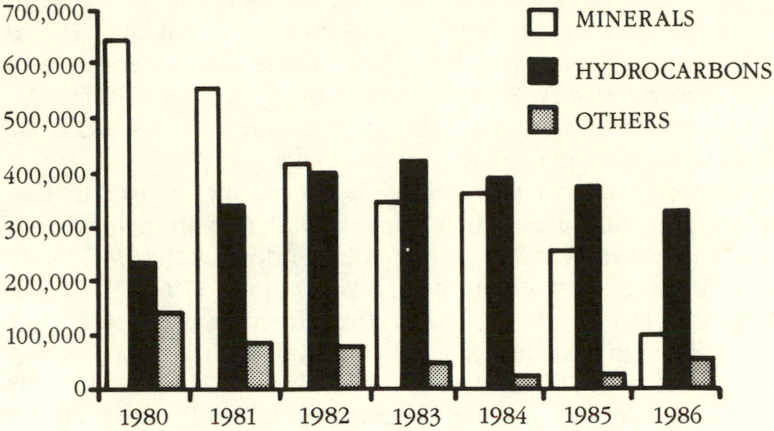

Source: UNITAS 1987.

The state-owned mining company was therefore in a vulnerable position when the world tin market collapsed in October 1985. Tin prices plummeted when the twenty-two–nation International Tin Cartel (ITC) ran out of money and was unable to meet its debt obligations (Crabtree, Duffy, and Pearce 1986). The ITC's economic situation deteriorated because aluminum tin-free steelplate was substituted for tin in the production process and new low-cost producers, such as Brazil and China, undermined the cartel's price and production quotas.

Because of this fall in tin prices and COMIBOL's high production costs, Bolivia's exports decreased from $1.04 billion in 1980 to one-half billion in 1986 (UNITAS 1987). And, as shown in Figure 6.2, no other (formal) economic sector compensated for this dramatic loss in mining revenue. Instead, the unregulated economy played a central role in compensating for the collapse of the formal economy. In particular, the cocaine industry replaced tin as the country's economic primary commodity by generating an estimated US$600 million in foreign exchange. (Malloy 1987; Flores and Blanes 1984; Doria Medina 1986). Similarly, many rural and urban Bolivians increasingly obtained their primary source of income through the sale of contraband goods from Chile, Peru, Argentina, and Brazil.

A DROP IN GNP AND HYPERINFLATION

The impact of this economic crisis on Bolivia's economy was a reduction in per capita GNP and income, along with a dramatic escalation of inflation rates. From 1980 to 1984, per capita GNP dropped by 27.5

percent. The balance of payments turned from a $4 million surplus in 1970 to a $282 million deficit in 1985 (*World Development Report* 1987). However, the most vivid reflection of the country's economic crisis is the inflation rate, the most rapid increase in Latin America and one of the highest in world history. Prices increased by 20,000 percent from August 1984 to August 1985; and from May 1985 to August 1985 hyperinflation climbed to a 60,000 percent annual rate (Sachs 1987).

Harvard economist Jeffrey Sachs, the economic advisor to the Paz administration, attributes Bolivia's hyperinflation to an increase in international interest rates and to the cutoff in lending by the IMF, the World Bank, and private creditors in the first years of the 1980s. The net effect of these two factors was to reverse the direction of resource transfer between Bolivian and international financial institutions. There was a net resource flow of $178 million toward Bolivia in 1980, but by 1983 the transfer flowed in the opposite direction by $190 million (Sachs 1987). The government, thus, had to meet this net drop in international financing with an inflation tax, the printing of new money. This so devalued the Bolivian peso that it was a common sight to see waist-high stacks of bills in front of gas stations and workers carrying home their wages in large flour sacks.

This economic instability placed a huge social cost on the Bolivian population. Inflation reduced the value of currency by half from one day to the next, making wages useless. Central government social-service expenditures also dropped considerably. For example, government expenditures on health care, as a percent of total expenditures, dropped from 6.2 percent in 1972 to 1.5 percent in 1985 and the education budget fell from 31 percent to 12.2 percent (*World Development Report* 1987).

To cope with the severe problems in the tin industry and in the economy as a whole, President Paz Estenssoro[4] announced the New Economic Policy (NEP). It was essentially designed to reduce the disequilibrium in the balance of payments, to put a halt to hyperinflation, to allow the country to meet its debt payments, and to restore the country's credit rating, which had been severely damaged during the previous governments of Luis García Meza and Tejada Siles.

Paz Estenssoro's neoliberal solution included a number of measures that are commonly included in IMF structural adjustment programs. The strategy centered on bringing money into the economy by raising petroleum prices, eliminating restrictions on foreign exchange circulation, and instead implementing a free-floating system to allow for frequent reevaluation of the exchange rate. A central part of this program involved recycling coca-dollars into the legal sector, a feat largely accomplished by prohibiting local, departmental, or national officials from investigating the origins of residents' fortunes. The decree also included a tax reform, a massive currency devaluation, and the replacement of the worthless peso by the boliviano (Sanchez de Lozada 1985; Grebe 1985; UNITAS 1987).

THE RESTRUCTURING OF THE TIN INDUSTRY

The central component of the restructuring program was to reduce the size of the state sector by privatizing firms and cutting subsidies and payrolls in public offices. Although the largest public firm in Bolivia was the nationalized tin industry, this state-sector reduction strategy centered on the denationalization of COMIBOL. Through Decree 21137 unproductive mines were closed, productive mines were turned over to the private sector, and cooperatives were encouraged to exploit a few mines with potential for profit.[5] The president's analysis of the tin crisis was in step with a World Bank study placing much of the blame for the industry's problems on the high degree of worker militancy, their involvement in COMIBOL's administration of the mines, and the high cost of the food subsidies, health, and education provided by the nationalized industry to its workers (Ayub and Hashimoto 1985). In the end, 23,000 of COMIBOL's 30,000 workers lost their jobs between August 1985 and January 1987 as a result of the adjustment program designed to deal with these problems. And when workers from the private mines are included, the unemployed approached 27,000 (*Presencia,* August 29, 1987; Arauco 1988).

THE MINERS' RESPONSE TO ADJUSTMENT

Not surprisingly, the miners were fervently against the closings of the mines, which represented their and their ancestors' lifework and constituted an important part of their cultural heritage. They had produced the nation's primary source of wealth since the beginning of the century and were the largest segment of the public labor force. Because of this economic importance, they constituted a powerful political force— heavily influenced by various streams of Marxist ideology, including Trotskyism, Marxist-Leninism and Maoism[6]—that through the Federated Syndicate of Mining Workers (FSTMB) dominated the COB since Bolivia's revolution in 1952. During the following three decades, when military regimes ruled the country, the miners were the victims of repression through massacres, imprisonment, and torture because of their resistance and protest against harsh working and living conditions (Dunkerley 1984; Lora 1977; Nash 1979; Barrios de Chungara 1978).

These harsh experiences also turned the miners' wives into a distinctively militant group of women. Organized in the Federación de Amas de Casas Mineras (the Federation of Mining Housewives) the women organized hunger strikes, road blockades, sit-ins, and marches to release their husbands from jail or to obtain cheaper prices and better goods in the *pulperias,* the subsidized company stores (Barrios de Chungara 1979).[7]

With this as their historical experience, men and women from the mining districts responded strongly to Paz Estenssoro's adjustment plans. In contrast to the president's neoliberal diagnosis, as a group the miners believed that although the tin industry did face severe economic problems, the restructuring of COMIBOL involved a fundamentally political agenda on the part of the Paz Estenssoro government because the miners were such powerful political foes. Victor López, leader of the FSTMB in 1986, explained the miners' perception of the restructuring plans:

> Drops in production, high costs, inflation, lack of investment that prevented any effective remedy—this was the situation encountered by the New Economic Program that saw a need to minimize the state mining sector operations without taking into consideration the serious problems which were already apparent. The policy of the neo-liberal government was thus to dissect the corporation into various small firms; because this socially weakened the organization of workers and separated the global context of the corporation into smaller units which would be profitable for private firms.
>
> We understand perfectly well what has happened and it is true that we have to make an Emergency Plan to introduce the adjustments which are necessary, costs, methods of production, etc., to keep the majority of the people working. We're against laying off the people because we see the political problems that are behind it and, secondly, because no job alternatives exist. (Interview by author, January 1988)

The miners and the government evidently differed both in their perceptions of and solutions to the crisis. Paz Estenssoro saw problems in the high costs of production, labor instability, and low production, and as a result, he was determined to straighten out the company's balance sheets. His neoliberal solution was to eliminate state control of the mines and to transfer the mines to the control of the private sector. The miners, in contrast, saw the industry's crisis as a result of mismanagement by authoritarian administrations and argued that only a nationalized firm would provide miners with jobs. They did not believe that the private sector would take up the slack left by the closing of the nationalized mines and reasoned that it would be reluctant to incorporate militant miners. Tin, the miners argued, could be an economically viable source of wealth for the nation if investments were made in the mines to increase production. Essentially, they believed that the issue at hand was not whether tin was a profitable commodity. Rather, the issue was who owns the ore and controls the work process.

In spite of their general consensus against COMIBOL's restructuring, the miners were not united against Paz Estenssoro's measures, a fact that would seriously affect their mobilization efforts. One group that took a more radical stance was the Eje de Convergencia Patriotica, a coalition of left-wing political parties under the direction of labor leader Juan Lechín Oquendo. The Eje resisted the closing of the mines at any cost and directed a series of general strikes that paralyzed the country, as it had done in response to Siles's measures. In its alternative plan, *Unidad al pueblo para derrotar a la oligarquia y al imperialismo* ("Unity of the people to defeat the oligarchy and imperialism"), the Eje called instead for the nationalization of all of the medium-sized mines that were privately owned. The other group, El Grupo de los 17, under the leadership of former Trotskyist leader Federico Escobar and Simón Reyes from the Bolivian Communist Party (PCB), took a more conciliatory stance with the Paz Estenssoro program. Escobar presented his own emergency rehabilitation plan, the Catavi Thesis, which was overwhelmingly selected as the official platform of the FSTMB. It involved a strategy to confront COMIBOL's economic problems. The miners would reduce the mine's top-heavy administrative costs by making themselves administrators of the mines and would increase production through forty-five days of uninterrupted work. Escobar elaborated this plan for the Catavi mine to include all other COMIBOL mines and presented this alternative Emergency Plan to Paz Estenssoro.

La Marcha por La Vida

To pressure Paz Estenssoro to approve this Emergency Plan, the miners' union organized the March for Life (*La Marcha por la Vida*) on August 22, 1986—the week that the president was expected to announce the details of his restructuring program. This event was the most significant labor mobilization against COMIBOL's restructuring after a long series of unsuccessful hunger and general strikes. It was an opportunity for the miners to show their strength and unity and to let Paz Estenssoro know that they would not allow the mines to close. Five thousand miners marched 150 miles along the arid flatland between the cities of Oruro and La Paz. The Housewives' Federation members marched with their children along the route and provided food for all of the participants, proceeding ahead of the crowd to prepare communal meals and drinks. They were encouraged by the strong popular support of students, teachers, and peasants, who joined the line or cheered them on from the side. Many of these supporters had also been affected by government budget cuts and saw the mobilization as an opportunity to make their interests known to the Paz administration and to improve their respective conditions (Crabtree, Duffy, and Pearce 1986).

Although the event was peaceful, Paz Estenssoro saw a great potential for social unrest and militant resistance to his plan. Learning from Siles's experience, he was determined not to allow the miners to compromise his restructuring plans. On August 26, Paz rejected the miners' Emergency Plan and announced Decree 21137, his own rehabilitation plan for COMIBOL: Administrative, mining, and smelting activities were to be decentralized and the most profitable mines turned over to the private mining companies. The following day, when the miners were in the town of Calamarca, thirty-five miles outside of the city of La Paz, the president declared a state of siege and ordered the army to surround the marchers with tanks and to arrest labor leaders.

The union was again divided in its response to Estenssoro's show of force. The Eje favored trying to continue the march and argued that the miners' bargaining power would be weakened if they negotiated and abandoned the march. The Grupo de Los 17, in contrast, decided to negotiate with the government. They argued that it was necessary to negotiate in order to avoid further repression and because they believed that grass-roots support for a confrontation with the military was weak, since thousands of workers had already resigned and accepted severance pay.

The resulting agreement reached with the FSTMB leaders and the government on September 13 virtually maintained Decree 21137 as written. The government's only compromise was that it agreed to reconsider its plan for turning some of the mines into cooperatives, but it soon backed out on its promise. Imprisoned mining leaders were released, and the FSTMB agreed to put an end to its pressure on the government.

After the March for Life

The state of siege was a defeat for the Mining Federation and signaled the end to their dominance within the Bolivian political arena. After the March for Life, the marchers returned to the mining districts, greatly disillusioned and with little hope for a future as miners. The severance pay offered by the government seemed to offer the most promise. The relocation process, begun in February of 1986, sped up as a result. When all figures were counted, the number of COMIBOL *relocalizados,* 23,000, was almost twice the 14,000 that the Rehabilitation Plan had foreseen. It was an astonishing and inconceivable development that so many miners, who are known for their militancy and rebellion, would "voluntarily" hand in their resignation notices. Table 6.1 shows the number of unemployed estimated by COMIBOL as of May 1987.

TABLE 6.1 Unemployed COMIBOL Workers, August 1985 to May 1987

Mine	Employed August 1985	Unemployed May 5, 1987	Percent Reduction of Staff in Mine	Percent of Total Unemployed
Quechisla	4,818	4,604	96	20
Catavi	4,509	3,961	88	18
Colquiri	2,514	1,977	79	9
Huanuni	2,243	1,317	59	6
Uniflcada	2,028	1,632	80	7
San José	1,850	1,309	71	6
Caracoles	1,176	1,028	87	5
Santa Fe	1,038	830	80	4
Corocoro	989	963	97	4
Viloco	787	627	79	3
Matilde	635	606	95	3
Bolivar	614	206	34	1
Colquechaca	417	407	98	2
Colavi	402	378	94	2
Ferro Corp.	288	65	23	0
Pulacajo	322	146	45	1
Rio Yura	288	141	49	1
Metalurgia Oruro	120	89	74	0
La Palca Plant	583	541	93	2
Machamarca	150	131	87	0
La Paz Central Office	658	478	73	2
Oruro Office	975	914	94	4
Bolsa Negra	23	–	–	–
Kami	11	4	37	–
Other COMIBOL establishments	130	41	31	0
Total	27,568	22,310		100

Source: Presencia, August 29, 1987 (based on National Tin Company [COMIBOL] and Centro de Promoción Minero [CEPROMIN] data).

Without employment or subsidies and evicted from the company houses, mining households were faced with the task of starting new lives. Most decided to leave the mining districts and migrated to the large urban centers—Sucre, Potosí, Oruro, and especially La Paz and Cochabamba—because of greater opportunities for employment (see Table 6.2). Others decided to remain in the mining areas and organize themselves into cooperatives, according to the government's controversial plan;[8] a small number of households returned to the agrarian communities where they still had family or land; and in a lesser number of households, the males colonized the tropical frontier.

TABLE 6.2   Destination of Mining Households

City	Number of COMIBOL Workers	Percent of Total
La Paz	5,394	26
Oruro	6,552	32
Cochabamba	2,763	13
Potosi	2,373	11
Llallagua	1,498	7
Tarija	672	3
Sucre	236	1
Santa Cruz	181	1
Puerto Suarez	1	0
Robore	2	0
Camiri	1	0
Villazon	100	0
Tupiza	594	3
Atocha	389	2
Total	20,756	100

Includes only laid-off workers registered in banks for their severance pay as of January 1988. The total laid-off workers (from public and private mines) reached 28,489. Data elaborated by the Programa de Asentamiento Minero in 1988.

Source: Quoted in Sandoval Z. Godofredo and M. Fernando Sostres, La Ciudad Prometida, Pobladores v Organizacions Sociales en El Alto. La Paz: Instituto Latinoamericano de Investigaciones Sociales (ILDIS), 1989.

Approximately 4,250 of these relocalizado families migrated to La Paz. Most of the migrants settled in El Alto. This residential area of approximately 405,000 people has grown rapidly over the last decade with the influx of rural migrants seeking employment in the cities or escaping drought and flooding on the Altiplano. The settlement of this semiurban, semirural area, which spreads out toward the expanse of the Altiplano, has been virtually unplanned, making the provision of basic services extremely difficult. Over half the population does not have electricity, running water, or access to a sewage system, which even its City Hall lacks.

SURVIVAL STRATEGIES OF RELOCALIZADOS IN TWO EL ALTO NEIGHBORHOODS

How did this transition from economic dependence in the mines to economic autonomy affect mining households that migrated to El Alto? In the mining districts their experiences had been both positive and negative. On the one hand, living and working conditions for men and women had been generally horrendous, as Domitila Barrios de Chungara graphically describes in her book *Let Me Speak* (1979). On the other hand, over the years their political clout and mobilization had turned the miners into a relatively privileged group of Bolivian workers. From the state-owned company they received housing and subsidized food, although of poor quality, and their children had access to a good educational system. However, because they were geographically isolated and COMIBOL provided these necessities, mining families were entirely dependent on the company for their livelihood—a fact that was often used to keep them in line. Uprooted from their mining communities, the relocated mining families therefore had to face both the negative and positive consequences of unprotected economic independence.

In an effort to learn how this crisis affected a group of mining households and how they responded, I conducted case study research in three El Alto villas: Katari, Apaza, and Espinal. I interviewed both male and female community leaders, asking about their perception of the crisis, their efforts to generate resources for the community, and the problems they faced. I was particularly interested in the role of women leaders within the community and in how they viewed their experience as women and as members of the mining community. With thirty women from the villas, I then conducted structured interviews designed to obtain information on how households generated income and made use of limited resources.[9]

In addition, I carried out a series of interviews with officials: I met with the president of the Municipal Council of El Alto and with city planners to learn about the resources available at a local level and about how the miners, with their particular form of organization, fit into the local government structure. I also interviewed representatives of private and governmental organizations—specifically those working with women—to gather information on the resources and project-level assistance available to the *relocalizados.* And finally, I met with national FSTMB and COB union leaders to understand how factions within the labor movement perceived the adjustment process.

What follows is a story of the divergent experiences of two of the El Alto settlements—Katari and Apaza—in compensating for declining resources and in generating income. All these migrant families were suffering the effects of the same crisis: They had lost their jobs for the same reasons—the debt crisis, the drop in tin prices, COMIBOL's production problems, and corresponding adjustment measures. They all received severance pay and were trying to survive in the same constrained economy. However, a number of factors differentiated how these households and communities experienced relocation. First, the nature of the development projects and the support systems available to them defined

their experiences. Second, women's roles in obtaining resources determined household and community well-being because women provide
most of the food, clothing, and shelter for their families. Communities
that were able to best mobilize these resources at a community level had
women with leadership experience and, just as importantly, male leaders
who did not feel threatened by the women's independent actions. Gender
and political ideology, as we will see, played an important mediating
role in how migrant households responded to their relocation.

Katari

In November 1986, Margarita Rosa de Montoya's[10] husband lost
his job in the Catavi mine. He was one of the first workers to be laid off
because he had been with the company for only seven years. After all of
his debts to COMIBOL were paid, he was left with $500 in severance
pay, plus $40 per month for ten months.[11] Feeling that they had no
alternative, the Montoyas decided to leave Catavi with Margarita's eight
children plus two from her husband's previous marriage. While he
traveled to Cochabamba to investigate settlement opportunities, Margarita moved to La Paz and found temporary shelter in the COB and Mining
Federation Offices, where other *relocalizados* were regrouping and organizing against the government. She was restless to settle in a permanent
home and to obtain a job, especially since her severance payments were
depleted from expenditures on transportation and food. When a friend
told her of a large complex of abandoned row houses in the Katari region
of El Alto, Margarita saw an opportunity to move:

> I found out that these houses had been constructed for low-income people
> and they were now abandoned. They had closed the doors, the toilets, the
> windows and everything. I found out about them from second parties when
> I was staying at the COB office with my eight children. I got excited and
> applied to move into the buildings. The first day they neither refused nor
> accepted me. The second day they accepted me and told me they would
> help me out. I waited sixteen days, in the meantime spending my US$500,
> which was disappearing fast. So I decided to take my things and move in
> without authorization. I was the first one of everybody who lives here now.
> In the beginning I had many problems with the previous neighbors.
> They even tried to throw me out with the 110 (police). The colonel came
> to threaten me into leaving. But I stood my ground and told him that no, I
> wouldn't leave. "If you want me to leave, take my things out of here and
> I'll build a tent over there."

The colonel let her stay in the abandoned house, and other families
sheltered in the union offices soon followed. They were a diverse group

coming from various mines, including Catavi, Vilocos, and San José, and belonged to different political parties. When a sufficient number of them had moved into the abandoned units, the migrants decided to register their organization legally. They replicated the mining syndicate structure, electing as their *dirigente* and president of the Housewives' Federation a husband-and-wife team who were both affiliated with the Eje de Convergencia Patriótica. Men from the syndicate and women from the Housewives' Committee began to meet regularly, gathering jointly to organize the new community and to strategize on how to obtain income and food. Their past experiences in the mines made this joint action a possibility. In spite of the initial resistance, the miners had reluctantly learned that the women's ability to act politically was central to their struggle for basic needs as well as to their resistance against the military.

Carmen, who was also a national leader of the Housewives' Federation, describes how women became involved in the Siglo XX mine in 1961:

> In those times the men were so *machista* that they would whistle at the women when they first organized in the *pulpería* of Siglo XX. Seeing the marching women—there were always men surrounding them, whistling at them—they'd say: "Let's see if these women will do anything. What will women be able to do anyway?" They shouted all types of things at us, but the women became strong and marched to La Paz. Don Federico Escobar was the leader at that time. The women's husbands were being held in the penitentiary. And then the men heard that the women had organized and were fighting for their husband's freedom: They went on hunger strikes and were able to obtain the freedom of their *compañeros*.
>
> Since then, the Housewives' Committee has grown in all the other mining districts where they had always been shunted before. And ever since, the women have been changing. We have progressed a lot, haven't we? But it has cost us a lot fighting in the companies, in the mines. Mostly, we fight for the *pulpería*. In the beginning, in 1961, they gave us eight items, including meat, bread, sugar, rice, noodles, oil, and lard. Then they took away four articles and we were left with meat, bread, sugar, and rice— nothing else as staples. And we have always fought for weight—so that the bread would be 120 grams. Mostly we struggled for salary, supplies in the *pulperías*, improved housing conditions, and education. So we helped and coordinated with the syndicates, never paralleling their activities. We have always been unified.[12]

It was therefore not out of gender character for Margarita and Carmen to take the initiative and find a source of income from the community. Through their class-based struggles, it had become increasingly acceptable for women to participate in mining community decisionmaking, although only as long as the men perceived a common sense of struggle.

In Katari, their efforts were supported by the male leadership who did share this common understanding based on class identification. They hoped for a permanent source of income through project funding from the growing number of development organizations receiving a large inflow of money after La Marcha por la Vida. Margarita and Carmen developed proposals to start a chicken coop and a handicrafts project and presented their ideas to a few organizations, including the Social Emergency Fund (SEF). This institution was established with the stated intention of offsetting the social costs of the adjustment with money that began to flow into Bolivia from the UN, the United States, and European governments after the miners' defeat. The SEF was designed to pay for infrastructure projects, such as road and sewage construction, that would put the *relocalizados* to work.

However, the SEF and a number of private development organizations rejected the women's income-generating projects because the market for projects such as sewing, mechanics, and artisan shops was glutted. And because the SEF preferred infrastructure projects, it suggested that the Katari families expand their homes through a self-help construction project, called *autoconstrucción:*[13]

> We wanted to start a factory, but the Fund rejected us and said they couldn't give us a loan for a knitting or a sewing factory, or anything. Instead they suggested that we expand our homes. So that's where the idea came from. So then Carmen and I got a proposal together and fortunately it has all worked out.

As part of the project, the Katari families purchased the original two-room units for $2,180. They also took out a $2,000 loan, at 8-percent interest, to pay for the materials for the additions. In teams of five families, the community members worked together to complete one house at a time. An engineer gave them construction instructions, and all materials were brought in by truck. Usually one member of the family worked in a team making adobes, mixing the cement, and laying the corrugated steel roof. For this labor each worker received $40 per month, which provided a minimal amount of subsistence while they constructed the houses. Once one house was finished, the team moved on to construct another.

An important dimension of men and women's participation was their attitude toward this self-help housing project. They expressed skepticism about the project's funding, arguing that the money international institutions donated to the SEF was now controlled by Banzer's conservative party because Banzer had made a pact with Paz Estenssoro during the presidential elections. They felt that this donated money was theirs because of the years of labor spent in the mines and their contribution to the nation's foreign exchange earnings. They stated that it was an insult that these funds were returned in the form of loans and therefore they did not intend to pay back the loans.

For constructing their homes, community members were fortunate to receive a salary, although meager. Otherwise, employment was very difficult to find. Full-time jobs were especially hard to come by, for both men and women, because the adjustment measures had cut the government public jobs and the economic crisis had constrained the growth of the private sector. Adjustment created a 25-percent national unemployment rate in 1987 (*Presencia,* Sept. 29, 1987). And a national-level study of *relocalizado* households found that in July 1987 only 25 percent of all migrants had found paid employment. Of these, 74 percent had temporary and 25 percent had permanent positions (Arauco 1988).

The political dimensions of the restructuring process also became clear when the miners searched for work. Employers were reluctant to hire miners, especially in groups, because of their past militancy, as Margarita noted:

> If they get a whiff that someone is a miner, they no longer want to give us work. There are temporary jobs, but that only lasts three to four days. I think it must be because of the fear that the miners are subversive. But in my opinion, it's not subversion because we only claim our rights.

Virtually their only possible source of income was, therefore, through public works projects, which provided part-time, temporary, and extremely low-paying employment. In Katari most families worked laying cobblestones in the adjacent villa of Brasil during their first few months of residency. As Carmen describes, her entire family worked for a USAID-funded Food for Work project:

> We were relocated from the San José mine. We came with $200, we didn't have food and we no longer had the subsidized stores. So we arrived and started to work. My husband, my children and I worked, all of us. We laid stones in this whole area. With all six of us working, we collected a lot of flour, enough to sell some of it. But the wheat and the milk were harder to sell, so to a large extent that wheat sustained us.

Income from this work was minimal and women, as a result, had to find ways to feed their families while the men worked part time or looked for employment, a task that took most of their time. The women washed clothes, knitted sweaters, and sold food and clothing on the streets. But income-earning opportunities were limited because El Alto's informal market was oversupplied with the wares of other miners or peasant migrants. One woman in the study also stated that for a time she transported contraband goods across the Peruvian border, but she was caught and lost $200 worth of goods. To supplement household income some children also worked, primarily shining shoes or selling candy. Older girls worked as maids in La Paz. However, it is interesting to note that in spite of the great financial need most children stayed in school and did not work. The women stated that their children's school attendance was partly due to El Alto's saturated informal market, but mostly it was due to the parents' determination to keep them in school and continue the education they had received in the mines.

With a limited income, women therefore had to make do with very little, as Carmen describes:

> I would wash clothes, and sometimes clean houses, like the large houses of the gringos. For that they paid me a little bit of money. I'd bring home about 20, 30 pesos a day.
>
> So with that we could buy a little rice, noodles, or sugar, which would last for a few days, and then we were back to eating bread with tea. Our diet was based on flour. We make a meal we call *piri,* from white flour. You toast the flour while you heat a little water, salt, and oil in a pot. You add the flour, you cover it and put a little hole in the top. And that rises like a little volcano, spilling over the pot. And then a kind of curd begins to form and you make a big ball of dough and you eat it like bread, as it is. It's a good substitute for bread, isn't it?

Family meals were thus very simple, as Margarita describes:

> For lunch we have rice, or noodles, or *lagua* (cornmeal soup). Or, if God wills, wheat. If we have money left over, sometimes we buy meat. Not really meat though. We might be able to buy hooves, or the head.

To help compensate for these meager diets, Margarita and Carmen obtained funds from a private nonvoluntary organization to start the sixth of El Alto's seven *olla comúnes* or community kitchens (literally "common pot"), which are similar to the Peruvian *comedores populares.* These kitchens played an important buffering role for El Alto *relocalizado* communities during the crisis. Communal cooking allowed women to provide their families with low-priced and well-balanced meals: soup and a main course with meat and vegetables. The system involved a pooling of cooking labor, costs, and of benefits. Women in the villa purchased ingredients together and took turns preparing the food in large pots, which were either donated or bought with grants from private development organizations. Each individual was then charged for his or her meal and the collected money was recycled to buy ingredients for the next meal.

This idea, Carmen explains, was borrowed from Peruvian mining women who communally provided milk to miners marching in protest from Canaria to Lima:

> In Peru, a form of obtaining sustenance existed called *vaso de leche,* a glass of milk. In a protest march from Canaria to Lima, women along the way organized themselves to prepare glasses of milk. So every place they went they took their pots, their stoves and cooked in large pots. They distributed this milk to all of the people attending the march. That's how we have organized the *ollas comúnes.* And we also did this in the March for Life. Every place we arrived, we rested, the women gathered and in large pots we cooked in the same way. So what difference was it for us, once we left our mines, to organize ourselves in the same way, and to stay organized, so as to not disperse and each go our own way?

In addition to providing a pooled food source, the *olla* was therefore a strategy for the El Alto *relocalizadas* to organize, essentially fulfilling the same function as the *pulperías* of their mining districts.

However, in spite of its important political purpose and buffering role, the *olla* did not function regularly. The first reason was economic. Because income generation was sporadic, some households could not afford to pay the 50 bolivianos for a meal. Households that had longer-term work or had more working-age members preferred to pay an extra 75 bolivianos for an extra dessert and a drink; they bought their meals in the market or from women who cooked meals for sale in their homes. The second reason was political. The *olla* often closed down because Carmen and her successor as leader of the Housewives' Federation had severe ideological differences. The women judged their neighbors according to their political affiliation. Eje members regarded their PCB neighbors as reformists who were easily co-opted. In turn, those with the PCB saw the Eje as inflexible and excessively tied to dogma. These group-level ideological differences greatly affected the functioning of the *olla* as Carmen belonged to the Eje and Isabel to the PCB:

> We would fight with Isabel and the very same people she controlled. She wanted to run things in her own way, like we were little girls. But there are *compañeras* that also have a clear vision—right? and cannot be fooled so easily. If we have fought for so many things, if we have fought against the government, then against these people it's peanuts. We hit it off terribly and have tremendous political disagreements.

These politically based differences were important for the women because of the highly politicized nature of their daily existence in the mining districts and the central role parties had always played in setting the agenda for organizing and mobilization. Political affiliations were also significant because development activities are highly politicized in Bolivia. Aid organizations, both governmental and nongovernmental, are associated with parties because groups in power often take over their control and exchange aid for party loyalty. As a result, ideology often guided the leaders to the institutions from which they obtained assistance. As a result, women judged others according to the institutional contacts made; most assistance to the *relocalizados* takes place at a project level.

Yet, despite these differences between left-wing groups, both male and female leaders in Katari interpreted their displacement as a result of their position in the class structure and Bolivia's dependent relationship to industrialized countries. The day-to-day choices they made and the attitudes they held about their condition were always placed in relation to some broader framework, as reflected in this statement by the villa's male leader:

> If yesterday you were "relocated," today you are living that crisis or the consequences of that relocation. Now tomorrow, what are your objectives? Are you satisfied with simply looking for jobs, or do you really have other objectives?

It is clear that both political and gender ideology combined with economic needs to define the survival strategies of Katari settlers. By the creative use of limited food and shelter, Katari households were largely successful in their efforts to make up for the decline in income and services. This success was largely due to past mobilizing experience, which had a number of effects on their actions. First, this experience led them to see external and structural causes for their economic condition, thereby having a great psychological effect—the Katari *relocalizados* did not internalize the blame for their poverty. Second, this past experience gave them skills to generate the resources they needed. In particular, women's mobilizing experience around basic needs issues and against military repression greatly facilitated their efforts to obtain resources for community consumption. Women are responsible for feeding and clothing their families, so their ability to act affected the well-being of the community as a whole. Yet, I must also stress that men's growing, although initially reluctant, acceptance (founded on a perception of a common struggle) of women's mobilizing efforts enabled the women to put these important skills to work.

Apaza

Don Ernesto and Don Nicolás learned of a large tract of flatland located on the border of El Alto, at the place where the earth slides into a green valley of the La Paz canyon. This valley is known by a few for the abandoned bullet-ridden church where General Banzer's political prisoners were tortured. Even though the available land is perhaps 500 feet above the church, the terrain is different: flat, barren, and is, in fact, the garbage dump for that corner of El Alto. In spite of this unpleasant location, and the fact that the soil is quickly eroding into the valley, the site seemed an ideal place for a new settlement, essentially because no one seemed to know who the owners were.

The two men requested official permission to settle the area from the mayor of El Alto, a member of Banzer's Acción Democrática Nacionalista (ADN) party. The mayor consented, on the condition that the new community support him in the coming elections. The leaders, who were eager to settle, agreed with these terms, and in July 1987 the Apaza miners' settlement was established. News of the open tracts spread quickly throughout the COB and FSTMB offices, and families approached the two men, asking if they could be part of the cooperative that was being organized. Don Ernesto was elected as the *dirigente* and Doña Maria was selected to be the Housewives' Committee representative.

By August, over one hundred families had settled onto the smelly and fly-infested refuse. A dozen people crowded into one makeshift tent made by tying together sheets of plastic and attaching them to wooden poles. The conditions became slightly more tolerable when Caritas, a Catholic relief organization, donated large canvas tents and offered the Apaza *relocalizados* a self-help housing project. Caritas promised to supply all building materials, truck in dirt from nearby public work projects for the adobes, and provide technical support for the construction. The responsibility of the *relocalizados* was to provide the labor for their own houses and to complete the construction before the Pope's visit in May.

Construction work was arduous, especially for the women who worked on the project while their husbands looked for jobs. First they had to clear the garbage with shovels. The trucked-in soil had to be sifted before it was ready for making adobes. And because much of this dirt was from road projects and had large stones, the residents were forced to use the soil below the garbage, which was finer and suitable for making the bricks. Especially for smaller and female-headed families, progress was slow because work was organized on an individual family basis. In these families, women and children who were old enough to pick up a shovel did most of the construction while the men went to work in temporary public works projects or sought employment. These families barely managed to clear the land, while those with more available labor completed thousands of adobes.

In contrast to the Katari self-help project, families in Apaza did not receive a salary for their work so they were faced with the dilemma of expending their energy finding sustenance or building their homes. With no income, they struggled simply to feed themselves. If they met the construction schedule, Caritas gave them food supplies, otherwise each family was on its own and had to survive with its own resources.

Also, in contrast to Katari's experience, the community was unable to offer the households any support services, largely because the women were poorly organized and felt inhibited to act independently from the male syndicate. Victoria, for example, wanted to organize a Mother's Club in Apaza. But she desisted because the male leaders felt that her organizing attempts threatened their political control over the community. This lack of support, she believes, is based on the men's political affiliation with the conservative ADN, in contrast to her left-leaning ideas:[14]

> We wanted to meet with some women's organizations, we wanted to ask for projects. But the leaders would not let us. They said that they would do it and that we couldn't leave the camp without their permission. The housewives' committee is headed by another woman and the syndicate leaders don't let her do anything. So I would say to her, let's form a Mothers Club, and the president would say, "Don Nicolás and Don Ernesto won't like it. You know that they don't like us to act without their authority."
>
> I'm not sure why the leaders haven't gotten a Mother's Club. I think it's because they have given in to the politics of the ADN. Yesterday, the president of the Housewives' Committee told me that they had applied for a project but hadn't gotten it because they had done it through an ADN contact. And the funding institution was bothered upon seeing those recommendations.
>
> So I told her that even if it bothers the men, we have to do something. Because there are people here who are really in need, like me. At least for a little flour, a little oil, a little wheat that we could use when we don't have anything to eat. So I told her that we had to organize because without those organizations, what will we do if our husbands haven't found jobs to bring home food to us?

Victoria also wanted to start an *olla común* similar to those in other El Alto *relocalizado* communities because of the serious problems Apaza households had obtaining enough food. However, she was again unable to convince the president of the Apaza Housewives' Committee to take action:

We [the La Paz Housewives' Federation] have been organizing *ollas comúnes* in all of the areas in El Alto. It would be to my advantage to have one here, right? But the *dirigentes* don't want one. Sometimes not even the bases themselves. At first they wanted one. But not many people lived here at the time, and now that we've started working on the houses it's necessary. I don't know, I said that to the Housewives' leader. "Talk to the bases, organize them. Call a meeting." But she doesn't act with authority because the *dirigentes* don't like it. If she's the leader of the Housewives' Federation then she should call a meeting of women, at least so that we can talk about what we will survive on, what we are going to do or what groups we can form.

In spite of her efforts, Victoria was not successful in getting a Mother's Club or *olla común*. Although she had been politically active in her mining districts and participated in the La Paz Housewives' Federation in Apaza, she was restrained from generating resources on behalf of the community. Unfortunately, Apaza households negatively felt the repercussions of these political and gender-based conflicts because they could not rely on the community for consumption pooling. Household members, as a result, faced tremendous constraints, with a great part of the burden falling on women. In spite of their persistence, they found it virtually impossible to provide for their families' most basic needs. For example, most of the women in Apaza described the following as a typical day's diet: for breakfast an herbal tea (*mate*), sometimes with bread; for lunch a flour soup and an occasional main dish, a *segundo,* that only rarely included meat; and tea for dinner.

We can draw an important lesson about a community's ability to respond to economic crisis from Apaza's experience. Although potential female leaders, such as Victoria, who could generate necessary resources lived in the community, politically based gender conflicts barred them from taking actions that would benefit the community as a whole. In contrast, women's participation in Katari highlights the fact that empowerment is a central dimension of household and community survival strategies in that community. This empowerment had its roots in class-based mobilization, which perhaps unexpectedly, has had an effect on gender roles within the mining community. Empowerment is thus a factor that differentiates—both qualitatively and in terms of the physical resources obtained—the villas of Apaza and Katari. These seeds of empowerment are also evident, although dormant, in Apaza. There is a growing understanding by at least some women that their inability to act had serious repercussions on the community as a whole. As Victoria very clearly states:

Machismo is no longer viable. We women also need to have the right to organize ourselves, to be able and to know how to support ourselves, to survive. We have to have our own direction, to know how to lead ourselves and not be led by men. . . . We also have ideas, and maybe they are better ones. There are times when we women express our feelings honestly, clearly. But men can't do that because they are men. Because they can't allow themselves to be humiliated.

I believe that we cannot continue to be led by the *machismo* of men. We have to free ourselves from our husbands and we as *dirigentas* have freed ourselves. We don't know how, but we have convinced many men and there are many men who understand us and support us. And there are others who don't allow us to organize ourselves. Many women are afraid to liberate themselves because they are afraid of isolating themselves from their husbands. But it's not isolating oneself. Instead it's entering into an agreement, talking, we helping them like them helping us. Mutually. And it's not just for us. It's for our children and for all of the girls and boys who are to be born. It's for the future of this country.

This statement illuminates the important role that both consciousness and empowerment play in individual and group strategies to respond to economic crisis. Women's experience and education have made them aware of their important role in the development process. Although in Katari women's mobilization is not explicitly based on gender-defined issues, this understanding of the important role that they play has been translated into action. In Apaza, ideas such as those expressed by Victoria will remain only a seed until male leaders change their attitudes and/or until the women translate Victoria's statement into a political platform for change.

CONCLUSION

These two case studies highlight a number of important points about Bolivia's experience with economic adjustment. First, the design of development projects, such as self-help housing and public works projects, greatly affected the quality of life of the *relocalizados.* Second, in light of declining income, women of Bolivian mining households played a central role in the household and the community, providing income and finding creative ways to compensate for declining resources. Third, their ability to take action was largely due to their past organizing experience in the mining districts, which provided them with skills, confidence, and motivation to act on behalf of their families and communities. This empowerment greatly influenced the well-being of *relocalizados* in their new El Alto communities. These two case studies also demonstrate, however, that women's past experience is insufficient, as gender and political ideology played an important mediating role in both Apaza and Katari. As we have seen, women with leadership skills still encountered roadblocks in their resource mobilization efforts, largely because of political differences with male leaders. And as a final comment, the experience of the *relocalizados* makes it clear that we must understand the historical experiences and ideological factors that define groups affected by economic crises in order to identify sources of and barriers to change that will make survival strategies into transformative ones, as Elson highlights in Chapter 2.

NOTES

1. Interdisciplinary studies on the impact of structural adjustment measures on the Latin American poor have overcome many of the limitations of discipline-bound research. Since the late 1970s, researchers have focused on household survival strategies to examine the relationship between changing forms of production and the domestic group formations through which basic material needs are met (Schmink 1984). This integrated micro and macro focus is an advancement over past analyses of poverty, which focused either at the macro or at the micro level and did not consider the direct interaction of the two. Anthropological studies, for example, did not relate the household unit to wider political and economic processes (Guyer and Peters 1987). At the other extreme, macroeconomic analyses ignored the human dimension of global economic restructuring. Each approach therefore limited understanding of how structural and global economic conditions—such as changes in demand for primary and manufactured goods, recessions, and the debt crisis—affected the poor.

2. Siles's party, the Popular Democratic Union (UDP), was a coalition party composed of the Leftist National Revolutionary Movement (MNRI), the Bolivian Communist Party (PCB), and the Leftist Revolutionary Movement (MIR).

3. Van de Hoeven and Richards (1987) write that primary goods were more vulnerable to the recession in industrialized countries because of lower substitution possibilities and low-income elasticities. In contrast, for manufacturing production, the recession did not have such a negative impact, primarily because in the total consumption of industrialized countries, the share of manufactured exports from developing countries is very small.

4. The conservative forces of Bolivian politics won the elections of 1985. Paz Estenssoro of the National Revolutionary Movement (MNR) was inaugurated on August 6, 1985, having barely won the presidency from former dictator Hugo Banzer Suárez. Banzer actually won the popular elections by a close margin, but the conclusive decision was made by Congress, which voted in favor of the MNR leader. In a political maneuver that assured his control of Congress and his support by the military, Paz signed an historic agreement, the Pact for Democracy, with Banzer's ADN. In exchange, the MNR assured Banzer that he would control key public sector corporations (Malloy and Gamarra 1988).

5. The cooperatives were previously a strategy of workers to circumvent exploitation by firms, but under the NEP they became government-encouraged

work units that took away the government's responsibility to provide tools, capital, wages, social security, housing, or other benefits to the work force, while placing risk on the cooperativist.

6. As Nash writes, this class consciousness first began to emerge in the mid-1880s, with the opening of Patiño's industrial mines, and developed because of the "transplanting of anarcho-syndicalist and socialist conceptions of society by European emigrant workers from Argentina and Chile coming into Bolivia about 1910" (Nash 1979:320). Their modern industrialized consciousness, she adds, solidified with the labor strikes in 1918 and a massacre at the Uncla mine in 1923.

7. The Housewives' Federation was founded in the Siglo XX mine of Oruro in 1961 and throughout the following decades spread to all other mining districts.

8. Many within this group also became *jucos,* stealing ores from the mines at night for sale to the private companies.

9. The following typology of household strategies developed by Cornia (1987a, b) is useful in conceptualizing which grass-roots adjustments buffer the poor and vulnerable during crisis periods:

1. Income generating strategies: Households seek to maintain the level of income in response to a decline in real wages, employment, or other income-earning potential. Households respond by increasing the supply of labor to the economy; women and children are drawn into the formal and informal market to offset the decline in male employment. They also might increase self-production, growing their own food, building their own shelters and providing their own health care. Another strategy is to change the assets and liabilities of the household through the sale of assets or by taking out loans. Finally, households may increase the flow of income transfers by obtaining official aid, unemployment benefits, or supplementary feeding for children.

2. Improving the efficiency of existing resources: Households reduce food costs by changing their purchasing habits—that is, they join together with other families and buy food in bulk. Or households modify how they prepare food such as in the experience of Peruvian *comedores populares* where families obtain balanced meals by purchasing food and cooking communally. Households also change their dietary patterns or modify their overall consumption patterns.

3. Migration and extended family: Cornia distinguishes three forms of migration. The first involves the temporary labor-seeking migration of household members who are not head of the household; the second is relief-seeking migration of the head of household; and the third is the migration of the entire family, normally under severe crisis conditions. And finally, households may reduce living costs by incorporating new adult members into the household or by sending dependent children to better-off relatives or families.

10. Note that all names are pseudonyms.

11. Throughout various periods of the *relocalización,* the government increased the amount of severance pay as an incentive for miners to hand in their

notices. The amounts received therefore did not always reflect the number of years worked in the mines. This divergence created considerable resentment amongst miners' households who retired when the amount promised was not at a maximum.

12. *Compañero* means both "partner" and "comrade." *Pulperías* are the company stores.

13. An official of a local nonprofit organization told me that he had dozens of proposals stacked on his desk for mechanic shops, bakeries, knitting cooperatives, and sewing shops. He automatically turned them down because the glutted market made them economically unfeasible.

14. The *dirigentes'* affiliation with the ADN was also detrimental because many church, nonprofit, or women's organizations who sympathized with more progressive political positions shied away from the community.

REFERENCES

Arauco, Isabel. 1988. "Una Approximación al Análisis de la Relocalización," *Tennas Laborales* (La Paz) 5:7–30.

Ayub, Mahmood Ali, and Hideo Hashimoto. 1985. *The Economics of Tin Mining in Bolivia.* Washington, D.C.: The World Bank.

Barrios de Chungara, Domitila. 1978. *Let Me Speak: Testimony of Domitila, a Woman of the Bolivian Mines.* New York: Monthly Review Press.

CEPROMIN (Centro de Promoción Minero). 1987. Plan de Reactivación Productiva de la Corporación Minera de Bolivia, Empresa Minera Catavi. La Paz: CEPROMIN.

Cornia, Giovanni Andrea. 1987a. "Adjustment at the Household Level. Potentials and Limitations of Survival Strategies." In Giovanni Andrea Cornia, Richard Jolly, and Frances Stewart (eds.), *Adjustment with a Human Face: Vol. I, Protecting the Vulnerable and Promoting Growth.* New York: Oxford University Press.

———. 1987b. "Economic Decline and Human Welfare in the First Half of the 1980s." In Giovanni Andrea Cornia, Richard Jolly, and Frances Stewart (eds.), *Adjustment with a Human Face: Vol. I, Protecting the Vulnerable and Promoting Growth.* New York: Oxford University Press.

Crabtree, John, Gavan Duffy, and Jenny Pearce. 1986. *The Great Tin Crash: Bolivia and the World Tin Market.* New York: Monthly Review Press.

Doria Medina, Samuel. 1986. *La Economía Informal en Bolivia.* La Paz: Editorial Offset Boliviana (EDOBOL).

Dunkerley, James. 1984. *Rebellion in the Veins: Political Struggle in Bolivia, 1952–1982.* London: Verso Editions.

Flores, Gonzalo, and Jose Blanes. 1984. *Dónde va el Chapare?* Cochabamba Bolivia: Centro de Estudios de Realidad Económico (CERES).

Grebe, Horst. 1985."La Nueva Política Económica" in *Seminario sobre la Nueva Política Económica,* La Paz.

Guyer, Jane I., and Pauline E. Peters. 1987. "Conceptualizing the Household: Issues of Theory and Policy in Africa." Special issue of *Development and Change* 18 (2):197–214.

Lora, Guillermo. 1977. *A History of the Bolivian Labor Movement, 1948–1971.* New York: Cambridge University Press.

Malloy, James. 1987. "Bolivia's Economic Crisis." *Current History* (January):9–38.

Malloy, James, and Eduardo Gamarra. 1988. *Revolution and Reaction: Bolivia 1964–1985.* New Brunswick: Transaction Books.

McFarren, Wendy. 1989. The Politics of Adaptation: Survival Strategies of Bolivian Mining Households. Master's Thesis, Cornell University, Ithaca, N.Y.

Nash, June. 1979. *We Eat the Mines and the Mines Eat Us: Dependency and Exploitation in Bolivian Tin Mines.* New York: Columbia University Press.

Sachs, Jeffrey. 1987. "The Bolivian Hyperinflation and Stabilization." *The American Economic Review* (May):279–283.

Sanchez de Lozada. 1985. "La Nueva Política Economica." In *Seminario sobre la Nueva Política Económica.* La Paz: UNITAS, Documentos de Análisis #1.

Schmink, Marianne. 1984. Household Economic Strategies: Review and Research Agenda. *Latin American Research Review (LARR)* 19 (3):87–101.

Tin Statistics. 1987. *Tin Statistics.* London: International Tin Council.

UNITAS. 1987. *La Crisis del Sector Minero y Sus Efectos Socio-Económicos.* La Paz: UNITAS, Documentos de Análisis #3.

Van de Hoeven, R., and P. J. Richards. 1987. "Depression and Adjustment." *World Recession and Global Interdependence.* Geneva: International Labour Organization.

World Development Report. 1987. New York: Oxford University Press (published for the World Bank).

7

The Impact of Crisis &
Economic Reform on Women
in Urban Tanzania

☙ AILI MARI TRIPP

An economic crisis, manifested in sharply declining real wages, forced Tanzanian workers in the 1980s to gradually cease their dependence on formal jobs as the primary source of livelihood and to increase their reliance on informal income-generating activities. Because men represented more than 80 percent of the employed work force in Dar es Salaam (Tanzania 1986), these changes frequently made children, the elderly, and especially women important, if not the most important, contributors to the household economy through their involvement in "projects" or *miradi,* as they are referred to in Swahili. For women these projects ranged from making and selling pastries, fried fish, beer, paper bags, and crafts, to braiding hair, tailoring, animal husbandry, and agricultural production. Operators of small projects were required to obtain licenses, but the majority of women chose not to bring their projects under such government controls, which means that these income-generating activities could be considered part of the informal economy.

Just as the crisis that began in the late 1970s placed new burdens on urban women to pursue projects, economic reforms adopted in the mid-1980s merely perpetuated women's new economic responsibilities through measures that led to increased layoffs and a continuing decline in real wages. These developments made urban women even more important to the economic well-being of the household, much the same way rural women historically had assumed the main responsibility for agricultural production.

It is curious that given these dramatic changes, Tanzania's structural adjustment programs—like most economic restructuring programs—have not incorporated policies that address the different ways in which these reforms have affected or ought to affect different sectors of society, for example, women, children, and the elderly. In the official statements regarding the reform measures, society is largely treated as an undifferentiated whole. Such common oversights not only disregard how policies have differential impact on various sectors of society, they also overlook the effect of policy on economic activities outside the purview of standard statistical data, frequently ignoring some of the most important forms of market and nonmarket activity.

However, it is not only the architects of structural adjustment policies who are guilty of overlooking the differential impact of such programs on different sectors of society. Even those who have been critical of reform measures advocated by the International Monetary Fund (IMF) and World Bank for not protecting the "weak" groups have also tended to treat the household as a monolithic unit (Cornia 1987). Their policy recommendations, therefore, frequently do not take into account the different roles played by household members in the struggle to survive. They may accurately portray women and children as "vulnerable" with respect to health, education, and various social services but overlook these same sectors for their strengths in having been the ones who so often kept their families and societies afloat amidst unprecedented hardships. Because the burden of supporting the family has fallen largely on women, this makes women especially important not only as recipients of social services, but also as potential beneficiaries of credit, training, and technical assistance. Crudely put, policies that render support to the household or to the informal sector in general do not automatically translate into support for the entire household. In many African societies like urban Tanzania, because of women's key role as the ones who provide and distribute resources throughout the household, support for women, in particular, is more likely to have an impact on larger numbers of household members.

Before pursuing these points further I will briefly outline the context of crisis and reform within which the changes in the household are occurring. The rest of the chapter will look at how the new and emerging economic importance of women to the survival of the urban household in Tanzania challenges many of the assumptions held by liberal and Marxist theorists that tend to marginalize and peripheralize the economic activities of women. Given the major shift within workers' households, from relying primarily on wage earnings in the 1970s to relying mainly on informal incomes in the 1980s, the discussion in this chapter will focus on this relationship between informal income-generating activities and formal wage employment and how perceptions or misperceptions of this relationship affect our view of women's economic contributions.

The chapter will explore the household as one arena where the relationship between formal wage labor and women's informal labor is frequently obscured by theories that do not distinguish among varying economic interests and actors within a household. The chapter goes on to argue that when women's work is considered, it is often discussed as a "lesser" form of economic activity, supplementing the returns of wage laborers or reducing the costs of wage labor. This is reflected in the preoccupation of policymakers and social scientists with wage labor, leading to some distorted conclusions regarding, for example, income differentiation or the relative importance of large-scale industry to small-scale production in a country like Tanzania. The chapter argues that the experience of Tanzania in the late 1970s and 1980s forces one to take a hard look at the meaning of these conventional notions of work and production that tend to elevate certain forms of economic activity over others, thereby ignoring economic activities of entire population groups like women.

THE ECONOMIC CRISIS

In order to focus on the impact of the changes on women, I will give only a thumbnail sketch of the evolution of Tanzania's economic crisis and reform programs. Like many African countries, Tanzania suffered in the 1970s from drops in export commodity prices as a result of world recession. The fall in exports was compounded by increases in import prices, especially of oil. Other factors that contributed to the crisis included drought and rising interest rates that hurt debt repayment efforts.

These external causes of the crisis were exacerbated by government policies, like the rapid expansion of state expenditure and state-initiated social and political programs that could not be sustained by the economy. When the government nationalized the banks and key industries and established hundreds of parastatals (state companies), it frequently did not have the capacity to efficiently manage these institutions, which all too often became a drain on the country's resources. There was a tendency to invest heavily in industrial programs at the expense of agriculture in a country where agricultural production is the main source of domestic revenue and the base supporting other sectors. This urban bias against rural producers was also manifested in the low producer prices paid to them by state-run crop authorities. These policies resulted in shifts away from the production of export crops to the production of food crops and to sales of both export and domestic crops on parallel or unofficial markets rather than sales through state-run crop authorities. The trade balance, which had been in surplus in the 1960s, experienced a deficit in the 1970s. In the late 1970s Tanzania fell into a severe and chronic foreign exchange crisis. This, in turn, affected agricultural and industrial performance, which are heavily dependent on imported inputs.

Thus, both external and internal factors contributed to the economic crisis Tanzania faced. In the 1960s Tanzania had the highest rate of increase in domestic food production for the entire African continent and was exporting grain to neighboring countries. By the mid-1970s, Tanzania's agricultural production had declined to the point where it was forced to import food (Lofchie 1988:144). By 1981 commercial agriculture and cash crop exports declined to half of what they had been in the 1970s. Industrial production had fallen to an annual −11 percent growth rate in 1981. Inflation was soaring and the urban cost of living had increased by 400 percent each year from 1978 to 1984, based on official statistics (Lofchie 1988:147–148). By 1987 Tanzania's debt stood at $4.3 billion and its annual debt-service ratio (that is, the ratio of debt to export earnings) had reached almost 18.5 percent (World Bank 1989:253). The country plunged into a severe and chronic foreign exchange crisis, which affected agricultural and industrial performance because of their heavy dependence on imported inputs.

RESPONSES TO THE CRISIS

After an unsuccessful attempt to obtain IMF support in 1980, differences between the IMF and the Tanzanian government effectively kept Tanzania from signing an agreement with the Fund until 1986. Meanwhile Tanzania adopted its own stabilization program in 1981 and a structural adjustment program in 1982, neither of which did much to reverse the deterioration of the economy. In June 1986 a three-year Economic Recovery Programme (ERP) was initiated in anticipation of the agreement signed shortly thereafter with the IMF. Some of the ERP measures included exchange rate adjustments, the raising of official producer prices, lifting of price controls, improving foreign exchange allocations, and efforts to raise the level of domestic savings, to improve the infrastructure and to launch major rehabilitation projects.

The initiation of the ERP alone, however, could not solve Tanzania's foreign exchange crisis. As foreign exchange supplies dried up, Tanzania had little choice but to reach an agreement with the IMF in July 1986. Had Tanzania failed to reach an agreement, it would have faced drastic cuts in aid from the Nordic countries and other Western donors who made their continued support contingent upon the signing of an agreement with the IMF. In addition, Tanzania would not have been able to reschedule its previous loan payments.

The IMF agreed to a standby arrangement subject to various criteria, which included substantial devaluations, restrictions on the amount of credit that could be transferred from the banking system to government institutions, limits on the accumulation of new debt, and controls on new external borrowing and on the overall budget deficit. In signing an agreement with the IMF, Tanzania also came under considerable pressure to adopt various measures opposed by the country's leaders. These included: the fast pace of currency devaluations, constraints on wage increases, and cuts in public services.

The government launched a second three-year Economic Recovery Program in 1989 along the same lines as the first, but included a Priority Social Action Programme to begin reversing the deterioration of social services that had occurred in the previous decade of reforms. Social, public, and welfare services as a percentage of government expenditure had decreased substantially in the 1980s, and by 1986 they had dropped to their lowest point in twenty years. The amount spent on health, education, housing, public, community, and social services was cut in half between 1981 and 1986, from 21 to 11 percent of total government expenditure (calculated from data provided in the Tanzanian Government's Annual Economic Surveys, 1970–1986).

Apart from the serious decline in social and public services, one of the main consequences of the ERP has been a rise in growth rates, with the GDP increasing from −4 percent in 1981 to 4 percent in 1989. Although still below peak production levels, crops like coffee, tea, cashew nuts, tobacco, and sisal made a recovery and did, in fact, respond to price incentives. However, the program had little positive impact on industry, which continued to register negative growth rates throughout the 1980s and continued to operate at 20–30 percent capacity (Lipumba 1989:11–12; Mbelle 1989:7–9).

IMPACT ON LIVING STANDARDS

In order to better understand the impact of the crisis and the economic reforms on the population, I carried out a study in Dar es Salaam between 1987 and 1988. The study involved a cluster survey of 287 people (145 men and 142 women) in Buguruni and Manzese, two parts of the city populated by workers and self-employed entrepreneurs. I also carried out 300 unstructured interviews with small entrepreneurs throughout the city along with a snowball survey of 51 middle- and upper-income household members.[1] The study also included interviews with leading local figures, including 300 party leaders at the lowest level of the cell in addition to party and government leaders at all levels up to the Central Committee and Cabinet. These interviews were conducted in Swahili.

Between 1974 and 1988 Tanzanian workers experienced a 65-percent drop in real wages (Stein 1988). This figure is calculated from official prices, which were significantly lower than actual prices, so the drop in real wages was even greater. This dramatic decline in living standards was one of the reasons the Tanzanian government consistently resisted IMF pressures to freeze wages. Instead, the government adopted small wage increases each year after 1986 to compensate for the difficulties workers were facing. In the 1989–1990 budget, for example, the government raised the minimum wage 26 percent from the previous year and slashed income tax by 5 percent. But even such measures made little difference because the basic inability of the average worker to keep up with the cost of living had not changed.

In 1988 one worker's monthly salary could cover the cost of only three days of food a month for an average household of six, according to my survey. For the rest of the month, the income had to come from other sources. In 1976, wages constituted approximately 77 percent of the total household income. In contrast, by 1988, my study shows that wage earnings made up roughly only 10 percent of the household income, with informal incomes making up the remaining 90 percent.

The inability of wages to keep up with the cost of living was felt especially in the area of food purchases, which made up roughly 85 percent of all purchases for low-income households (Bryceson 1987:174). Even though they began to stabilize with the introduction of various economic reform measures, food prices remained prohibitive. Nevertheless, the measures signaled a step in the right direction. The gradual lifting of restrictions on domestic trade and the raising of producer prices in the mid-1980s was partially responsible for moving the country from food deficit to food surplus between 1986 and 1988. Restrictions were removed on the interregional movement of food, including permits, roadblocks, and limits on the quantity of crops that could be transported. In addition, maize prices were decontrolled. The measures had positive results almost immediately. Production increased, especially for rice and maize, and open-market consumer prices for rice and maize stabilized. Liberalizing internal trade eroded the high-scarcity premiums of some traders, especially those who had profited from diverting cheap maize from the state-owned National Milling Corporation and selling it at hiked prices. Similarly, the risk factor was eliminated from domestic trade and this also helped reduce the price of grains.

The new availability of food and the stabilization of food prices had a positive impact on low-income households not only for purposes of consumption, but also because numerous women's baking projects relied

TABLE 7.1 Occupational Distribution of 287 Men and Women in the Sample, 1988

	Women *(percent)*	*Men* *(percent)*	*Total*[a] *(percent)*
Informal work[b]	66	68	67
Employed	9	36	23
Retired	0	8	4
Farming	72	44	59
No occupation	13	0	7

[a]The percentages do not total 100 percent because people often engaged in two or more activities simultaneously (see Table 7.2).
[b]Includes all own account workers: mostly self-employed but also those in family enterprises, partnerships.

Source: Tripp 1990:43.

on flour and rice. Between 1983 and 1986 open-market prices for key components of the typical food basket (maize, rice, beans, coconut) increased by approximately 143 percent in Dar es Salaam. That rate of increase was lowered to roughly 50 percent between 1986 and 1989 due to trade liberalization, according to Marketing Development Bureau figures. But even with these developments, women found the prices of foods steep. By 1988 daily food costs for the average household in the areas I surveyed came to 325 Tanzanian shillings (Tsh) or eight times the daily minimum wage.

WOMEN'S RESPONSES TO CRISIS AND ECONOMIC REFORM

One of the main responses of women to the declining real wages and standards of living was the increased pursuit of income-generating projects in addition to their child-rearing and housework responsibilities. Sabot's 1971 study found only 7 percent of urban women self-employed (1979:29). In contrast, seventeen years later approximately 66 percent of women I surveyed in Dar es Salaam were self-employed (Tables 7.1 and 7.2). Other surveys taken in the late 1980s corroborate this finding (Kulaba 1989; Tibaijuka 1988).

The particular impact of the crisis on women is evident from the fact that women began their projects more recently than men, with about 80 percent of women starting their businesses between 1982 and 1987, compared to only 50 percent of men who started businesses in the same period (Table 7.3). For most women with small projects this was their first one.

TABLE 7.2   Disaggregation of 287 Male and Female Occupational Categories, 1988

	Women (percent)	Men (percent)	Total (percent)
Employed full time	3	11	7
Informal work full time[a]	13	32	23
Farming full time	22	8	15
Retired full time	0	0	0
Employed/informal work	1	8	5
Employed/farming	2	9	5
Employed/informal work/farming	3	5	4
Informal work/farming	45	17	31
Informal work/retired	0	1	1
Informal work/retired/farming	0	3	2
Retired/farming	0	3	1
Cooperative	0	2	1
No occupation	11	0	5
	100	100	100

[a]Includes all own account workers: mostly self-employed but also those in family enterprises and partnerships.

Source: Tripp 1990:43.

When asked why it was only in recent years women had become involved in projects, Mama Hamza, a pastry maker, answered without hesitation: "*Jua Kali!*" (the hot sun!), implying that the conditions of life had become harder. She said she could no longer depend on her husband, who worked at a government store, and therefore she had started selling chapati pastries. She would wake up at 3 or 4 in the morning and make about 50 to 80 chapatis. She took them to the nearby Changombe industrial area, where she sold them to workers at 6 Tsh apiece. She

TABLE 7.3   Year in Which Worker Began Self-Employment Activity

Year Started Self-Employment	Women (percent)	Men (percent)	Total (percent)
Employed full time	3	11	7
1940–1949	1	2	2
1950–1959	0	4	2
1960–1969	3	7	5
1970–1979	10	21	15
1980–1987	86	66	76
	100	100	100

N = 190

Source: Tripp 1990:73.

made between 200 and 340 Tsh profit a day (approximately US$2.00 to $3.40 at 1988 exchange rates).[2] She would have liked to sell fried fish but needed more capital than she had to start such a project. Mama Hamza explained:

> You can't wait for your husband to bring home money. They don't take care of the family, wife and children. . . . That is why women have started doing projects—to save money. Every woman has some project. They are now building houses. I am building a four-room house.

In addition to building a house near her farm on the outskirts of the city, Mama Hamza used her earnings to educate her son Hamza, one of four children. She was visibly proud of Hamza, explaining how he had been a top student and was now in Form Two in Secondary School. In order to save, she participated in two rotating credit associations, one with neighborhood women and another with fifty-seven market sellers.

The centrality of women to the economic survival of the household was underscored by another woman, a bank clerk who at the same time had a project raising chickens. She pointed out:

> Women are trying their best. They are affected most by the hardships and want to see to the well-being of their children. It is their responsibility to the family. They don't expect much help from their husbands. Women care more for their homes because of the children. For this reason it is necessary that they do projects rather than wait for the assistance of their husbands. My husband gave me capital to start my project, but most of the effort is the woman's.

One of the ironies of the situation in the late 1980s is that women who might have prided themselves for having a job as a teacher, nurse, secretary, or even a factory worker, were frequently finding themselves better off leaving their jobs to become self-employed on a full-time basis. Of those women who had left jobs, 67 percent had done so between 1980 and 1987 (Table 7.4). Not surprisingly, the most common reason they gave for leaving their jobs was low pay.

In the 1980s, women not only engaged in projects for cash, they also increased their involvement in urban farming projects. Over 70 percent of the women I interviewed farmed, most in the areas surrounding the city on plots averaging around 3 acres (1.2 hectares). The majority had started farming within the five years prior to the survey. They grew primarily cassava, rice, and maize in addition to fruits and vegetables. Most cultivated for consumption, but one-half of those who farmed reported that they sold their produce. Some women and children would

TABLE 7.4   Year During Which Worker Left Formal Employment

Year Left Employment	Women (percent)	Men (percent)	Total (percent)
Employed full time	3	11	7
1950–1959	0	1	1
1960–1969	0	7	5
1970–1979	33	30	31
1980–1987	67	62	63
Total	100	100	100

N = 93

Source: Tripp 1990:60.

travel long distances to their rural home areas during the harvest season. Others had returned to the rural areas on a permanent basis. There was a growing perception that rural life was more attractive than urban life because in the city you need cash to eat whereas in the countryside you can grow your own food. My survey and the 1988 census both suggest that migration to the cities had slowed down considerably since the 1960s and 1970s and that birth rates accounted for most of the city's growth in the 1980s, rather than migration, which was the main factor in Dar es Salaam's growth in the 1960s and 1970s (Tanzania 1989). The main reason for the emigration from urban to rural areas and the slowing down of migration to the cities was clearly the increased attractiveness of farming relative to life in urban areas, where new jobs were virtually nonexistent, wage earnings were below subsistence levels, and self-employment offered a precarious existence, especially for those with little capital to begin with.

WOMEN'S WORK AND THE HOUSEHOLD

The developments in Tanzania illustrate in a striking manner the importance of looking at ways in which such crises affect differentially various members of the household. A growing body of literature has given credence to the argument that the household cannot be analyzed as an unvaried whole, in challenging economic theories like the new household economics (Bruce and Dwyer 1988; Clark 1989; Fapohunda 1988a; Guyer and Peters 1987).

Implicit in this new understanding of economic dynamics at the microlevel is a critique of an idealized notion of household borrowed from preindustrial Europe. This prototype household, as depicted in the works of Marshall Sahlins, A. V. Chayanov, and Karl Polanyi, is seen as living together in a single house, pooling its labor and capital resources for consumption and production. Resources are managed centrally either through consensus or in an authoritarian manner. The household is considered the dominant economic unit even where various household members might work for wages. More recently, but in the same vein, theorists have sought a more universal prototype, depicting the household as a resource sharing unit (Clark 1989).

Instead of trying to identify the household in this manner, Guyer and Peters suggest we look at what are the significant units of production, consumption, and investment in a region or among a certain group of people and "what are the major flows and transfers of resources between individuals and units" (1987:208, 210). This approach would, for example, allow us to look at the manifold economic interactions between women and family members, kin, neighbors, and other groups and individuals surrounding them. The patterns of these relationships become infinitely more complex than the fictionalized ideal household within which the role of women as independent economic actors can be so easily obscured.

For example, urban women in Tanzania, as in other parts of Africa, do not generally pool their income with that of their husband nor do they always let their husbands know what their real income is (Robertson and Berger 1986:10). Women usually operate income-generating projects separate from those of their husbands. Most of the projects are individually owned, but 60 percent of the women interviewed reported that they were helped by their children. Similarly, when they go to a food stall or the market to sell their produce, they frequently will be accompanied by a female friend, neighbor, or relation who is also engaged in a similar project. Often the husband's only contribution to the project is to provide the starting capital. In fact, up to 44 percent of women with projects reported that they received starting capital from their husbands. Although some couples shared projects, most often the project belonged to the wife and in some cases the husband assisted her when he came from work.

In one typical family, the husband, who was a welder, gave his wife 3,000 Tsh with which she started a project making and selling *mbege,* an alcoholic beverage made of bananas. With the starting capital she bought cups, pans, and a barrel in addition to bananas and *ulezi* (millet for fermenting). Less than one year after she began the project she was making about 1,130 Tsh a day (26 times her husband's wage), selling to people in the neighborhood.

One way women keep their incomes separate from those of their husbands or other household members is to save it in *upato* rotating credit societies. Close to half of all women with projects participated in

such societies, pooling on the average one-third of their income into the
kitty. Interviewees reported that the numbers of women participating in
such credit societies had increased to an unprecedented level with the
growth of women's income-generating activities. Women used their earnings to buy clothes for their children, pay for their education and health
costs, and some were able to save to build houses.

Although it is too early to say how or whether women's expanding
economic role will translate into political leverage or other forms of
power and influence, the implications of these changes in the household
economy have not been lost on men, or on women for that matter. Gender
relations and perceptions are clearly in flux. Urban men would frequently
downplay Tanzanian women's role as important economic actors with
independent sources of income, by saying that women "just make a few
cents" with their projects. Refusing to acknowledge women's actual
contribution to the household became a way of minimizing their activities
and thereby making them appear less threatening. Other men, fearing
their wives would become too independent or leave them, were more
openly hostile to women's income-generating projects. They might refuse
to let their wives even become involved in a project or would restrict the
kinds of projects they could engage in. In Buguruni, one of the areas I
studied, one Lutheran pastor told me that one of the new problems he
encountered among members of his congregation was husbands coming
to him complaining that they did not want their wives involved in projects
because this would reflect on them and their own ability to support the
family. Nevertheless, economic necessity had apparently convinced most
men to encourage their wives' projects. One woman hairdresser explained it this way:

> Some women get money from their projects and it makes them less
> respectful of their husbands. They say, "I am free and can budget on my
> own, I can buy what I want. I don't have to ask my husband for money for
> everything." For them it may have caused more problems. But for most
> women these projects have meant solving the budgetary problems in their
> family. So they have made family life easier. . . . We would not have worked
> to have projects in the 1970s. Then you could live on the salary of the
> husband and it would have caused problems if the wife had a project. But
> today because of hiked prices and shortages, if it was only the husband
> working, most of us would go crazy. (Tripp 1989:613)

Another woman who had started a women's fishing cooperative on the
outskirts of Dar es Salaam explained how the twenty-one women in the
cooperative also had their own individual projects transporting and
selling coconuts to the city, growing and selling vegetables, making and

selling pastries, and frying fish for sale. She noted that since women had become increasingly active in such activities, the men would have liked to object to these projects

> but they keep quiet. They know they can't support the family and they need the woman's income. Some men are even getting ambitious and are trying to find businesses for themselves.

Some men had gone so far as to calculate the value of a woman as a wife by her ability to manage a successful project. One young man described half-jokingly the kind of woman he wanted to marry:

> I want an intelligent woman with brains who will know how to find a project. She can take care of the project better than I. I can't manage to look after a large amount of money because I will end up drinking a lot. But if my wife is bright, she can take care of the project and we will do well. (Tripp 1989:612)

RELATIONSHIP BETWEEN FORMAL WAGE LABOR AND INFORMAL LABOR

Various conceptualizations of the household tend to conceal varying interests and resource flows within the household, and many conceptions of labor can also lead to such oversights of women's work. Benería (1981), for example, has shown how conventional definitions of "active labor" have excluded women's household production or "use value production" by focusing primarily on exchange value production. In fact, the focus on formal wage labor obscures not only noncommoditized activities, but also market activity within the informal economy. The preoccupation with conventional statistical data in the Tanzanian case all too often leads to serious distortions and oversights of some of the most important dynamics taking place within the society as a whole. Undue importance is frequently placed on the role of wage labor in economies where this represents only a fraction of all economic activity, and wage labor tends to be seen as the point of reference for self-employment.

For example, the Marxist notion that household production lessens the cost of maintaining and reproducing the labor force is often alluded to. This notion was applied to analyses of the informal sector in the 1970s and was extended to analyses of women's work in the 1980s. Basically, the argument is as follows: Capitalist enterprises in the periphery need to pay workers low wages in order to give the enterprises the competitive edge in the international market. The informal sector/economy reduces the costs of labor in formal capitalist enterprises in peripheral countries by enabling the capitalist sector to maintain low wages by producing cheap goods and services through the use of cheap informal labor (Portes 1978:37). Portes later modified this position and explained that the main cost-saving feature of informality is not the direct lowering of wages but rather the capitalists' ability to avoid the provision of social benefits and employee-related payments to the state (Castells and Portes 1989:30–31). Gender studies, in particular, have explored other ways in which the informal sector lowers wages. Bujra, for example, suggests that "in petty commodity production and commerce, then, as well as in subsistence cultivation, women's labor underwrites the reproduction of labor power for capitalist enterprises" (1986:126). She argues that the process of capitalist transformation and proletarianization in Africa has therefore expanded women's role in subsistence and small-scale production for the market.

These arguments are a logical extension of the notion that in order for capitalists in many Third World countries to maximize their profits they need to minimize wages. Unlike in the industrialized countries, where pressures to expand the internal market necessitate higher wages and the gradual incorporation of subsistence activities, this necessity is not present in peripheral countries because commodities are produced for external consumption and profits are realized in international markets (Portes 1978:35–36). The parsimony of these arguments is appealing and at a very general level they can be found to be useful; their actual application to particular situations suggests some limitations, especially as they relate to gender issues.

In Tanzania, where the government controls 65 percent of wage employment and 70 percent of the wage bill (Mtatifikolo 1988:35), it was primarily the state that benefited from maintaining such depressed wages. Private wages and salaries, which were also controlled by the government, were not substantially higher. Since the late 1960s the government had used its control of wages and salaries, prices, and taxes in a concerted effort to ensure the equal distribution of incomes among households, regions, and between rural and urban areas in both the public and private sectors (Valentine 1983:52). The government argued that because employed workers had improved their standard of living at the expense of peasants, wage and salary restraints were necessary to narrow the rural-urban income gap. They adopted a two-part strategy: first, to suppress all wage and salary earnings, especially after 1974, when agricultural producer prices were being raised, and second, to reduce the gap between high salaries and low wages (Mtatifikolo 1988:35).

The force of the crisis of the late 1970s, however, overtook these equalizing strategies, and increasingly the government's policy was dictated by the fact that many state-run industries were operating at a loss and government expenditure was at a deficit. This meant that resources simply were not there to pay adequate wages and salaries. As President Mwinyi said in his 1990 May Day speech: "No salary increase would enable us to meet all requirements [of labor]. . . . Therefore, I would like to repeat my appeal to fellow workers to initiate small projects which would supplement their income" (*Daily News,* 25 May 1990).

The prospect of the government increasing wages to keep up with inflation is so slim that workers have long since given up on their demands for meaningful wage increases. Up until the 1960s Tanzania had a vibrant labor movement that fought vigorously and successfully to raise wages to keep them in line with the cost of living. The ruling party's elimination of an independent labor movement since the 1960s coupled with economic crisis has made the issue of meaningful wage raises virtually irrelevant. Today, workers' energies are focused on how to increase their incomes off the job rather than on how to mobilize for pay increases on the job. In Tanzania today the increase in small-scale production has occurred in the context of economic decline and in the midst of the deindustrialization of large-scale enterprises.

The government has repeatedly acknowledged that higher wages would improve productivity, lessen the time workers take off from work to pursue their own projects, and reduce both white-collar crime as well as pilfering and bribery—all of which became rampant in the 1980s. Low government wages, however, are not intended to maximize profits but to avert complete and total bankruptcy. This is not to say that within the context of a healthier economy the Tanzanian government might not resort to suppressing wages in order to maximize profits. However, restoring wages to subsistence levels has been the goal of the Tanzanian government since the mid-1980s.

Thus the increase in women's economic activities in urban Tanzania has not arisen out of the expansion of capitalism or out of the need for capital in the "periphery" to maximize profits by lowering wages, but rather out of the attempt by industry to stay afloat amidst economic disaster. Wages do not even come close to covering the cost of reproducing the labor power of the individual worker, not to mention the cost of reproducing the entire household. As mentioned earlier, the average worker cannot cover the food expenses of his/her household for more than three days of the month on his/her monthly salary.

Looking at the women's informal economic activity in this context as merely supplementing the formal wage sector or as providing cheap goods to reproduce labor (mainly male labor) cheaply is to diminish the significance of women's economic activities and see their importance only in relation to formal wage labor. In Tanzania, at least, these informal activities of both men and women have sustained the entire urban economy throughout years of unprecedented hardship. They are crucial to the survival of the entire fabric of the society. For example, from the point of view of women involved in these informal projects, they do not "supplement" wage earnings, as economists frequently put it. If anything, the salary at the end of the month supplements the small businesses and serves as a source of capital that can be dipped into if the business runs into difficulties. This observation holds true regardless of income group and is even more true of middle- and upper-income employees. A woman engaged in an ongoing project, even one bringing in little revenue, almost invariably exceeds the income of her employed husband or family member. Thus, to focus only on the dynamics of the formal wage sector is to see societies like urban Tanzania through the lens of an industrialized country, where wage labor plays a proportionately greater role.

It is obvious why workers and their households rely on informal incomes, but a more appropriate question under the circumstances would be: Why do they even bother to work as wage employees when they could potentially make more money if they went into managing their projects full time? Instead they often straddle their jobs and projects, keeping their options open in both the formal and informal spheres of the economy.

It has long been recognized that Africa's urban dwellers rarely depended solely on one source of income, either as individuals or as a household. Some argue that it is the security of the formal income rather than the size of the income that keeps workers on the job (Berry 1978; Hart 1973:78; Peil 1972; Pfefferman 1968). This risk aversion is evident in the reasons some of Dar es Salaam's workers chose to remain employed while pursuing more lucrative income-generating projects. Some workers had not been in business long enough to be certain they would succeed. For others the job provided a dependable source of back-up capital to invest in their businesses, especially if it was in a slump, or as a reserve fund if they were forced to spend their working capital on daily necessities.

In one household, a man employed as a messenger gave his wife capital obtained from sales of cotton from their farm in Tanga to build a restaurant. The wife supported their seven children and his parents from what she made selling porridge, meat, beans, bread, and tea at the restaurant. The restaurant was primarily the responsibility of the wife, who made 20,000 Tsh a month from her work in the project. Her husband's job brought in only 1,070 Tsh a month, which after deductions (e.g., taxes, insurance) amounted to only 900 Tsh take-home pay. Although they had the restaurant since 1972 and considered it a fairly stable source of income, the husband saw no reason to leave the job as long as his wife could manage the business and they could use his wages as back-up capital if the business ran into problems. For example, once a health officer closed down their restaurant for half a year on grounds that it was not sanitary because the walls were not painted, the building was too small, and the toilet not up to standard. Unable to afford the so-called "requirements" for their restaurant, they finally gave the officer what he really wanted—a bribe. In the meantime, while their restaurant was closed, they claimed that the husband's wages helped tide the family over (it is doubtful that they actually complied with the inspector for more than a few days).

The job could provide a ready market for goods produced in informal projects or serve as a source of contacts, resources, and information that could be useful to one's project. For professionals, the job frequently provided access to cheap housing, a car, or a phone. They also found employment useful in order to maintain the status that corresponded with the position, even though the status was not reflected monetarily in their salaries. Others believed they would become bored if they worked only on their project. One woman in her early forties who raised cows and pigs and worked with the Ministry of Education said she felt obligated to the Ministry. "At my age," she said, "I still have more to offer." A nurse who made 80,000 Tsh a month raising chickens—sixteen times her own salary and eight times her husband's salary—was asked why she did not leave her job. She responded emphatically that she would never leave her job as a nurse because she enjoyed it so much.

INCOME POLARIZATION AND WOMEN'S ENTERPRISES

The preoccupation with formal wage labor and data pertaining to wage labor has also obscured a major consequence of the economic reforms: the role of women's informal incomes and the widening gap between income groups. The Tanzanian government's policy had been to narrow official wage differences through its control of pay scales, increasing the minimum wage earner's income while keeping the top salaries relatively stable. The highest salary for a government official, for example, had been reduced to only around four times that of the minimum wage worker by the late 1980s.

Because of party prohibitions against "sideline" businesses and because of attempts to avoid taxation, many economic activities, often rather lucrative businesses, went unlicensed, untaxed, and therefore unregistered. Up until the early 1970s official statistics on wages bore some relation to reality. But the pervasiveness of such unlicensed activities at every level and the large disparities that existed between real incomes made the official statistics on income levels little more than a fiction in the late 1980s. It would seem obvious that a meaningful discussion of income equality in the 1980s would have to account for informal incomes, which make the gap significantly larger than official wage differentials. Yet economists continue to focus on formal wage indicators when they discuss income differentiation in a country like Tanzania.

For example, in an otherwise interesting piece by Mtatifikolo on Tanzania's incomes policy, he hints in his conclusion that growth of the informal sector may make wages irrelevant, yet he argues that "by the early 80s a large degree of income equality had been achieved" as a result of the government's wage policy because the ratio of lowest to highest public sector wages had been lowered from 1:20 in 1967 to 1:5 in 1986 (1988:35).

One of the reasons for such glaring oversights of real incomes is the neglect not only of women's economic activities but of the informal economy as well. Income polarization between poor women and the middle- and upper-income women has never been greater. In a snowball survey I made of fifty-one households in the middle and upper income brackets, these women were making on the average 51,130 Tsh a month, ranging from almost ten times what the poorer women made from their small businesses, and on the average ten times their own formal salaries as professionals or semiprofessionals. In terms of official incomes, how- ever, these same middle- to upper-income women brought in only twice or at the most three times what the average woman worker made (Tripp 1989). Those women with access to greater capital, know-how, and resources to start businesses kept chickens, tended pigs and cows, opened hairdressing salons, operated flour mills and bakeries, exported prawns to Botswana, and imported chicks from Zambia. A few had accumulated sufficient capital from illegal projects of this sort and had been able to set up larger legal businesses, including shipping and receiving compa- nies, secretarial service companies, private schools, textile factories, and dry cleaning businesses. Such ownership of major businesses by women was virtually unheard of in Tanzania in the early 1980s.

Even though some women have managed to enter into more lucrative enterprises, most women, for whom access to capital is a serious problem, have little hope of expanding beyond a small microenterprise, selling pastries or porridge.

LARGE-SCALE AND SMALL-SCALE PRODUCTION

The focus on employed labor to the neglect of informal eco- nomic activities is paralleled in the focus on large-scale industrial development; small-scale production is seen as a peripheral activity to the operation of the entire economy. The broader liberalization and privatization measures, for example, have not included policies that would have created an environment more conducive to forms of small-scale production. Instead, the policies have been aimed at the more visible and large-scale industries. Women continue to operate under considerable constraints in an environment that does not encourage small income-generating activities. They face licensing and tax disincentives (paying such fees necessitates paying bribes) and then they face militia harassment because they do not have licenses. Moreover, taxes on produced goods can go as high as 200 percent with no differentiation made with respect to the size of the production unit. Women's projects are generally so new and precarious that taxes of this kind could destroy them altogether. Women's access to formal credit for small businesses is virtually nonexistent in urban areas. Women, who generally buy small quantities of inputs or equipment, frequently have to pay for them at illegally hiked prices, unlike those operating in the formal sector, who have greater access to inputs at official low prices because they can buy in bulk or are well connected.

Nevertheless, even throughout the worst years of the crisis, small-scale production proved remarkably resilient at a time when large state-run industries and enterprises deteriorated. Small-scale manufacturing operations were among the most lucrative forms of work in the city, while factory employment offered below-subsistence wages. Small-scale production provided cheap goods using local inputs while production in the import-dependent large industries suffered from machine breakdowns, frequent power cuts, lack of spares and raw materials, declining working capital, and delays in importing inputs in part due to foreign exchange shortages. Large-scale industry, for example, registered negative growth rates throughout the 1980s and was operating at 20 percent capacity in the late 1980s. Meanwhile, small-scale production was growing at an unprecedented rate, accommodating markets that the formal industry could no longer serve, offering more affordable goods, and providing individuals with work and livable incomes that large-scale manufacturers could no longer sustain. Because small-scale production depends on local resources and technology and is not dependent on imports, it is less vulnerable to external shocks. Moreover, small-scale production in Tanzania, according to Kwan Kim, is "at least five times as effective as its large-scale counterpart in terms of output measured per unit investment" (1988:96). Thus, while the formal industrial sector experienced the worst declines in the history of Tanzania, small-scale producers were increasing in numbers and expanding their businesses.

CONCLUSION

The way in which we conceptualize women's work has both theoretical and policy implications. The role of women in the economy can easily be obscured, as I have shown in the case of Tanzania, by focusing on an idealized notion of the household, by operating with conventional conceptualizations of the importance of wages and large-scale industrial production, and by looking simply at official statistics on income differentiation. These concepts need to be redefined in a way that allows us to see more of the complexities of economic life. Women's economic interactions, however small-scale and petty they may appear, have in the case of Tanzania proven to be the backbone sustaining entire urban populations in the face of industrial decline.

More concretely, as women are the focal point in the flow of resources through the household, they are key to leveraging assistance to larger numbers of household members, including children and youth. No matter how poor the household, women attempt to save a portion of their income and have proven to be remarkably successful in doing so. Mothers not only engage their children in their income-generating projects, but they are the ones primarily responsible for making sure that the children are fed, clothed, and have school supplies and medicine. At the same time women have shown ingenuity and flexibility in responding to the adverse effects of the crisis and economic reform on their living standards by pursuing income-generating projects. They have done so regardless of their meager capital, resources, and know-how. Policymakers and donors would do well to learn from these women on how to survive under extreme austerity. Policies directed at urban women would need to start from women's own strategies, forms of organization, and priorities. By asking women about their own needs and plans, policymakers could better address women's needs for credit, loans, transport, child care, and skills.

NOTES

The author is grateful to the United Nations World Institute for Development Economic Research in Helsinki for its financial support of the fieldwork on which this chapter is based. Special thanks to Salome Mjema, who assisted in the field research, and to Karen Hansen and Sita Ranchod for their helpful comments on an earlier draft of the chapter.

1. I adopted the snowball survey method since people of this income bracket frequently were civil servants, who feared losing their jobs if found by the party to have a second income. They were more hesitant to talk about their activities since the Party Leadership Code forbade employees from having second incomes,

even if the business was carried out by the spouse of the employee. One interviewee would refer us to a friend, and that friend referred us to another. By establishing trust in this way, we were able to find out more about their additional sources of income.

2. The exchange rates fluctuated dramatically after major devaluations in 1986. For example, from June to December 1988, the exchange rate increased from US$1 = 97 Tsh to $1 = 124 Tsh. Therefore, all references to dollar amounts in this chapter are necessarily approximations. They are offered merely as rough indicators.

REFERENCES

Benería, L. 1981. "Conceptualizing the Labor Force: The Underestimation of Women's Economic Activities." In N. Nelson (ed.), *African Women in the Development Process*. London: Cass.

Berry, S. 1978. *Custom, Class and the "Informal Sector" or Why Marginality Is Not Likely to Pay*. Working Paper No. 1, African Studies Center, Boston University.

Bruce, J. and D. Dwyer (eds.). 1988. *A Home Divided: Women and Income in the Third World*. Stanford: Stanford University Press.

Bryceson, D. F. 1987. "A Century of Food Supply in Dar es Salaam: From Sumptuous Suppers for the Sultan to Maize Meal for a Million." In J. I. Guyer (ed.), *Feeding African Cities: Studies in Regional Social History*. Manchester: Manchester University Press.

Bujra, J. M. 1986. " 'Urging Women to Redouble Their Efforts . . . ': Class, Gender, and Capitalist Transformation in Africa." In C. Robertson and I. Berger (eds.), *Women and Class in Africa*. New York: Africana Publishing Company.

Castells, M., and A. Portes. 1989. "World Underneath: The Origins, Dynamics, and Effects of the Informal Economy." In A. Portes, M. Castells, and L. A. Benton (eds.), *The Informal Economy*. Baltimore: Johns Hopkins University Press.

Clark, G. 1989. "Separation Between Trading and Home for Asante Women in Kumasi Central Market, Ghana." Paper presented at African Studies Association meeting, Atlanta, Georgia, 1989.

Cornia, G. A. 1987. "Adjustment at the Household Level: Potentials and Limitations of Survival Strategies." In G. A. Cornia, R. Jolly, and F. Stewart (eds.), *Adjustment with a Human Face: Protecting the Vulnerable and Promoting Growth*. Oxford: Oxford University Press.

Fapohunda, E. R. 1988a. "The Nonpooling Household: A Challenge to Theory." In J. Bruce and D. Dwyer (eds.), *A Home Divided: Women and Income in the Third World*. Stanford: Stanford University Press.

————. 1988b. "Dynamic Approaches to Domestic Budgeting: Cases and Methods from Africa." In J. Bruce and D. Dwyer (eds.), *A Home Divided: Women and Income in the Third World*. Stanford: Stanford University Press.

Guyer, J. I., and P. E. Peters. 1987. "Introduction." *Development and Change* 18:197–214.

Hart, K. 1973. "Informal Income Opportunities in Urban Employment in Ghana." *Journal of Modern African Studies* 11 (1):61–89.

Kim, K. 1988. "Issues and Perspectives in Tanzanian Industrial Development with Special Reference to the Role of SADCC." In M. Hodd (ed.), *Tanzania After Nyerere*. London: Pinter Publishers.

Kulaba, S. 1989. "Local Government and the Management of Urban Services in Tanzania." In R. E. Stren and R. R. White (eds.), *African Cities in Crisis: Managing Rapid Urban Growth*. Boulder, Colo.: Westview Press.

Lipumba, N.H.I. 1989. "Long Term Trends in Exports." *Tanzania Economic Trends* 2 (1):11–23.

Lofchie, M. F. 1988. "Tanzania's Agricultural Decline." In N. Chazan and T. M. Shaw (eds.), *Coping with Africa's Food Crisis*. Boulder, Colo.: Lynne Rienner.

Mbelle, A. 1989. "Industrial (Manufacturing) Performance in the ERP Context in Tanzania." *Tanzania Economic Trends* 2 (1):7–10.

Mtatifikolo, F. P. 1988. "Tanzania's Incomes Policy: An Analysis of Trends with Proposals for the Future." *African Studies Review* 31 (1):33–46.

Peil, M. 1972. *The Ghanaian Factory Worker*. Cambridge: Cambridge University Press.

Pfefferman, G. 1968. *Industrial Labor in Senegal*. New York: Praeger.

Portes, A. 1978. "The Informal Sector and the World Economy: Notes on the Structure of Subsidised Labour." *IDS Bulletin* 9 (4):35–40.

Robertson, C., and I. Berger. 1986. "Introduction: Analyzing Class and Gender— African Perspectives." In C. Robertson and I. Berger (eds.), *Women and Class in Africa*. New York: Africana Publishing Company.

Sabot, Richard H. 1979. *Economic Development and Urban Migration: Tanzania 1900–1971*. Oxford: Clarendon Press.

Stein, H. 1988. "The Economics of the State and the IMF in Tanzania." Paper presented at the 1988 annual African Studies Association Meeting in Chicago, Illinois.

Tanzania. 1986. *Statistical Abstract 1984*. Dar es Salaam: Ministry of Finance, Planning and Economic Affairs, Bureau of Statistics.

————. 1989. *1988 Population Census: Preliminary Report*. Dar es Salaam: Ministry of Finance, Planning and Economic Affairs, Bureau of Statistics.

Tibaijuka, A. K. 1988. "The Impact of Structural Adjustment Programmes on Women: The Case of Tanzania's Economic Recovery Programme. Economic Research Bureau, University of Dar es Salaam." Report prepared for the Canadian International Development Agency (CIDA).

Tripp, A. M. 1989. "Women and the Changing Urban Household Economy in Tanzania." *Journal of Modern African Studies* 27 (4):601–623.

————. 1990. *The Urban Informal Economy and the State in Tanzania*. Ph.D. diss., Northwestern University, Evanston, Ill.

Valentine, T. R. 1983. "Wage Adjustments, Progressive Tax Rates, and Accelerated Inflation: Issues of Equity in the Wage Sector of Tanzania." *African Studies Review* 21 (1):51–71.

World Bank. 1989. *Sub-Saharan Africa: From Crisis to Sustainable Growth*. Washington, D.C.: The International Bank for Reconstruction.

8

Gender Relations & Food Security: Coping with Seasonality, Drought, & Famine in South Asia

☙ BINA AGARWAL

Rooted in public policies and programs directed at ensuring food security in Third World countries are certain assumptions about the family: the responsibility of its members toward each other's well-being, and their capability and willingness to fulfill that responsibility. For instance, government programs that direct resources and employment at male household heads assume implicitly that the associated benefits will be shared equitably with women and children. Are such assumptions valid in practice? Even more important, are they valid in food crisis situations?

To answer this question, we need to examine how poor agricultural families in South Asia themselves respond to the problem of food insecurity associated with seasonal troughs in the agricultural production cycle and with calamities such as drought and famine. How, for instance, is the burden of coping shared between male and female family members, and what does this reveal about intrafamily gender relations?

An understanding of these dimensions is important for designing public policy interventions for food security, whether by the State[1] or by non-State agencies, to ensure their appropriateness on at least two counts: (1) in strengthening the survival mechanisms not only of the most vulnerable families but also of their most vulnerable members by explicitly focusing on any intrafamily inequalities in the impact of contingencies; and (2) in complementing rather than undermining people's own efforts at dealing with contingencies, with people being seen as actors in the process of change rather than as passive recipients of aid and relief.

I consider the issue of food security here in the sense of ensuring maintenance of food consumption levels in the context of specific contingencies rather than in the sense of providing adequate food intake for all. Broadly, a household is seen as effectively coping with seasonality and calamity where, as a result, it suffers no irreversible damage to the productive capacity of its members or to its net asset position. The terms "household" and "family" have been used here interchangeably to connote commensal units.

The chapter is divided into five sections. Section 1 outlines an analytical approach for conceptualizing the family: the bargaining approach, which would be useful for examining not merely these concerns but a range of concerns that stem from or impinge on intrafamily gender relations. Sections 2 and 3 examine how poor rural families cope with seasonality, drought, and famine. Section 4 focuses on some regional variations in women's position as they impinge on the gender consequences of food crises, and Section 5 discusses policy implications.

Although the illustrative examples are drawn from South Asia, especially India, the analytical framework suggested here has wider relevance, both geographically and in terms of issues.

CONCEPTUALIZING THE FAMILY: THE BARGAINING APPROACH

In an examination of the relationship between seasonality, calamity, and the family, a critical question is: How do we conceptualize the family? This is a question that much of standard economic theory either ignores, or sees as unproblematic, treating the family as an undifferentiated unit. Indeed, as some recent feminist critiques have pointed out, there is a noteworthy similarity between neoclassical and Marxist economic theories on this count (Folbre 1988; Hart 1990). Yet the growing evidence of persistent intrafamily inequalities in the distribution of resources and tasks as well as cross-cultural anthropological descriptions of intrafamily interactions and decisionmaking indicate the need for a very different conceptualization of the household: one that takes account of multiple actors, with varying preferences and interests, and differential abilities to pursue and fulfill those interests.[2]

In the context of the present discussion, I would like to suggest here that it is useful to conceptualize the family as a complex mesh of relationships across which there is ongoing (often implicit) negotiation, subject to the constraints set by gender, age, type of relationship (kinship association), and what could be termed "undisputed tradition" (elaborated later).

The nature of this intrafamily negotiation could then usefully be described as one of cooperative conflict, as A. K. Sen (1983, 1990) has done in his critique and extension of standard economic bargaining approaches. Many cooperative outcomes are possible in relation to who does what, who gets what goods and services, and how different family members are treated—outcomes that are beneficial to the negotiating members relative to noncooperation. But among the set of such possible cooperative outcomes, some are more favorable to one party than others, hence the underlying conflict of interests between those cooperating. Which outcome emerges depends on the relative bargaining power of the different family members, and a member's bargaining power within the family would depend especially on the strength of the person's fall-back position, should cooperation fail.

A person's fall-back position (and associated bargaining strength within the family vis-à-vis, say, subsistence needs) would depend, in turn, on a range of factors, of which I would like to highlight four:[3]

- ownership and control over assets, especially land
- access to employment and other income-earning means
- access to communal resources (village commons, forests)
- access to external social support systems (such as of patronage, kinship, and friendship) embodying relationships in which factors other than the mere economic take precedence, that is, they fall under the rubric of what has been termed by some as the "moral economy" (e.g., Scott 1976; Greenough 1982)

These four factors impinge directly on a person's ability to fulfill subsistence needs outside the family. The premise here is that the greater a person's ability to physically survive outside the family, the greater would be his/her bargaining power (at least in relation to resource sharing for subsistence) within the family.[4] (A fifth factor could be access to support from state or nonstate organizations, but this is discussed toward the end of the paper.) Inequalities among family members in respect of these factors would place some members in a weaker bargaining position relative to others. Gender is one such basis of inequality, age another.

Crises of seasonality and calamity can negatively affect asset ownership, income-earning opportunities, and the strength of external support systems for both sexes, but insofar as men and women are affected *unequally,* it would alter their relative intrafamily bargaining strengths as well. A collapse of the wife's fall-back position (as could happen, for instance, in a famine) while that of the husband is sustained (in relative terms) could weaken her bargaining position even to a point where noncooperation is found more beneficial by the man, creating a tendency toward his abandoning of his spouse and the disintegration of the family.

Whether or not an actual breakdown occurs would be subject, of course, to other considerations as well, such as the ties of love and affection holding a family together and the structural placement of the family (stemming from its class, caste, and ethnic position) within the larger society.

In addition, I may add that not all family decisions are explicitly bargained over. At any given time, for a given society, some decisions would fall in the realm of what the French sociologist Bourdieu (1977) terms "doxa"—that which is accepted as natural and self-evident, as part of undisputed tradition. In the context of the present discussion, this could include practices that favor group over individual interests (such as strategic marriage alliances) or favor some groups over others (such as a given gender division of labor or women eating last and eating the least nutritious foods in many regions of South Asia). Such practices also reflect the dominant perceptions of the needs and rights of people (say of women in relation to men) prevailing in a society,[5] perceptions that may well be internalized through a socialization process by the disadvantaged persons/groups themselves, or to which the persons/groups may submit because of a lack of choice.[6] But, over time, what constitutes doxa may itself be subject to challenge and change, with processes of politicization (of the disadvantaged), shifts in cultural meanings, and structural changes in the economy.

When we examine actual responses of families to food crises in the context of South Asia, and especially India, we find that seasonality reveals the face of the family as one of unequal cooperation, and famine mirrors one of disintegration. Consider first the issue of seasonality.

COPING WITH SEASONALITY

Typically, poor agricultural households are found to cope with seasonal variations in the crop cycle, and associated variations in food availability, employment, wages, prices, and so on, in five main ways: (1) diversifying income sources, including by seasonal migration; (2) drawing upon communal resources—village common lands, forests; (3) drawing upon social relationships—patronage, kinship, friendship—or informal credit sources such as moneylenders; (4) adjusting consumption patterns; and (5) mortgaging or selling assets. These are not mutually exclusive and are typically adopted in combination, although selling productive assets is usually a last resort.

Although the particular mix of measures adopted can vary by region according to the prevailing economic, technological, ecological, and social possibilities, the implications are mediated by some common underlying features. When we examine these mechanisms three aspects, in particular, emerge as noteworthy:

1. Intrahousehold cooperation between men, women, and children is critical in enabling poor households to tide over seasonal troughs.
2. Women of poor households cooperate within the family from a weaker bargaining position than men in several respects:

   - They have virtually no direct access to productive resources such as land, and limited access to personal assets such as cash and jewelry (Agarwal 1988).
   - Their access to incomes is circumscribed by fewer employment opportunities, lesser occupational mobility, lower levels of training, and lower payments for the same or similar work.[7] They also face much greater seasonal fluctuations in employment and earnings than do men due to the greater task specificity of their work, have sharper peaks and longer slack periods in many regions, and have less chance of finding employment in the slack seasons.[8]
   - Moreover, there are noteworthy inequalities in the allocation of tasks and of resources for basic needs within the household: typically women work longer hours, have poorer health care, and in several regions have lower food intakes relative to needs than men in the same families.[9]

3. There are differences in the roles played and burdens borne by male and female family members in relation to these coping mechanisms, with women on balance bearing the major load.

Consider some examples. Landless and land-poor families seek to reduce the subsistence risk that traditional farming systems entail by diversifying income sources, such as by seeking employment where available, multiple cropping and intercropping where the household has some land, keeping a variety of livestock and poultry, trading, and seasonally migrating either individually or as families.[10] (This last could be seen as a kind of spatial diversification.) In all these coping mechanisms, the labor of women is critical, along with that of men and children, for the following reasons:

- Women's absolute contributions to household subsistence from their wage earnings in poor households are typically significant, often equal to men's, and sometimes greater than those of men.[11]

- Livestock, poultry, etc., which significantly help the household diversify incomes, are usually cared for by women and children.[12]
- Although individual male out-migration is the most common pattern of seasonal migration, women also sometimes migrate as individuals or in families,[13] and when they stay behind they assume additional workloads and responsibilities as de facto female heads, which facilitates male migration.[14]

Women's contribution is apparent again when households draw upon village commons (VCs) and State forests to obtain food and other essential items for daily use. All rural households use VCs in some degree, but the dependence of the poor is especially high. A study covering semiarid regions in seven states of India found that among the rural landless and land-poor households, VCs accounted for up to 20 percent or more of total income, over 90 percent of their firewood, and over 65 percent of their grazing (Jodha 1986; Dasgupta 1987; and Ryan et al., 1984). Forests serve a similar function.[15] The dependence on communal sources for firewood is especially critical because firewood is the single most important source of domestic fuel in rural South Asia and is largely gathered, not purchased.[16] This dependence on gathered food and fuel gets accentuated seasonally. To the extent that periods of slack in crop production do not entirely coincide with lean periods of VCs and forest output, this helps sustain the poor during troughs in agricultural employment (Jodha 1986). Tribal populations in particular depend critically on gathered food during certain seasons (Pingle 1975; Banerjee 1988).

Typically, it is women and children who play the primary role in the collection of produce from VCs and forests (Dasgupta 1987; Brara 1987; Agarwal 1987, 1989). Also, as the main foragers and gatherers, they often have a valuable reserve knowledge of edible forest produce, which can help tide poor families over prolonged seasonal shortages.[17]

What is of particular note here is that VCs and forests provide women, children, and even the aged with an independent source of subsistence *unmediated* by dependency relationships on young male adults. For instance, women have rights to use the VCs by virtue of their membership (through birth or marriage) in the village community, whereas their access to the cash economy, to markets, and (in areas of strong female seclusion) to the marketplace itself is constrained and usually dependent on the mediation of male relatives.[18]

However, the rapid decline in forests and VCs, especially in semiarid areas, is effectively eroding this significant source of protection against food shortages for the poor. In much of Pakistan and Bangladesh less than 10 percent of the geo-area is under forest (Table 8.1). In India, by

TABLE 8.1 Percent of Geo-Area Under Forest in South Asia

Country	Reference Year	Percent Geo-Area Under Forest
Bangladesh	1985–1986	15.7[a]
India	1985–1987	19.5
Nepal	1978–1979	37.6
Pakistan	1986–1987	5.4[b]
Sri Lanka	1982–1985	39.0

[a]The figures are over 10.0 in only four districts: Noakhali, Chittagong, Chittagong (hill tracts), and Khulna.
[b]The figures are over 10.0 in only one province: North West Frontier Province.

Sources: Bangladesh 1988; India 1990; Nepal 1988; Pakistan figures compiled by the International Union for the Conservation of Nature and Natural Resources, Karachi, 1990; Sri Lanka/World Bank 1986.

the 1985–1987 satellite survey, only 64 mha (million hectares) or 19.5 percent of the geographic area is today under forests, and this is estimated to be declining at the rate of 1.3 mha a year (Table 8.2).

Ironically, State policy, first under colonial rule and subsequently in the postindependence period, has been a major contributor to this decline: The commercial logging of forests and the clearing of land for large hydroelectric-cum-irrigation projects are two of the principal causes of deforestation in India.[19] Likewise, as Jodha's (1986) study indicates,

TABLE 8.2   India: Percent of Geo-Area Under Forest, by State, 1985–1987

State	Percent Geo-Area Under Forest[a]	State	Percent Geo-Area Under Forest[a]
Andhra Pradesh	17.3	Manipur	80.0
Arunachal Pradesh	82.3	Meghalaya	69.8
Assam	33.2	Mizoram	86.2
Bihar	15.5	Nagaland	86.8
Gujarat	6.0	Orissa	30.3
Haryana	1.3	Punjab	2.3
Himachal Pradesh	24.0	Rajasthan	3.8
Jammu and Kashmir	9.1	Sikkim	42.8
Karnataka	16.7	Tamil Nadu	13.6
Kerala	26.1	Tripura	50.1
Madhya Pradesh	30.1	Uttar Pradesh	11.5
Maharashtra	14.3	West Bengal	9.6
		All India	19.5

[a]Based on 1985–1987 satellite imagery.

Source: India 1990.

the most significant cause of the decline in VCs has been land privatization as a result of State policy. For instance, large tracts of VCs have been distributed to individuals by the government since the 1950s, under various land reform and antipoverty schemes, ostensibly to benefit the landless but effectively endowing the already landed. In some parts of India, as in Jalore District of Rajasthan, as much as 86 percent of VC land so distributed has gone to those already owning land. *The poor have thus lost out collectively while very few of them have gained individually.* Parts of VCs have also been auctioned by the government to private contractors for commercial exploitation. Illegal encroachments by larger farmers, subsequently made legal, have compounded the decline in VCs (Jodha 1986; Cernea 1981). The gender implications of this loss are particularly adverse, given the noted greater dependency of women on these resources and their responsibility for fetching fuel, fodder, and water. Ironically, many new tree-planting schemes have often worsened matters by promoting largely commercial varieties such as eucalyptus, sometimes at the cost of species used by the poor (Agarwal 1986b, 1987, 1991).

Apart from the loss of communal resources, erosion is also apparent in social support systems of patronage, kinship, caste groupings, and even friendships built up in different ways by male and female family members, which have traditionally helped tide families over periods of shortage.[20] The decline in kin support is especially apparent among communities and groups that have become poorer over time, making it increasingly difficult for families to support kin. As a result, widows and the aged are left the worst off (Dreze 1990; Fernandes and Menon 1987; Jansen 1986). This erosion is especially dramatic in tribal communities traditionally characterized by a high degree of communal and cross-gender cooperation in work and social life. It is linked partly to the shift from communal, swidden cultivation to settled individual farming (a shift to which State policies toward land use and forests have contributed in critical ways)[21] and partly to the growing impoverishment of these tribal populations.[22]

The decline in customary systems of patronage, however, is associated particularly with the growth of capitalist farming, and it needs to be distinguished from emerging interlinked credit-labor systems that do not provide any of the subsistence guarantees and rights associated with the old, while often being just as exploitative (Breman 1985; Bhalla 1977; Banerjee 1988).

In this scenario of eroding traditional support systems, strategies of borrowing between families as well as free collection are becoming less viable. This situation has some specific gender implications: (a) because women's dependence on these support systems is greater than that of men, given their lesser access to the cash economy, this erosion means a weakening of women's fall-back position over time; (b) to the extent that earnings, borrowings, free collection, and the running down of inventories prove inadequate, families seasonally adjust consumption by changing the content of the diet and reducing total intake. A disproportionate burden of reducing consumption falls on women and female children. This is because, even in normal times (as noted), in several parts of the subcontinent (and especially in the northwest), there is an antifemale bias in food distribution and health care within the family. This bias often gets accentuated during food shortages.[23] Pregnant and lactating women and preschool children are especially vulnerable to body weight changes and seasonal malnutrition.[24]

Finally, usually as a last resort, a household may be forced to draw upon productive assets. The sale of land and draft animals affects its long-term productive capacity and can lead to what Chambers (1981) terms "poverty ratchets," where seasonal troughs leave the household worse off each year in relation to the previous one.

In overview then, three dimensions have been highlighted in our examination of seasonal coping mechanisms:

1. There are specific gender implications in the ways families cope: Although the inputs of all family members are critical for tiding the family over the troughs, the burden of coping appears to fall disproportionately on women, be it in terms of the work adjustments needed to diversify incomes and to draw upon communal resources or in terms of consumption adjustments (see the summary in Table 8.3). Hence, although it is beneficial for wives to cooperate with husbands because cooperation leaves them better off than non-cooperation, in relative terms they get the worse deal.

2. There is also a class, caste, and regional dimension to the effects of seasonality. While some households may suffer only temporary hardships, others face a downward slide with each sharp trough. These are more likely to be the assetless, belonging to low castes or tribes and located in semiarid regions.

3. Communal resources such as VCs and forests are particularly important in reducing the vulnerability of poor households and especially of women in such households. These resources thus need to be protected (through institutional and legal means) to ensure their communal control and access rather than being privatized.

COPING WITH DROUGHT AND FAMINE

Household responses to contingencies such as drought and famine are not dissimilar to those noted for seasonality in their *content*.

TABLE 8.3   Seasonal Coping Mechanisms in South Asia: Relative Gender Contributions (summary)[a]

Coping Mechanism	Relative Gender Contributions (F=female; M=male)
1. Diversifying income sources	
• seasonal migration	F < M
• keeping livestock, vegetable gardens, and so on	F > M
• adjusting workloads accordingly	F > M
2. Drawing on communal resources	F > M
3. Drawing on social relationships	
• patronage	F < M
• husband's kin	F < M
• wife's kin	F > M
• neighbors/friends	Equally
4. Adjusting consumption	F > M
5. Drawing on assets: mortgaging or selling	Unclear

[a]This summary should be taken as only a very rough assessment based on the discussion in the text.

Indeed, seasonality, drought, and famine may appear as three points in a continuum. But there is a significant difference in *context:* (a) in the relative *predictability* of seasonality as versus calamity, and (b) in the relative *intensity* of the food shortages experienced in the three situations. Hence, despite the noted weakening of traditional social security arrangements, they still work in some degree during seasonal troughs. This is not so during severe calamities such as drought and famine, when most such arrangements begin to collapse.

Indeed, what calamities bring into sharp focus is the critical limitations of arrangements that may work during seasonal troughs. Conflicts over access to village commons intensify;[25] help from relatives, friends, and neighbors (especially if they are similarly afflicted) begins to dry up,[26] as does credit from moneylenders;[27] patron-client relationships, already weak, may virtually snap;[28] families shift to famine foods and cut back on consumption[29]—women, children, and the old usually bearing the brunt of the cuts;[30] and assets are often sold.[31]

In this context, three aspects in particular are noteworthy: (1) in areas of recurrent droughts, families may make long-term work and demographic adjustments as a protective measure; (2) there is a pattern in family asset disposal with specific implications for women; and (3) families may themselves begin to break up. The form and extent of these responses and especially their gender consequences vary cross-regionally, as I will discuss shortly, but there are overall commonalities in the directions of these responses. Let us consider each of these in turn.

On Long-Term Adjustments

The most common method for farming families, in agricul-
turally risk-prone contexts, is to undertake income diversification. The
nature and content of this diversification can vary by region, depending
on available economic opportunities as well as cultural contexts. But
broadly, two types of responses stand out. First, diversification into urban,
less risk-prone contexts, such as by educating children for urban jobs,
choosing city-based sons-in-law, or forming other strategic marriage
alliances. This may also lead to fertility decline, as families begin to
invest less in numbers of children and more in their education (Caldwell,
Reddy, and Caldwell 1986). Second, diversification in the rural context,
including by marrying daughters into more distant, environmentally less
risk-prone villages, and by building up joint families (Maclachlan 1983).

The last case is especially interesting and needs some elaboration. In
a village of Karnataka state in South India, Maclachlan (1983) compared
the severe drought of 1965 when no deaths occurred with that of 1976
when a large number died and asked: Why didn't they starve in the
1960s? His answer: agricultural intensification, which was made possible
by deploying large amounts of family labor to dig open surface wells,
tend the fields, and cultivate gardens.

The strategy included building up large joint families with a careful
selection of brides (especially cross-cousins and first daughters) from
poorer hardworking families, and a strong ideological emphasis on the
joint family as the ideal and most productive family form, with the
concept of *dharma* (duty) being used to order a certain gender and age
division of labor and behavior.

Maclachlan found that joint families (defined as those with more than
one male adult), relative to others, indeed had higher yields per acre and
per capita; they were favored by landlords when seeking tenants, derived
economies in the division of farm tasks, had higher savings, used equipment more intensively, and had the advantages of interactive decisionmaking and the advice of the elders. Again, households with more than
one woman had distinct advantages in terms of diversification into
livestock, dairy, and sericulture handled by women and saved time
through work sharing in domestic tasks.

However, the typical family in South Asia today is no longer joint but
nuclear, especially among the poor and low castes (Kolenda 1987; A.
Chowdhury 1987). The question this raises is: Are there institutional
arrangements that can re-create cooperative labor deployment networks
or other advantages of extended families successfully *outside the context
of the family*? (a point to which I will return). Also, would other
institutional arrangements change the form and nature of intrafamily
relations?

The Sequence of Asset Disposal

It has been noted that under extreme food-shortage situations, rural households first reduce current consumption and deplete inventories of food, and so on; then they sell nonproductive assets such as utensils and jewelry, protecting draft animals and (particularly) land to the last (Jodha 1978; Borkar and Nadkarni 1975). The sale of draft animals, and especially land, thus becomes a barometer of the degree of distress.

Holding onto productive assets to the last makes economic sense because it affects the household's long-term survival capacity. However, in the noted sequencing of asset sales, what appears to have passed without comment in the discussion is that the first casualties are typically assets owned and controlled by women, namely, utensils and jewelry (Jodha 1978; Borkar and Nadkarni 1975; Singh 1975; Greenough 1982; Currey 1978). The sale of jewelry is perhaps not surprising as it is a much more liquid asset than land, serves as a store of value for a crisis, and, unlike cattle, is less prone to price plummeting (Jodha 1978; Borkar and Nadkarni 1975). However, utensils and jewelry, and possibly small animals, are usually the *only* assets possessed by women, who rarely own land. Once these are disposed of, even if the household is able to protect its productive assets, women would be left with nothing to fall back on, leaving them especially vulnerable during a severe calamity such as famine, when families may themselves begin to fragment and disintegrate.

Indeed, as noted earlier, while seasonality reveals a face of the family that is essentially one of (unequal) cooperation, famine often reflects one of disintegration. We come then to the third major aspect of calamity response, namely, the break-up of families.

The Disintegrating Family

Famine poses in the most stark terms the economic and moral dilemmas relating to intrahousehold food sharing and mirrors intrafamily relations that few other contexts can.

For illustrative purposes consider the Bengal famine of 1943, which serves as an especially poignant case study in this respect. This famine was characterized by the virtual absence of government employment relief works and, as is now well accepted, it was a result of entitlement failure rather than of overall food shortages (Sen 1981). In occupational terms those most severely affected were agricultural laborers, paddy huskers, fisherfolk, and transport and craft workers. However, my focus here is on the relatively lesser examined *gender dimensions* of this entitlement failure, which calls for a reinterpretation of some of the existing facts about the famine from a gender perspective.

A variety of evidence points to some of the specific disadvantages and deprivations suffered by women and children of poor households during this famine. First, estimates by Mahalanobis, Mokerjee, and Ghosh (1946) reveal a predominance of young and middle-aged females among those made destitute by famine in rural Bengal. In January 1943, 55 percent of all destitute and 66 percent of the destitute in the 15–50 age group were female. Women of this age group also constituted the largest number of *new* additions to the destitute between January 1943 and May 1944, the worst period of the famine, and were twice the number of new male destitutes of this age group.[32] Children of both sexes in the 5–15 age category were next largest in number.

Second, most of those who came to the government relief centers during the most intense months of the famine and were able to pay cash for food tended to be male adults. In contrast, most of those who were absolutely destitute and dependent entirely on gratis relief tended to be females (mostly adult): 84 percent of the female destitutes needed gratis aid at the relief centers compared to 43 percent of the male destitutes.[33]

Third, consider the famine mortality figures.[34] The general pattern appears to have been one of relative female advantage, in that for all ages taken together the excess mortality due to famine was greater for males than females (as measured both in terms of the absolute and proportionate increases in mortality rates attributable to the famine). However, this was not true of the 20–40 age grouping. For this age grouping, the estimated absolute number of famine deaths during the critical year of 1943, as well as the absolute increase in mortality rates, were higher for women than men. In fact, men of this age group showed the least excess mortality (in absolute terms) of all age groups of either sex. The greater mortality disadvantage in absolute terms suffered by women compared with the men in the 20–40 age grouping is particularly noteworthy, as this is despite the reduction in childbirth and childbearing-associated risk due to famine-induced reduction in birthrates. Also the majority of women in this age grouping would have been within marital relationships at that time, women who would normally be expected to have the support of husbands and families (on which more later).

Fourth, a survey of some 2,500 destitute living on the pavements of Calcutta in September 1943 found that 53 percent were females, and among the married destitute 64 percent were female. The pavement dwellers had earlier belonged to 820 families, of whom half had recently broken up, 70 percent as a result of husbands and wives separating. The women, on being asked why they had left the village for Calcutta, said that their husbands had been unable to maintain them and had either deserted them or asked them to go elsewhere in search of food (Green-ough 1982).

Fifth, there is a variety of anecdotal evidence of women being aban-doned by husbands, including where the husband had migrated for work elsewhere or had decided to use the family's subsistence plot of land solely for himself; of women being forced into begging or prostitution; of parents selling children into bondage, especially girl children, even 2–13-year-olds, into prostitution, and so on (Greenough 1982). The evidence of familial disintegration and of the abandonment of women and children, while largely indirect (and from which the scale of it cannot be assessed) is a sufficient indication that this was not an isolated phenomenon but fairly widespread. (Accounts of several other famines in Asia and Africa also describe the abandonment of women and children, such as in Bangladesh in 1974 and Malawi in the 1970s.)[35]

What does this indicate about intrafamily relations? Paul Greenough (1982) argues that this disintegration of families in the 1943 Bengal famine did not occur randomly but was the result of a deliberate decision by the male head of household to exclude the less valued family members (women and children) from domestic subsistence, and further that this decision was in keeping with the powerful Bengali ideal of family continuity, equated with the continuity of the patriline through the adult male, whose survival thus counts over that of women and children. In other words, no contradiction is seen here between male self-interest and the culture-specific moral order.

I would like to suggest that an alternative way of viewing this process of female victimization would be in terms of shifts in the relative male/female entitlements and fall-back positions, and so in their relative bargaining strengths within the family, along the lines discussed in Section 1 of this chapter. The decision of the man to abandon his wife and children appears to occur at a point when the wife's entitlements have collapsed completely, while those of the husband are weakened but not entirely gone. For instance, first, it is a telling point that, during the worst months of the calamity, 57 percent of the men compared with only 16 percent of the women chief recipients of relief at the government relief centers were able to pay cash for food. Second, the least excess mortality (in absolute terms) occurred among men of 20–40 years of age. Third, one of the traditionally few fall-back occupations of women in Bengal—paddy husking—was not sustained. Paddy huskers ranked among the first four categories of those hardest hit. Fourth, there is the noted anecdotal evidence on the circumstances under which the women and children were abandoned.

On average, men's fall-back position appears to have been stronger than women's on at least two counts: one, their greater mobility and ability to migrate over longer distances for a job, without the burden of children or the fear of sexual exploitation that women faced; and two, the possibility of leftover assets after women's jewelry, and so on, had already been disposed of. Basically, therefore, during the Bengal famine, women of affected households would have been left with virtually no economic bargaining strength within the family *at a much earlier stage* in the process of famine impoverishment than the men.

Within the bargaining view of the family, at this point noncooperation by the husband would make sense in the interest of his individual physical survival and do him no harm in terms of his social survival (he could marry again). If additionally he had an ideological justification that this was in keeping with the moral code it would merely have eased the decision.

Essentially, Greenough's view of the family comes close to what A. K. Sen (1983) has described as the "despotic" family, in which the male family head makes all decisions and others just obey (indeed, "acquiesce even as victims"), although Greenough sees the male head as essentially a benevolent despot, guided by moral considerations. What I am suggesting here is that the victimization process could be equally, indeed better, explained by the bargaining view of the family.

The point, however, is that what view we take of the family—the despotic one or the bargaining one—could point to different policy conclusions. Under the former, we could, for instance, make a case for strengthening the economic position of the benevolent male head of household to better support his wife and children (the passive recipients of his bounty or rejection). Under the latter view, where women are seen as active (if disadvantaged) agents in the arrangements of reciprocity within the family, we would make a case for strengthening their fall-back positions and bargaining power. The present analysis points to the importance of strengthening women's bargaining power to improve both intrahousehold gender allocations and the family's coping ability. The question then is: How can this be done?

To answer this, it is useful to recall the four factors emphasized at the beginning of the chapter as likely to affect a person's bargaining power within the family and his/her overall ability to fulfill subsistence needs. These were: ownership and control of assets, especially land; access to employment and other income-earning means; access to communal resources such as VCs and forests; and access to social, especially kin, support networks.

Map 8.1   Traditional Practices of Land Inheritance

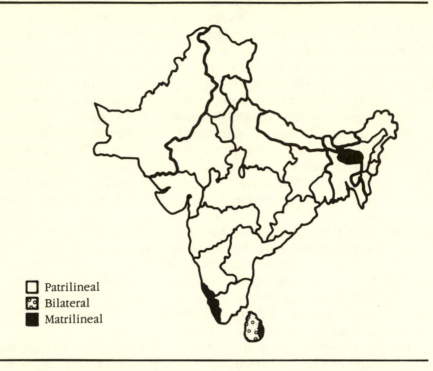

□ Patrilineal
▨ Bilateral
■ Matrilineal

I have sought below to map these factors (or proxies for them) as they vary regionally across South Asia.

REGIONAL DIMENSIONS

Women's position in relation to these four factors varies strikingly both across regions within India and between countries across South Asia (see Maps 8.1 to 8.4).

Land Inheritance (Map 8.1)

Traditionally the pattern of land inheritance in India (legally and in practice) was overwhelmingly patrilineal (inheritance through the male line). The exceptions were a few pockets of matriliny (only daughters inheriting) or of bilaterality (both daughters and sons inheriting) among some tribal and Hindu communities located in southwest and northeast India. Among Muslim communities scattered across India, and in Pakistan and Bangladesh, although women were legally entitled

Map 8.2   Female Labor-Force Participation Rates

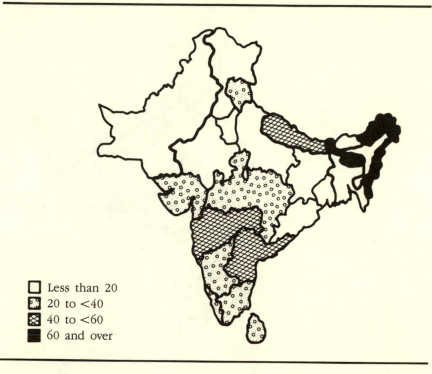

☐ Less than 20
▨ 20 to <40
▨ 40 to <60
■ 60 and over

to half their brothers' shares under Islamic law (and could therefore be termed weakly bilateral), in practice these rights were seldom realized. Sri Lanka, however, has always been strongly bilateral (by customary law *and* practice) among both the Buddhist Sinhalese and the Hindu Tamils, with Muslim Moors in the Eastern Province inheriting matrilineally (Agarwal 1990c). Today women have legal rights to inherit parental land among most communities and regions of South Asia. However, these largely remain rights on paper. In practice they are seldom realized for a complex set of reasons. These include the reluctance of male kin to voluntarily part with the land and their intimidation of women who seek to assert their claims;[36] patrilocal postmarital residence (especially in northern India, women generally move to a distant village on marriage, which makes it difficult for them both to claim their rights and to self-manage any land they may inherit); norms of seclusion, which constrain their mobility and ability to self-manage land, and so on. Hence they usually waive their claims (or are compelled to do so) in favor of brothers (Agarwal 1988 and forthcoming).

Map 8.3   Percent of Geo-Area Under Forests

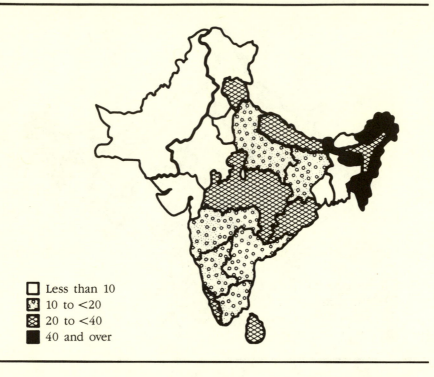

☐ Less than 10
▨ 10 to <20
▧ 20 to <40
■ 40 and over

Income-Earning Means (Map 8.2)

Female labor-force participation rates (FLPRs) have been used here as a crude proxy for this—crude because these do not capture the intensity of work effort or actual earnings. However, in the absence of more direct cross-regional information on women earners, these are illustrative (Tables 8.4 and 8.5).[37] As seen in Map 8.2, FLPRs also reveal noteworthy variations across regions; the rates are significantly higher in the southern (South India and Sri Lanka) and northeastern parts of the subcontinent than in the northwest.

Access to Communal Resources (Map 8.3)

The percentage area under forests has been used as a proxy for this, in the absence of adequate information on the regional distribution of VCs. Again we note a regional pattern, with the northeast, south, and central regions being more favorably placed than the northwest (Tables 8.1 and 8.2).

Map 8.4   Distance (in miles) of Woman's Postmarital Residence from Her Natal Village

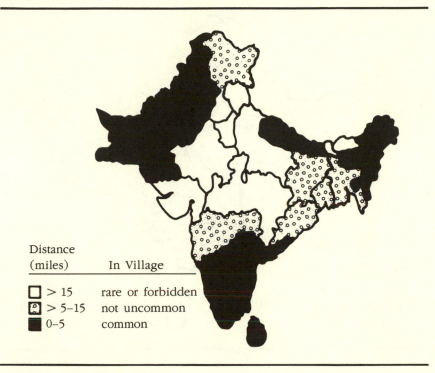

Distance (miles)	In Village
□ > 15	rare or forbidden
▣ > 5–15	not uncommon
■ 0–5	common

Source: Agarwal (forthcoming).

Access to Kin Support Systems (Map 8.4)

Postmarital residence could be used as a proxy for the degree to which women can draw upon kin support. Where women marry within or close to their natal villages, their ability to draw upon such support is greater than where they marry into distant villages. Women in northwest India are the most disadvantaged in this respect. The prevalence of close-kin marriages also strengthens the likelihood of kin support. In this respect too, in northern India, and especially in the northwest where close-kin marriages are typically forbidden, women are in a disadvantaged position (see also Agarwal 1988 and forthcoming).

The four factors mapped do not always overlap regionally, but the strength of some can compensate for the weakness of others, and vice versa. In particular, because communal resources and kin support systems are noted to be eroding, access to land and income-earning opportunities acquires particular importance.

Map 8.5   Sex Ratios: Number of Females per 100 Males

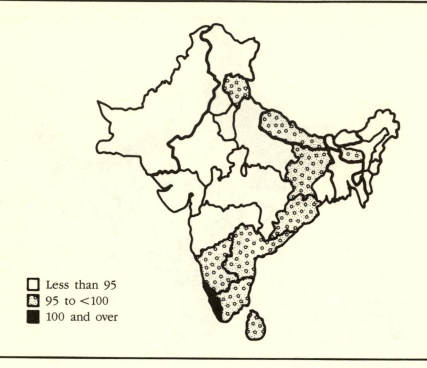

☐ Less than 95
▨ 95 to <100
■ 100 and over

TABLE 8.4   Rural Female Labor-Force Participation Rates in South Asia (percentages)

Country	Age Group (in years)	Reference Year	Rates[a]
Bangladesh	10 and above	1981 census	4.2
India	15 and above	1981 census	24.4
Nepal	10 and above	1981 census	47.2
Pakistan	10 and above	1981 census	3.0
	10 and above	1985–86 LFS[b]	11.5
Sri Lanka	10 and above	1981 census	23.7

[a]Economically active population in a given age group as a percent of total population in that age group. For India the figures relate to "main workers" only.

[b]LFS = *Labour Force Survey 1985–86.* For Map 8.2 it was assumed that the figure would be somewhere between the census and the LFS figures.

Sources: Bangladesh 1988:97; India 1987:134–135; Nepal 1987:210; for Pakistan, see World Bank 1989a:28; Sri Lanka 1986:164.

TABLE 8.5   India: Rural Female Labor-Force Participation Rates (FLPRs) by State, 1981

State	FLPRs[a]	State	FLPRs[a]
Andhra Pradesh	46.6	Manipur	61.4
Arunachal Pradesh	67.7	Meghalaya	60.8
Assam	NA[b]	Mizoram	60.9
Bihar	15.3	Nagaland	72.3
Gujarat	20.2	Orissa	16.7
Haryana	7.6	Punjab	2.6
Himachal Pradesh	29.2	Rajasthan	16.1
Jammu and Kashmir	8.5	Sikkim	61.4
Karnataka	33.4	Tamil Nadu	39.8
Kerala	20.2	Tripura	14.2
Madhya Pradesh	39.7	Uttar Pradesh	9.4
Maharashtra	47.3	West Bengal	10.0
		All India	24.4

[a]Main workers only; 15 years and above.
[b]NA = not available.

Source: India 1987:134–195.

    In very broad terms, at the intercountry level, these maps suggest that rural women would have a much greater bargaining strength in Sri Lanka, on all four counts, than elsewhere in South Asia. Within countries, say in India, the bargaining strength of women in Kerala, and more generally of women in the south and northeast, would be higher than in the northwest. The implications of these interregional differences in women's bargaining strength, on intrafamily resource sharing for subsistence, need more probing than possible in this chapter. But that such implications are likely to exist is suggested by the emerging empirical evidence quoted earlier in Note 4. It is also suggested, although in very broad terms, by a comparison of Map 8.5 (which regionally maps sex ratios: females/100 males)[38] with Maps 8.1 to 8.4. As seen from Map 8.5 (and Table 8.6), northwest India, which performs poorly in terms of women's bargaining strength by all the indicators, also has among the most female-adverse sex ratios.[39] And sex ratios are only an extreme indicator of intrafamily gender differentials in the distribution of subsistence resources (especially for food and health care); such inequalities need not necessarily manifest themselves in higher female to male mortality.

    In the context of the present discussion on food crises situations, it is important to recognize, of course, that the possibility of drought and famine itself varies across regions. Hence, to draw broad inferences about the regions where food security interventions, to reduce gender vulnerabilities, may be *most* acutely needed, we would require, among other

TABLE 8.6   Sex Ratios (Females/100 Males) in South Asia

Country	Sex Ratio[a] (1985)
Bangladesh	94
India	93
Nepal	95
Pakistan	91
Sri Lanka	98

India, by State, 1981			
State	Sex Ratio	State	Sex Ratio
Andhra Pradesh	9	Manipur	97
Arunachal Pradesh	86	Meghalaya	95
Assam	NA[b]	Mizoram	92
Bihar	95	Nagaland	86
Gujarat	94	Orissa	98
Haryana	87	Punjab	88
Himachal Pradesh	97	Rajasthan	92
Jammu and Kashmir	89	Sikkim	83
Karnataka	96	Tamil Nadu	98
Kerala	103	Tripura	95
Madhya Pradesh	94	Uttar Pradesh	88
Maharashtra	94	West Bengal	91

[a]Sex ratios relate to total population. Province-wise computation of sex ratios for Pakistan showed very little variation between provinces.
[b]NA = not available.

Sources: World Bank 1989b; India 1987.

things, a regional mapping of poor women's relative bargaining strength laid over a mapping of environmentally high-risk areas. That is clearly the task for a separate paper.

In any case, even though such a cross-mapping of environmental risk and gender vulnerability would clearly be useful for fine-tuning policy, the broad directions of such a policy remain unambiguous because irrespective of the relative regional position of women vis-à-vis one another, *in all regions* women of poor households are more vulnerable to destitution than the men of those households. This, then, brings us to the final question: What can be done to improve the situation?

ON POLICY AND EXTERNAL INTERVENTIONS

Given the range and complexity of factors that impinge on female food security within the family, not all are conducive to change via outside intervention. Cultural practices defining the gender division of labor within and outside the home, female seclusion, and patrilocal residence, all of which impinge on women's independent access to subsistence income, are likely to be particularly resistant. However, it is possible to act on women's economic circumstances to some extent by a better enforcement of their legal property rights, the expansion of their income-earning opportunities, and a strengthening of their communal control over the village commons and forest land. Such economic change could, in turn, induce changes in some of the cultural parameters over time. The question then is: What should be the forms and agencies for such interventions?

In much of the existing discussion on seasonality and calamity there is a strong emphasis on direct State intervention, especially in the form of public works, and relatively little on interventionist forms that do not depend directly on the State.

State success in preventing the 1970–1973 drought in Maharashtra (India) from escalating into large-scale famine and in significantly containing productive-asset depletion, nutritional distress, and excess mortality through guaranteed employment on a large scale via public works appears to have been particularly influential in pointing policy in this direction (Dreze 1988). The Maharashtra example is also significant in that up to half the labor force in the Maharashtra Employment Guarantee Scheme (EGS) has been female (Dandekar 1983). By providing women with direct (and not male-mediated) entitlements in the form of guaranteed employment, protection was given both to poor households and to the more vulnerable persons within those households.

In the present discussion, however, several factors caution against depending on the State alone for providing food security in contingencies. First, the State has a poor record of dealing with food deprivation situations less acute than famine, although it has been fairly effective in dealing with threats of large-scale famine, especially in India since independence. (Indeed, in situations verging on famine there may be few alternatives to government public works.)

Second, there are contradictions in State policies themselves. For instance, those relating to VCs and forests are noted to have systematically *weakened* the ability of the poor, and especially of women, to themselves cope with food crisis situations.

Third, the degree to which the State responds to the demands of the vulnerable sections depends not the least on the degree to which these sections can make their demands heard. The critical issue here is not only of being *entitled,* but of being able to enforce these entitlements effectively, through *empowerment.*

The term "empowerment" has been used variously in recent years by social action groups in South Asia, and in the present context may be defined as the ability of an individual or group to successfully challenge existing economic and political power relations and so ensure that decisions relating to entitlement are made in its favor (be it within the family, or of the family vis-à-vis the community or the State).

In South Asia, group organizing has been one of the significant means of empowering the vulnerable sections—the poor, the low caste, the women—not only to better enforce their legal entitlements within the community and family, but also to expand the scope of these through agitating for changes in the laws themselves.[40] Group approaches have been effective also in the provision of credit to the rural poor. Credit, in fact, is a good example because, as noted, it plays an important role in a family's coping mechanisms and has received considerable emphasis in State policies for poverty alleviation. Typically, however, government policies, pitched at the individual, have had little success in reaching the poorest.

In contrast are initiatives such as the Grameen Bank in Bangladesh. This was launched as an experiment by an individual in 1976 and, after its proven success, institutionalized by the Bangladesh government in 1983 as a specialized credit agency for the rural poor. Today it has 250 branches spread across five districts and a membership of 200,000 in 3,700 villages (Siddiqui 1984; Chandler 1986; Hossain 1988). Among its noteworthy features are:

- The *class homogeneous* nature of its clientele—it caters exclusively to the landless and near-landless (that is, those owning less than 0.5 acres)
- Its *group approach* to loan disbursement—borrowers form groups of five, and although loans are given to individuals there is implicit group pressure and responsibility for repayment
- Lending *without collateral*
- A special focus on loans for *women* (women borrowers form separate groups from male borrowers)
- *Convenience of repayment*—this is collected weekly by a bank worker from the village itself; this especially helps women, who have limited mobility because of the strictness of female seclusion in Bangladesh and because of women's primary responsibility for child care
- Various *social security* schemes

By all evaluations, the Grameen Bank reaches the target group (92 percent of the borrowers are landless or near-landless) and has more than a 97-percent recovery rate; it has substantially improved the incomes of the borrowers, particularly of women, who constitute 70 percent of the members. It has also improved the family's bargaining power vis-à-vis landlords and employers, and of women vis-à-vis men within the family, by strengthening their fall-back positions. Women say they are now treated with greater consideration at home (Hossain 1984, 1988; Siddiqui 1984; Rahman 1986; Rahaman 1986; Ahmed 1985; Chandler 1986).

The Self-Employed Women's Association in western India and the Working Women's Forum in south India, catering entirely to poor women, are additional examples of initiatives (Sebstad 1982; Noponen 1987; Kalpagam 1987).

All of these are also potentially effective substitutes for the declining traditional arrangements based on feudal patronage and exploitation. And where joint ventures are undertaken, these offer the potential advantages and economies of labor deployment and teamwork that joint families are noted to have in the Maclachlan example. We clearly need a more detailed review and evaluation of such initiatives from the point of view of social security for the poor and a comparison with existing State attempts at providing similar services.

Underlying such ventures is a recognition that the effective implementation of existing State laws, programs, and even relief measures can be contingent on group initiative and pressure from below. And they have an explicit thrust toward building group solidarity among those who are more homogeneous economically and often also socially (by caste, gender).[41]

Finally, whether interventions take the form of government programs and/or of nongovernmental group initiatives, the most general policy principle that emerges from our examination of coping mechanisms among poor rural families is the need for measures that would strengthen women's bargaining position within the household. This is likely to decrease intrafamily gender bias in subsistence resource allocations as well as strengthen the ability of the whole family to cope with calamity.

NOTES

This chapter was presented in the PEW/Cornell lecture series on Food and Nutrition Policy, Cornell University, November 13, 1990. It draws especially upon two earlier articles: "Social Security and the Family: Coping with Seasonality and Calamity in Rural India," *The Journal of Peasant Studies* (U.K.), April 1990; "Who Sows? Who Reaps? Women and Land Rights in India," *The Journal of Peasant Studies,* July 1988; and upon my ongoing work on a book on *Gender and Land Rights in South Asia.* I am grateful to Nancy Folbre, Janet Seiz, and Gail Hershatter for some useful suggestions on this version.

1. In India the term "state" relates to administrative divisions within the country and is not to be confused with "State" used in the chapter in the political economy sense of the word.

2. For an interesting discussion on some of the problems associated with a unitary conceptualization of the household, see Guyer and Peters (1987) and Hart (1990).

3. A. K. Sen (1981), in his entitlement approach to famine, highlights two factors as significant in determining a person's (or a family's) ability to command goods (including food) and services: his/her endowments (ownership of land, labor, etc.) and exchange entitlement mapping (that is, the exchange possibilities that exist through production and trade and that determine the consumption set available to a person with a given endowment). These would be covered broadly by the first two factors listed here. However, the approach can usefully be extended to cover two types of entitlements that neither fall within the purview of ownership nor are specifically exchange entitlements, namely, those stemming from traditional rights in communal resources and external social support systems. The last concerns relationships between social groups or persons in which considerations other than the solely economic take precedence. These typically relate to nonmarket exchanges such as relatives providing informal credit without interest during a drought.

4. Relative bargaining power is revealed, among other things, in who participates in decisionmaking in relation to what as well as whose interests prevail in the decisions finally made. Hence, in South Asia, communities in which women participate in decisionmaking relating to, say, agricultural production, may be said to have greater bargaining strength than those who are excluded from such decisionmaking altogether. But relative bargaining strength is also revealed in terms of final outcomes: for instance, in terms of intrafamily distribution of goods, services, and tasks as well as the nature of treatment received. These outcomes may or may not be the result of an explicit, *observable* process of discussion and negotiation. Nonetheless, they could be seen to result implicitly from relative bargaining strengths.

Empirically, although much more research is needed on this question, several recent studies indicate a positive correlation between women's access to independent income and their intrafamily bargaining power. See examples in Acharya and Bennett (1982) for Nepal, Bhatty (1980) for India, Islam (1981) for Bangladesh, and Roldán (1988) for Mexico.

5. On how discourses about women's needs tend to be structured by the power relations between women and men, see Fraser (1989).

6. For instance, Bourdieu (1977:164–165) notes: "As we have seen in the case of domestic conflicts to which marriages often give rise, social categories disadvantaged by the symbolic order, such as women and the young, cannot but recognize the legitimacy of the dominant classification in the very fact that their only chance of neutralizing those of its effects most contrary to their own interests lies in submitting to them in order to make use of them. . . ."

7. For India, see discussions in Agarwal (1986a), K. Bardhan (1977, 1985), Duvvury (1989), and Ryan and Wallace (1985); for Bangladesh, see Islam (1981).

8. See, for example, Agarwal 1984; J. Harriss 1977; and Ryan and Ghodake 1980, quoted in Lipton 1983.

9. On relative male-female workloads see Agarwal (1985a), Dasgupta and Maiti (1987), Acharya and Bennett (1981), and Nag, White, and Peet (1977). On gender biases in the intrafamily distribution of food and health care, see Agarwal (1986a), B. Harriss (1986), Dreze and Sen (1990), Kynch and Sen (1983), Sen and Sengupta (1983), Behrman (1986), Rosenzweig and Schultz (1982), and Chen, Huq, and D'Sousa (1981).

10. See, for example, Caldwell, Reddy, and Caldwell 1986; M. Chen 1988; Jodha 1979; Majumdar 1978; Hossain 1987; K. Bardhan 1977.

11. See Gulati (1978), Kumar (1978), Mencher and Saradamoni (1982), Mencher (1987), and Dasgupta and Maiti (1987). Other microstudies that have examined male and female expenditure patterns within poor households that have earners of both sexes also find that, typically, female earnings are spent on the family's basic needs of food, fuel, and so on, but a not insignificant percent of males earnings goes towards tobacco and liquor (see Gulati 1978; Sharma 1980; Mencher and Saradamoni 1982; and Mies 1983).

12. See, for example, Mitra 1985, Banerjee 1988, George 1988, and Acharya and Bennett 1981.

13. See, for example, K. Bardhan 1977, Banerjee 1988, and Breman 1979, 1985.

14. See, for example, R. Desai 1982, Jetly 1987, and Naveed-I-Rahat 1980.

15. In India, nontimber forest produce is estimated to account for 14–38 percent (varying by region) of total tribal income in Madhya Pradesh, 10–55 percent in Andhra Pradesh, and 35 percent in parts of Gujarat (India 1982). Roughly 30 million people in the country are estimated to depend on nontimber forest produce for a livelihood (Kulkarni 1983).

16. See Agarwal (1987) for a discussion and figures on the percentage of domestic energy that comes from fuelwood in various parts of South Asia.

17. See Burling (1963) on the Garos of the northeast; also my personal observation during fieldwork in Meghalaya state (northeast India).

18. The prevalence of "territorial purdah"—the effective segregation of village space by gender, whereby there are clearly identifiable spaces that essentially constitute male spaces, such as the marketplace, that women are expected to avoid—strongly disadvantages women in their search for employment and in managing land independently. Of course, seniority, age, whether she is a daughter or daughter-in-law, her class/caste all affect a woman's freedom of movement; hence, older women with grown-up sons, village daughters, and women of poor and low-caste families enjoy greater liberty. But even for them, spaces of predominantly male presence are to be avoided. These restrictions are apparent in northern India and are especially great in countries such as Bangladesh and Pakistan. For a more detailed discussion on India, see especially Afshar and Agarwal (1989) and Sharma (1980); for Bangladesh, see Ellickson (1972) and Arens and Van Beurden (1977); and for Pakistan, see Shaheed (1989).

19. For a detailed discussion on the causes of deforestation in the subcontinent, and especially in India, see Agarwal (1986b, 1991).

20. For a discussion on the erosion of patron-client relationships, see Breman (1985), M. Dasgupta (1987), and Commander (1983). For declining support from kin, see Fernandes and Menon (1987) and Dreze (1990) for India; and Cain, Khanam, and Nahar (1979) and Jansen (1986) for Bangladesh.

21. For a case study of the effects and causes of the shifts from swidden to settled farming among the Garo tribe in northeast India, see Agarwal (1990b).

22. For a graphic and poignant description of the adverse effects (especially on women) of growing impoverishment and associated erosion of intracommunity support among the tribal groups in Orissa, see Fernandes and Menon (1987).

23. See A. K. Sen (1981), Kynch and Maguire (1988), and Behrman (1986). Behrman, on the basis of an econometric exercise using data on child nutrition for South India, concludes that "parents display male preference, at least during the lean season, particularly in lower caste households" and that "the nutritionally most vulnerable—especially females—may be at considerable risk when food is scarcest."

24. See Rajgopalan, Kymal, and Pei (1981), Ryan et al. (1984), Brown, Black, and Becker (1982). For a more detailed discussion and evidence on the relationship between food intakes, body weights, and seasonality, also see Agarwal (1990a).

25. Chen 1987 and Reddy 1988.

26. Help from a woman's natal kin (where they are in a position to help) can be critical during such periods. See Caldwell, Reddy, and Caldwell (1986) or Prindle (1979) for Nepal.

27. See, for example, Borkar and Nadkarni 1975; Caldwell, Reddy, and Caldwell 1986; Singh 1975; and Jodha 1978.

28. See Lewis 1958; Reddy 1988; Jodha 1978; Caldwell, Reddy, and Caldwell 1986; Rao 1974; Borkar and Nadkarni 1975; Singh 1975; Epstein 1967; and Greenough 1982.

29. See Caldwell, Reddy, and Caldwell 1986; Reddy 1988; Jodha 1975, 1978; Currey 1978; Rangaswami 1985; Chowdhury and Bapat 1975; Desai, Singh, and Sah 1979; and Gangrade and Dhadda 1973; Maclachlan 1983; and Greenough 1982.

30. See Caldwell, Reddy, and Caldwell (1986); also see Campbell and Trechter (1982), who explicitly examined differences in gender responses to varying degrees of food shortages in North Cameroon. They found that under severe food shortages, while women's actions commonly included going hungry for the whole day, men's more typically included migration.

31. See Mahalanobis, Mokerjee, and Ghosh (1946); Jodha (1975, 1978); Singh (1975); Borkar and Nadkarni (1975); Greenough (1982); and Currey (1978). The types of assets sold, however, depend on the severity of the crisis, as discussed further on in the text.

32. For a disaggregation by occupation and gender, see Chattopadhyay and Mukerjee (1946).

33. This is taken from Greenough's (1982) construction, based on the Bengal Famine Committee's records of the social profile of those who came to the State relief centers.

34. See the figures in Greenough (1982:311) and also Agarwal's (1990a) calculations.

35. See, for example, Alamgir (1980:135) on the Bangladesh famine of 1974. He notes: "Besides, there were many cases of desertion. In Rangpur, special homes for deserted children were set up. In Dacca, there were many women who were deserted by their husbands among the inmates of vagrant homes." Likewise, Vaughan (1987:123) observes in her reconstruction of the 1949 famine in Malawi: "Women stress how frequently they were abandoned by men, how harrowing it was to be left responsible for their suffering and dying children."

36. Forms of intimidation include threats by brothers to break off all links with sisters who asserts their rights as well as direct violence (the last occurs especially where the interests of male relatives other than brothers are involved).

37. Typically, FLPRs based on data collected through national censuses underestimate women's productive contribution in the household, especially in South Asia (Agarwal 1985b; Sen and Sen 1985). This is due to several reasons, including the perception in most parts of South Asia that because much of women's productive work is unwaged (being done on the family farm) it is part of domestic work, a perception sometimes shared by the women themselves. This is compounded by cultural biases where women's involvement in work outside the home is seen as lowering family prestige, and by definitional biases that tend to explicitly or implicitly associate working with doing paid work. Hence, much of the productive work that women do is not reported as work by the male respondents, and often not even when the respondents are women.

However, our concern here is with capturing that component of a woman's work that brings her some income, since it is her access to earnings rather than her doing productive work *per se* (especially if that is not *perceived* as such) that is likely to impinge on women's bargaining strength in the family (on this also see A. K. Sen 1990). For this purpose the figures provided by national censuses are, in fact, quite useful because this is the very component of women's work they are most likely to capture. In Map 8.2 therefore I have used the FLPR figures provided by the censuses of the different countries. For Pakistan, Bangladesh, Nepal, and Sri Lanka the figures relate to female workers aged 10 and above as a percent of female population of the same age group. For India, the figures relate to female ("main") workers aged 15 and over as a percent of female population of that age group because data for female workers between ages 10–15 were not available. All figures relate to censuses undertaken in 1981.

38. In the absence of high-quality mortality statistics, sex ratios serve as a proxy for sex differential mortality. *Juvenile* sex ratios (that is, sex ratios of children under 10) are sometimes used for more refined cross-regional analysis. This is especially to reduce the possibility of biases attributable to sex-selective interstate migration. However, my purpose here is merely to illustrate the point in very broad terms. For a discussion based on interregional variations in juvenile sex ratios, see especially Miller (1981, 1983) and P. Bardhan (1982).

39. There is now a growing literature on factors underlying female-adverse sex ratios: see especially Miller (1981), P. Bardhan (1982), and A. K. Sen (1983, 1990). Sen and Miller both place a great deal of emphasis on FLPRs in this

regard. Miller's work suggests a close positive correlation between sex ratios and FLPRs across regions. The incidence of dowry is another factor she finds is linked (negatively) to sex ratios. However, for a cross–South Asia mapping, dowry incidence per se is less helpful because in Sri Lanka, among communities such as the Jaffna Tamils and the Muslim Moors, dowry has traditionally served to transfer inheritance (including land) to the daughter, has been typically in her control, and has not had the coercive aspect that characterizes the practice in northwest India. Here, the dowry has no apparent link with inheritance, is never in the form of land, usually passes from the bride's family to the groom and his family, with the woman herself exercising little control over it, and often (implicitly or explicitly) the marriage is made conditional on the dowry settlement. The giving of dowry in these conditions places a considerable burden on parents and would sharpen tendencies toward female child neglect. Also in northwest India, dowry (being outside her control) would not add to a woman's assets and so to her bargaining strength, but in Sri Lanka (and even in parts of South India) it usually would.

However, in my view, to understand regional differentials in sex ratios across South Asia, it does appear important to examine not only FLPRs but also other independent means of subsistence available to women, including those considered in this chapter, such as the ownership of land, access to communal resources, and access to social support systems.

In any case, female-adverse sex ratios may be one and by no means a necessary manifestation of intrafamily inequalities in subsistence distribution.

40. See especially Dhagamvar (1987) and various issues of *The Lawyer's Collective* (Bombay).

41. Social and economic homogeneity is typically found to be important in ensuring the successful functioning of such initiatives. See Dixon (1979), PIDT (1982), and particularly Wade (1987), whose examples of successful collective action by villagers for regulating the use of common property resources are of special interest in the present context. In addition, gender homogeneity becomes important, especially but not only in contexts where female seclusion norms are strong, to ensure that women speak out in group meetings without feeling intimidated.

REFERENCES

Acharya, M., and L. Bennett. 1981. *The Rural Women of Nepal: An Aggregate Analysis and Summary of Eight Village Studies, The Status of Women in Nepal,* Vol. 2, Part 9. Kathmandu, Nepal: Tribhuvan University, Center for Economic Development and Administration.

———. 1982. Women and the Subsistence Sector: Economic Participation and Household Decision-making in Nepal. World Bank Staff Working Paper No. 526. Washington, D.C.: World Bank.

Afshar, H., and B. Agarwal. 1989. "Introduction." In H. Afshar and B. Agarwal (eds.), *Women, Poverty and Ideology in Asia: Contradictory Pressures, Uneasy Resolutions.* London: Macmillan.

Agarwal, B. 1984. "Rural Women and the HYV Rice Technology." *Economic and Political Weekly* 9 (13), 31 March.

––––––. 1985a. "Women and Technological Change in Agriculture: Asian and African Experience." In I. Ahmed (ed.), *Technology and Rural Women: Conceptual and Empirical Issues.* London: George Allen and Unwin.

––––––. 1985b. "Work Participation of Rural Women in the Third World: Some Data and Conceptual Biases." *Economic and Political Weekly (Review of Agriculture)* 20 (51–52).

––––––. 1986a. "Women, Poverty and Agricultural Growth in India." *Journal of Peasant Studies* 14 (4), July.

––––––. 1986b. *Cold Hearths and Barren Slopes: The Woodfuel Crisis in the Third World.* Delhi: Allied Publishers.

––––––. 1987. "Under the Cooking Pot: The Political Economy of the Fuelwood Crisis in Rural South Asia." *IDS Bulletin* 18 (1).

––––––. 1988. "Who Sows? Who Reaps? Women and Land Rights in India." *Journal of Peasant Studies* 15 (4), July.

––––––. 1989. "Rural Women, Poverty and Natural Resources: Sustenance, Sustainability and Struggle for Change." *Economic and Political Weekly* (28 October). Also forthcoming in R. Cassen and S. Guhan (eds.), *Poverty in India.* Delhi: Oxford University Press.

––––––. 1990a. "Social Security and the Family: Coping with Seasonality and Calamity in Rural India." *Journal of Peasant Studies* 17 (3), April.

––––––. 1990b. "Tribal Matriliny in Transition: Gender, Property, and Production Relations in North-East India." Geneva: International Labour Office, World Employment Programme Research Working Paper No. WEP 10/WP 50.

––––––. 1990c. "Gender and Land Rights in Sri Lanka." Geneva: International Labour Office, World Employment Programme Research Working Paper No. WEP 10/WP49.

––––––. 1991. "Engendering the Environment Debate: Lessons from the Indian Subcontinent." CASID Distinguished Lecture Series, Discussion Paper 8, Michigan State University.

––––––. *Who Sows? Who Reaps? Gender and Land Rights in South Asia.* Cambridge: Cambridge University Press. Forthcoming.

Ahmed, M. 1985. "Status, Perception, Awareness and Marital Adjustment of Rural Women: The Role of Grameen Bank." Dhaka: Grameen Bank Publication.

Alamgir, M. 1980. *Famine in South Asia: Political Economy of Mass Starvation.* Cambridge, Mass.: Oelgeschlager & Hain.

Arens, J., and J. van Beurden. 1977. *Jhagrapur: Poor Peasants and Women in a Village in Bangladesh.* Amsterdam: Third World Publications.

Banerjee, N. 1988. "Women's Work and Family Strategies: A Case Study from Bankura, West Bengal." Center for Women's Development Studies, New Delhi, mimeo.

Bangladesh. 1988. *Statistical Yearbook of Bangladesh.* Dhaka: Bureau of Statistics.

Bardhan, K. 1977. "Rural Employment, Wages and Labour Markets in India—A survey of research." *Economic and Political Weekly,* 25 June, 2 July, 9 July.

––––––. 1985. "Women's Work, Welfare and Status: Forces of Tradition and Change in India." *Economic and Political Weekly* 20 (50–51), December 14–28.

Bardhan, P. 1982. "Little Girls and Death in India." *Economic and Political Weekly,* September 17.

Behrman, J. R. 1986. "Intrahousehold Allocation of Nutrients in Rural India: Are Boys Favoured? Do Parents Exhibit Inequality Aversion?" Center for Analysis of Developing Economies, University of Pennsylvania, mimeo.

Bhalla, S. 1977. "New Relations of Production in Haryana Agriculture." *Economic and Political Weekly (Review of Agriculture)* 11 (13), 27 March.

Bhatty, Z. 1980. "Economic Role and Status of Women: A Case Study of Women in the Beedi Industry in Allahabad." ILO Working Paper. Geneva: International Labour Office.

Borkar, V. V., and V. Nadkarni. 1975. *Impact of Drought on Rural Life.* Bombay: Popular Prakashan.

Bourdieu, P. 1977. *An Outline of the Theory of Practice.* Cambridge: Cambridge University Press.

Brara, R. 1987. "Shifting Sands: A Study of Rights in Common Pastures." Institute of Development Studies, Jaipur, mimeo.

Breman, J. 1979. "Seasonal Migration and Co-operative Capitalism: The Crushing of Cane and Labour by the Sugar Factories of Bardoli, South Gujarat." Paper presented at the ADC-ICRISAT Conference on Adjustment Mechanisms of Rural Labour Markets in Developing Areas, International Crop Research Institute for Semi-Arid Tropics (ICRISAT), Hyderabad, 22–24 August.

——— . 1985. *Of Peasants, Migrants and Paupers: Rural Labour Circulation and Capitalist Production in West India.* Delhi: Oxford University Press.

Brown, Kenneth, II, R. E. Black, and S. Becker. 1982. "Seasonal Change in Nutritional Status and the Prevalence of Malnutrition in a Longitudinal Study of Young Children in Rural Bangladesh." Abstract in *American Journal of Clinical Nutrition* 36.

Burling, R. 1963. *Rengsanggri: Family and Kinship in a Garo Village.* Philadelphia: University of Pennsylvania Press.

Cain, M. T., S. R. Khanam, and S. Nahar. 1979. "Class, Patriarchy and the Structure of Women's Work in Rural Bangladesh." New York: The Population Council, Center for Population Studies, Working Paper No. 4.

Caldwell, J. C., P. H. Reddy, and P. Caldwell. 1986. "Periodic High Risk as a Cause of Fertility Decline in a Changing Rural Environment: Survival Strategies in the 1980–83 South Indian Drought." *Economic Development and Cultural Change* 34.

Campbell, D. J., and D. D. Trechter. 1982. "Strategies for Coping with Food Consumption Shortage in the Mandara Mountains Region of North Cameroon." *Social Science and Medicine* 16.

Cernea, M. M. 1981. "Land Tenure Systems and Social Implications of Forestry Development Programmes." World Bank Staff Working Paper No. 452, April. Washington, D.C.: World Bank.

Chambers, R. 1981. "Introduction." In R. Chambers, R. Longhurst, and A. Pacey (eds.), *Seasonal Dimensions of Rural Poverty.* London: Frances Pinter.

Chandler, A.F.D. 1986. *Participation as Process: What We Can Learn from Grameen Bank, Bangladesh.* Dhaka: Grameen Bank.

Chattopadhyay, K. P., and R. K. Mukerjee. 1946. *A Plan for Rehabilitation*. Calcutta: Statistical Publishing House.

Chen, L. C., E. Huq, and S. D'Souza. 1981. "Sex Bias in the Family Allocation of Food and Health Care in Rural Bangladesh." *Population and Development Review* 7.

Chen, M. 1987. "Update on Drought Situation in Devdholera Village." Harvard Institute of International Development, mimeo.

————. 1988. "Women and Household Livelihood Systems." Harvard Institute of International Development, mimeo.

Chowdhury, A. 1987. *Studies in Socio-Cultural Change in Rural Villages in Bangladesh*. Tokyo: Tokyo University of Foreign Studies, Institute for the Study of Languages and Cultures of Asia and Africa, No. 5.

Chowdhury, K. M., and M. T. Bapat. 1975. "A Study of Impact of Famine and Relief Measures in Gujarat and Rajasthan." Ahemdabad: Sardar Patel University, Agro-Economic Research Center, Research Study No. 44.

Commander, S. 1983."The Jajmani System in North India: An Examination of its Logic and Status Across Two Centuries." *Modern Asian Studies* 17.

Currey, B. 1978. "Famine Symposium Report: The Famine Syndrome—Its Definition for Relief and Rehabilitation in Bangladesh." *Ecology of Food and Nutrition* 7.

Dandekar, K. 1983. *Employment Guarantee Scheme: An Employment Opportunity for Women*. Pune, India: Orient Longman.

Dasgupta, M. 1987. "Informal Security Mechanisms and Population Retention in Rural India." *Economic Development and Cultural Change*, July.

Dasgupta, S., and A. K. Maiti. 1987. "The Rural Energy Crisis, Poverty, and Women's Roles in Five Indian Villages." Geneva: International Labour Organisation, Technical Cooperation Report, World Employment Programme.

Desai, G. M., G. Singh, and D. C. Sah. 1979. "Impact of Scarcity on Farm Economy and Significance of Relief Operations." Ahemdabad: Indian Institute of Management, CMA (Center for Management of Agriculture) Monograph No. 84.

Desai, R. 1982. "Migrant Labour and Women: The Case of Ratnagiri." Geneva: International Labour Organisation, World Employment Programme, Research Working Paper WEP 10/WP28.

Dhagamvar, V. 1987. "The Disadvantaged and the Law." Paper presented at a Workshop on Poverty in India, Queen Elizabeth House, Oxford, U.K., October.

Dixon, R. M. 1979. *Rural Women at Work: Strategies for Development in South Asia*. Baltimore, Md.: Johns Hopkins University Press.

Dreze, J. 1988. "Famine Prevention in India." In J. P. Dreze and A. K. Sen (eds.), *The Political Economy of Hunger*. Oxford: Clarendon Press.

————. 1990. "Widows in Rural India." Discussion Paper No. 26, Development Economics Research Programme, London School of Economics.

Dreze, J., and A. K. Sen. 1990. *Hunger and Public Action*. Oxford: Clarendon Press.

Duvvury, N. 1989. "Work Participation of Women in India: A Study with Special Reference to Female Agricultural Labourers, 1961 to 1981." In A.V. Jose (ed.), *Limited Options: Women Workers in Rural India*. Delhi: Asian Regional Technology and Employment Programme (ARTEP)/ILO.

Ellickson, J. 1972. "Islamic Institutions: Perception and Practice in a Village in Bangladesh." *Contributions to Indian Sociology* 6, December.

Epstein, T. S. 1967. "Productive Efficiency and Customary Systems of Rewards in Rural South India." In R. Firth (ed.), *Themes in Economic Anthropology.* London: Tavistock Publications.

Fernandes, W., and G. Menon. 1987. *Tribal Women and Forest Economy: Deforestation, Exploitation and Status Change.* Delhi: Indian Social Institute.

Folbre, N. 1988. "The Black Four of Hearts: Towards a New Paradigm of Household Economics." In D. Dwyer and J. Bruce (eds.), *A Home Divided: Women and Income in the Third World.* Stanford: Stanford University Press.

Fraser, N. 1989. *Unruly Practices: Power, Discourse and Gender in Contemporary Social Theory.* Minneapolis: University of Minnesota Press.

Gangrade, K. D., and S. Dhadda. 1973. *Challenge and Responses: A Study of Famine in India.* Delhi: Rachana Publications.

George, S. 1988. "The Female of the Species: Women and Dairying in India." Paper presented at a workshop on Women in Agriculture, Center for Development Studies, Trivandrum, 15–17 February.

Greenough, P. R. 1982. *Prosperity and Misery in Modern Bengal: The Famine of 1943–44.* Oxford: Oxford University Press.

Gulati, L. 1978. "Profile of a Female Agricultural Labourer." *Economic and Political Weekly* 13 (12), 25 March.

Guyer, J. I., and P. E. Peters (eds.). 1987. "Conceptualizing the Household: Issues of Theory and Policy in Africa." *Development and Change* 18 (2), April (special issue).

Harriss, B. 1986. "The Intrafamily Distribution of Hunger in South Asia." In J. P. Dreze and A. K. Sen (eds.), *The Political Economy of Hunger.* Oxford: Clarendon Press.

Harriss, J. 1977. "Implications of Changes in Agriculture for Social Relations at the Village Level: The Case of Ramdan." In B. H. Farmer (ed.), *Green Revolution?* London: Macmillan.

Hart, G. 1990. "Imagined Unities: Constructions of 'the Household' in Economic Theory." Cambridge, Mass.: Massachusetts Institute of Technology, Dept. of Urban Studies and Planning, mimeo.

Hossain, M. 1984. "Credit for the Rural Poor: The Experience of Grameen Bank in Bangladesh." Dhaka: Bangladesh Institute of Development Studies, mimeo.

———. 1987. "The Assault that Failed: A Profile of Absolute Poverty in Six Villages of Bangladesh." Geneva: United Nations Research Institute for Social Development (UNRISD).

———. 1988. "Credit for Alleviation of Poverty: The Experience of Grameen Bank in Bangladesh." Bangladesh Institute of Development Studies, mimeo.

India. 1982. Report of Committee on Forests and Tribals in India. New Delhi: Ministry of Home Affairs.

———. 1987. *General Economic Tables, Census of India, 1981,* Series 1. New Delhi: Census Commissioner.

———. 1990. *Forest Survey of India.* New Delhi: National Remote Sensing Agency.

Islam, R. 1981. "Women, Work and Wages in Rural Bangladesh." The *Journal of Social Studies* 11.

Jansen, E. G. 1986. *Rural Bangladesh: Competition for Scarce Resources.* Oslo: Norwegian University Press.

Jetly, S. 1987. "Impact of Male Migration on Rural Families." *Economic and Political Weekly* 22 (44).

Jodha, N. S. 1975. "Famine and Famine Policies: Some Empirical Evidence." *Economic and Political Weekly* 10 (41).

———. 1978. "Effectiveness of Farmers' Adjustment to Risk." *Economic and Political Weekly* 13 (25).

———. 1979. "Intercropping in Traditional Farming Systems." Progress Report 3, Economics Programme, International Crop Research Institute for Semi-Arid Tropics (ICRISAT), April.

———. 1986. "Common Property Resources and Rural Poor." *Economic and Political Weekly* 21 (27), 5 July.

Kalpagam, U. 1987. "Working Women's Forum: A Concept and an Experiment in Mobilisation in the Third World." Madras Institute of Development Studies, Offprint 6.

Kolenda, P. 1987. *Regional Differences in Family Structures in India.* Jaipur: Rawat Publications.

Kulkarni, S. W. 1983. "Towards a Social Forestry Policy." *Economic and Political Weekly* 18 (6), 6 February.

Kumar, S. K. 1978. "Role of the Household Economy in Child Nutrition at Low Incomes." Cornell University, Dept. of Agricultural Economics, Occasional Paper No. 95.

Kynch, J., and M. Maguire. 1988. "Wasted Cultivators and Stunted Girls: Variations in Nutritional Status in a North Indian Village." Oxford: Institute of Economics and Statistics, mimeo.

Kynch, J., and A. K. Sen. 1983. "Indian Women: Well Being and Survival." *Cambridge Journal of Economics* 7.

Lewis, O. 1958. *Village Life in Northern India: Studies in a Delhi Village.* Urbana: University of Illinois Press.

Lipton, M. 1983. "Labor and Poverty." Washington, D.C.: The World Bank, Staff Working Paper No. 616.

Maclachlan, M. D. 1983. *Why They Did Not Starve: Biocultural Adaptation in a South Indian Village.* Philadelphia: Institute for the Study of Human Issues.

Mahalanobis, P. C., R. Mokerjee, and A. Ghosh. 1946. *A Survey of After-Effects of the Bengal Famine of 1943.* Calcutta: Statistical Publishing Society.

Majumdar, D. N. 1978. *Culture Change in Two Garo Villages.* Calcutta: Anthropological Survey of India.

Mencher, J. 1987. "Women's Work and Poverty: Women's Contribution to Household Maintenance in Two Regions of South India." In D. Dwyer and J. Bruce (eds.), *A Home Divided: Women and Income Control in the Third World.* Stanford: Stanford University Press.

Mencher, J., and K. Saradamoni. 1982. "Muddy Feet and Dirty Hands: Rice Production and Female Agricultural Labour." *Economic and Political Weekly* (Review of Agriculture), 25 December.

Mies, M. 1983."Landless Women Organise—A Case Study of an Organisation in Rural Andhra." *Manushi* 3.

Miller, B. 1981. *The Endangered Sex: Neglect of Female Children in Rural North India*. Ithaca: Cornell University Press.

———. 1983. "Son Preference, Daughter Neglect, and Juvenile Sex Ratios: Pakistan and Bangladesh Compared." East Lansing: Michigan State University, Working Paper No. 30.

Mitra, M. 1985. "Women and Work in the Livestock Economy: An Introduction." In *Women in Dairying: A Set of Case Studies and Recommendations*. Delhi: The Ford Foundation.

Nag, M., B.N.F. White, and R. C. Peet. 1977. "Economic Value of Children in Two Peasant Societies." In *International Population Conference, Mexico,* Vol. 1. Belgium: IUSSP.

Naveed-I-Rahat. 1980. "Male Outmigration, Matri-weighted Families and the Changing Role of Women: A Case Study of a Punjabi Village in Pakistan." Islamabad: Quaid-I-Azam University, Dept. of Anthropology, mimeo.

Nepal. 1987. Population Monograph of Nepal, Population Census 1981. Kathmandu: Central Bureau of Statistics.

———. 1988. *Statistical Pocket Book of Nepal*. Kathmandu: Central Bureau of Statistics.

Noponen, H. 1987. "Organising Petty Traders and Home-based Producers: A Case Study of Working Women's Forum, India." In A. M. Singh and A. Kelles-Vittamen (eds.), *Invisible Hands*. Delhi: Sage.

PIDT (People's Institute for Development and Training). 1982. *Towards Participation: Case Studies of Small Farmers Development Programme, Nepal*. New Delhi: PIDT.

Pingle, V. 1975. "Some Studies of Two Tribal Groups of Central India: Part 2: Importance of Foods Consumed in Two Different Seasons." *Plant Food for Man,* Vol. 1.

Prindle, P. H. 1979. "Peasant Society and Famines: A Nepalese Example." *Ethnology* 1.

Rahaman, A. 1986. "Impact of Grameen Bank Intervention on the Rural Power Structure." Grameen Bank Evaluation Project, Working Paper No. 2. Dhaka: Bangladesh Institute of Development Studies.

Rahman, R. I. 1986. "Impact of Grameen Bank on the Situation of Poor Rural Women." Dacca: Bangladesh Institute of Development Studies, Grameen Bank Evaluation Project, Working Paper No. 1.

Rajgopalan, S. K., P. H. Kymal, and P. Pei. 1981. "Births, Work and Nutrition in Tamil Nadu, India." In R. Chambers, R. Longhurst, and A. Pacey (eds.), *Seasonal Dimensions of Rural Poverty*. London: Frances Pinter.

Rangaswami, A. 1985. "Women's Roles and Strategies During Food Crisis and Famines." Paper presented at International Workshop on Women's Roles in Food Self-Sufficiency and Food Strategies, ORSTOM, Paris, 14–19 January.

Rao, N.V.K. 1974. "Impact of Drought on the Social System of a Telengana Village." *The Eastern Anthropologist* 27.

Reddy, G. P. 1988. "Drought and Famine: The Story of a Village in a Semi-Arid Region of Andhra Pradesh." Paper presented at a Workshop on Afro-Asian

Studies on Social Systems and Food Crises, India International Center, New Delhi, 26–29 March.

Roldán, M. 1988. "Renegotiating the Marital Contract: Intrahousehold Patterns of Money Allocation and Women's Subordination among Domestic Outworkers in Mexico City." In D. Dwyer and J. Bruce (eds.), *A Home Divided: Women and Income Control in the Third World.* Stanford: Stanford University Press.

Rosenzweig, M. R., and T. P. Schultz. 1982. "Market Opportunities, Genetic Endowment and Intrafamily Resource Distribution: Child Survival in Rural India." Yale University, Economic Growth Center, Paper No. 323.

Ryan, J. G., P. D. Bidinger, N. P. Rao, and P. Pushpamma. 1984. "The Determinants of Individual Diets and Nutritional Status in Six Villages of Southern India." Hyderabad: ICRISAT, Research Bulletin No. 7.

Ryan, J. G., and R. D. Ghodake. 1980. "Labour Market Behaviour in Rural Villages in South India: Effects of Season, Sex and Socio-Economic Status." Hyderabad: ICRISAT, Progress Report, Economic Programme 14.

Ryan, J. G., and T. D. Wallace. 1985. "Determinants of Labour Market Wages, Participation and Supply in Rural South India." Hyderabad: ICRISAT, Economics Group, Resource Management Program, Progress Report 73.

Scott, J. C. 1976. *The Moral Economy of the Peasant: Rebellion and Subsistence in Southeast Asia.* New Haven, Conn.: Yale University Press.

Sebstad, J. 1982. "Struggle and Development Among Self-Employed Women: A Report on the Self-Employed Women's Association Ahemdabad," Washington, D.C.: U.S. Agency for International Development (USAID).

Sen, A. K. 1981. *Poverty and Famines: An Essay on Entitlement and Deprivation.* Delhi: Oxford University Press.

———. 1983. "Economics and the Family." *Asian Development Review* 1.

———. 1990. "Gender and Co-Operative Conflicts." In I. Tinker (ed.), *Persistent Inequalities: Women and World Development.* New York: Oxford University Press.

Sen, A. K., and S. Sengupta. 1983. "Malnutrition of Rural Children and the Sex Bias." *Economic and Political Weekly* 19, Annual Number.

Sen, G., and C. Sen. 1985. "Women's Domestic Work and Economic Activity: Results from National Sample Survey." *Economic and Political Weekly* 20 (17), Review of Women's Studies.

Shaheed, F. 1989. "Purdah and Poverty in Pakistan." In H. Afshar and B. Agarwal (eds.), *Women, Poverty and Ideology in Asia.* London: Macmillan.

Sharma, U. 1980. *Women, Work and Property in North-West India.* London: Tavistock Publications.

Siddiqui, K. 1984. *An Evaluation of the Grameen Bank.* Dhaka: Grameen Bank Publication.

Singh, K. S. 1975. *The Indian Famine 1967: A Study in Crisis and Change.* Delhi: People's Publishing House.

Sri Lanka. 1986. *Census of Population and Housing, Population Census 1981. General Report.* Vol. 3. Colombo: Department of Census and Statistics.

Sri Lanka/World Bank. 1986. *Forestry Master Plan for Sri Lanka.* Colombo: Ministry of Land Development, Forest Resources Development Project.

Vaughan, M. 1987. *The Story of an African Famine: Gender and Famine in Twentieth Century Malawi.* Cambridge: Cambridge University Press.

Wade, R. 1987. "The Management of Common Property Resources: Finding a Cooperative Solution." *Research Observer* 2.

World Bank. 1989a. *Women in Pakistan: An Economic and Social Strategy,* Vol. II. Washington, D.C.

———. 1989b. *World Development Report.* Washington, D.C.

9

Women's Paid & Unpaid Work in Times of Economic Crisis

❧ CHIARA SARACENO

The complex concepts of women's work, household strategies, and economic crisis have been subject to a great deal of debate and often confusion. For purposes of this chapter, I will deal with women's work as the work of wives and/or mothers, paid and unpaid, in the formal as well as in the informal economy, as part of household strategies in situations of economic stress in Italy. My focus will be on the different degrees of choice, or on the variety of alternatives, open to individuals, particularly adult women with family responsibilities in one of the world's ten most industrialized countries. I will also focus on households on the basis of individual history, life cycle stage, local labor-market options, and access to social security provisions. Therefore, I will try to analyze how various mixes of resources and constraints give rise to specific crises and how they not only open the way to differing strategies, but also reveal different degrees of ability to direct one's own life.

In order to do this I will sketch various circumstances in contemporary Italy that create economic pressure on households. On the basis of available data, I will indicate which strategies are open to households in different situations, and when, in particular, and with which kind of work, wives' and mothers' contributions are called for, expected, offered, or possible. To illustrate, I will present a case study dealing with the experience of a structural economic crisis in an area relatively well protected by social security measures. This will allow me to briefly conclude with an analysis of how social policy measures, together with more general social-service provisions, might influence both the way in which households face an experience of economic stress and the way in which individuals—men and women—may develop strategies and make choices, and even perceive that they have a choice.

THE PROBABILITY OF ECONOMIC CRISIS
BY REGIONAL AND SOCIAL GROUP

Italy is a diverse country in terms of economic development and local labor markets as well as local political cultures and traditions. Researchers speak of the existence of three or even more "Italys," which cannot be described as stages along an ideal development continuum but must be understood as distinct social formations (see, for instance, Bagnasco 1977). Within them, different "packages" of resources are available to individuals and households, and therefore different opportunities to "construct" household income. The packages include labor market resources, social security benefits, informal economy resources, environmental resources, and social services and transfer benefits publicly provided by state and local governments (Saraceno 1981, 1987).

Although these formations somewhat coincide with specific geographical areas, there are neither neat boundaries nor internal homogeneity. Economic marginality may be found in enclaves of the most economically developed regions; highly developed and advanced areas may be found in the south; and productive decentralization, small-scale industry, and diffuse family enterprises may be found in the midst of the industrialized "triangle" of Turin, Milan, and Venice. Very roughly, the so-called "three Italys," and the geographically specific risks of economic crisis on households, may be described as follows.

THE INDUSTRIALIZED NORTH

In the culturally and politically diverse northwest, there is a concentration of large industries as well as both a traditional and a developing technologically advanced service sector. Therefore, both the offer of and the demand for women's paid work are comparatively high in the formal (official and covered by social security) labor market. It is in the service sector that the participation of adult women with family responsibilities in the labor market started to expand in the 1960s (Barile 1984).

The crisis in international markets, economic restructuring, and the oil crisis in the late 1970s and early 1980s severely affected such area industries as textiles and automobile manufacturing, and the number of jobs declined during the period. For many households and individuals, economic insecurity, almost nonexistent in the years of the "economic boom" and with concessions won by trade unions in social security and job security, once again became a reality. For example, in the Piedmonte Region, industrial jobs in 1980 were 48.9 percent of total jobs, as compared to 32.2 percent in Italy as a whole. Here the restructuring processes of the early 1980s and the overall reduction of industrial employment had more serious consequences than in developed regions, which had a strong and rapid expansion of the technologically advanced service sector. The result was that both adult men and women were exposed to unemployment risks. Although in the last decade women's employment has increased in Piedmonte, reaching 60 percent of all adult women, it has done so to a lesser degree than the Italian average and even less than the north-central average. Moreover, in the 1980–1987 period, although in Italy as a whole women's employment increased by 7.7 percent, in Piedmonte it decreased by 1.7 percent (IRES Piedmonte 1989).

In the short run, the better social-security coverage of jobs in large industries and the increasing demand for jobs from the developing service sector offered a buffer to risks at the household level. In the long run, they proved to be a resource for recovery at the macro level, the more so the more diversified the productive sectors (e.g., Lombardy). In fact, in the late 1980s the unemployment rate—including youth unemployment—has been rapidly declining in these regions. There is even a demand for labor in the less skilled jobs, a demand that is either not met or that is satisfied through migrant (Third World), often illegal, labor.

At the same time in these regions, there is, as there was in the past, a diversified informal labor market. The unofficial labor market offers secondary jobs and wages to workers with regular jobs, with the mutual benefits of under-the-table payment for workers and employees (with forfeited taxation and social security contributions); primary jobs to adult women and the young who do not have the qualifications to enter the official labor market or who prefer to forfeit social security in exchange for flexibility and lower household taxation; and primary jobs to adult immigrants who have little bargaining power. This informal economic sector also can be a transitional situation to developing new formal jobs.

Individuals and families in the northwest, therefore, may certainly be exposed to economic risk through redundancy and layoffs, but this risk is generally covered in economic, if not in psychological, terms. There are differences according to productive sector and the size of industry and firm. The best protected workers in terms of social security are public (state) employees and workers in plants where there are more than fifteen employees, particularly in larger ones. The least protected are those working in artisan workshops, small offices, and shops as well as those working in the unofficial, unprotected labor market.

Bettio (1988) has observed that it is impossible to detect a pattern of gender-specific risk to layoffs at the macro level. Instead, there are gender-specific patterns according to a particular sector and a particular firm. Because women are concentrated in productive sectors such as textiles, they are vulnerable to changes in labor demand in these sectors. But they are also present in a higher than average proportion in administrative jobs as well as social services—teaching positions, for example—which are often tenured, state jobs with little market variation. There are fewer adult women in the labor force than men, and, on average, they have more difficulty in obtaining a job. However, most of the jobs created in the past decade in Italy, which are heavily concentrated in this geographical area, have been filled by women—young and unmarried women, but particularly married women, who account for the increase in the total labor force from the 1970s to the present (Accornero 1987; Bettio 1988; IRES Piedmonte 1989).

Studies have shown that during the 1950s and 1960s, family well-being and standards of living were maintained and/or improved by adult women with family responsibilities by upgrading and intensifying their house and caring work (Zanuso 1984). In the 1970s, and particularly in the 1980s, women's combined paid and unpaid work became a buffer against economic crises as well as a crucial resource for upholding the family standard of living. Two studies based on a sample of Milan low-income families, for instance, have indicated how families with dual incomes are better protected against the costs of inflation (Negri and Santagata 1984; Negri, Ortona, and Santagata 1986), the second earner being most often the wife-mother. At the same time, in situations in which the household is under economic stress due to unemployment or to increasing economic needs, women-wives-mothers tend to increase their total housework output. Research has indicated that, even irrespective of real cuts in wages and monetary resources, married women who lose their jobs often give up the use of services that previously substituted for part of household work: They make less use of commercial laundries, keep their children home from day-care services, and generally devote more time to housework (IRES Piedmonte 1987; Bianchi and Saraceno 1988). This behavior may be due sometimes, or even often, to the preference of the woman who can now devote more time to activities and relations previously sacrificed to the demands of paid work. But i* also suggests that women feel justified in being partially replaced in their capacity as family workers only insofar as their time is occupied by paid work. Otherwise they resume their "natural" duties, the more so if this implies some kind of saving in a period of economic tension.

Although unemployment and layoffs have been a real threat—if not an actual experience—in these regions in the first half of the 1980s (to which the case study refers), they are much less so in the latter half of the decade. Households where the main provider is older, unskilled, or a woman (since in this last case she is also the only wage earner) run a greater risk. Even the opportunities offered by a diversified labor market and by a diversification of sectors may turn into economic risks and failures for individual households. The encouragement given, for instance, to dismissed workers to set up their own enterprises or to cooperatively organize has also exposed quite a few to failure and loss of capital. The turnover rate of small enterprises in provinces such as Turin and Milan in the 1980s is a good indicator of this kind of risk (see, for instance, Regione Piedmonte 1986; Bianchi and Saraceno 1988).

Another expanding group at risk is that composed of Third World immigrants, especially illegal ones (the majority), who come to north-central Italy. Attracted by the opportunities the large towns seem to offer, they instead experience underemployment and exploitation. The highly segregated migrant labor market, with women concentrated in live-in personal services as maids, and men working as street vendors or un-skilled manual workers, makes it difficult for immigrants to set up households, especially for female-headed households with young children. Also, social services available to the population in these areas—health care, child care, afterschool and cafeteria programs, home helpers for invalids and elderly people, including services and provisions for the indigent—are less likely to be used by immigrants. This lack of use is due to three reasons: They are in the country illegally or they do not know about the services, or are afraid of the social control attached to them (the same is partly true for the most marginal segments of the resident population). Although an average household incorporates these kinds of services and benefits as a normal part of its package of resources, those who are most in need might be unable to obtain them.

An economic crisis, however, may befall a household for other reasons than those directly linked to labor market conditions, such as the death of a husband-father. His low level of job seniority may leave his children and wife with a meager survivor pension. The widow is compelled to look for a job if she is not working, or to change jobs if she is working part time, and therefore face the constraints of a labor market unfavorable to middle-aged adults. Separation and divorce, which have their highest rates in the north-central region, may provoke a sharp decline in economic resources for a woman and her children. For example, in the tribunal of Milan the average settlement for a child or a nonearning ex-spouse is 150,000 lira a month (about $122 in 1991 U.S. dollars) (the "vital minimum" paid by social assistance was about 350,000 in 1988) (see Maggioni, Pocar, and Ronfani 1988). Research is lacking, but data collected at local social-assistance offices suggest that many such households have a more or less prolonged recourse to social assistance. In view of this, it is not surprising that on average the employment rate of women who eventually terminate their marriages is higher than the average and that within one or two years from the separation almost all have a job.[1]

Another cause of household economic stress, if not impoverishment, derives from the housing market, particularly in metropolitan areas. There is a system of rent control in Italy, but its concrete way of functioning and its rigidities subject individuals and families to the constraints of a tight housing market, to high unofficial rents that often more than double controlled rents as well as to high buying prices. Families who would otherwise have an adequate income may find themselves in a situation where they must spend over half their income for rent or for installment payments for an apartment, therefore cutting more or less severely their overall living standard (food, leisure, vacations). Garonna (1984a) indicates that this can create a "new," often invisible, poverty, calling for increased housework in order to save on purchases as well as for increased participation in paid work by family members: the wife-mother, but also daughters, who might be compelled to cut their education.

THE UNDERDEVELOPED SOUTH

Southern Italy (*Mezzogiorno*) has a more recent and less widespread and established industrialization; significant areas of subsistence agriculture remain. In the large towns only a small portion of the population work within the formal, official economy, while a substantial portion exist within different forms of the informal economy, including the underground economy. High rates of unemployment (making up over 50 percent of the national total) prevail, particularly among the young and among women.[2] Although official workers in major industries have the same social security coverage as their northern colleagues,[3] their proportion of the total economically active population—which is already lower than in other regions—is lower. Therefore, the overall social security coverage of the population and of households, in terms of protection from the risks of unemployment, is low. In other words, households in the south, compared to other regions, have on average fewer members who hold a regular job, and not all households contain at least one member who has a regular job covered by social security (Becchi Collidà 1979).

According to some studies, having only one (even regular) earner per household is increasingly becoming a "luxury" that only high-income households can afford; for middle- and low-income households there is a "cost," in terms of increased vulnerability to market variations, less protection from inflation, as indicated above, and income inadequacy, given the average wage (Garonna 1984b). If this is true, in the south we find that the majority of families have to incur and to pay for this risk, due to the double constraints of a tight labor market and a large number of children. Having more than two children is, in fact, negatively associated with holding a regular job for wives-mothers (Federici 1984). Longer time and more energy spent in housework by women, even if necessary and made harder by insufficient urban and residential infrastructures (where running water is often unavailable), cannot compensate for the lack of income. At the same time, here we find the households where there is both a plurality of incomes and of earners. Real activity rates may be high while regular employment and regular wages may be low.

Economic stress and the risk of experiencing an economic crisis are not so much linked to individual circumstances as to structural conditions. Single individuals and households, therefore, have both less resources and less alternatives than elsewhere to avoid, or buffer, "individual" crises or to tailor behavior to perceived needs. For instance, the low separation and divorce rate that is found in these regions cannot be simply explained in terms of stronger conjugal and family relations; the impossibility of surviving alone is a strong incentive for women not to separate (as well as for adult children not to leave their families).

Average consumption data by geographical areas indicate this situation well: Families in the south spend over 50 percent less for their consumption than those living in the northwest, although they are on average larger. The "Report on Poverty" by the Poverty Commission in 1984 found that over 60 percent of families that may be defined as poor[4]—that is, having access to half the average national consumption rate—lived in the south.

This geographical inequality is reinforced by state intervention (in terms of social services provided, benefits paid, and so on): The per capita public expenditure in 1988 was 3.8 million in the south, compared to 4.3 million in the other regions (SVIMEZ 1989). A comparative analysis of the distribution of expenditure for specific services and benefits, such as hospitals, schools, child-care services, school cafeterias, or pensions, confirms this overall picture (Saraceno 1981, 1990; Artoni 1989).

The scarcity of jobs in the official labor market (notwithstanding the somewhat abnormally large public service sector) causes adult men to compete with young, and often very young, people in the informal and underground labor markets. On the other hand, adult women, and often also young women, have difficulty both in supporting themselves and integrating household economic resources (*Inchiesta* 1986; Accornero 1987; Pugliese 1989). In the urban areas of the south the very poor work at home (for example, in garment and leather production), in the least protected, lowest paid, and often most unsafe conditions, sometimes with the help of their children. The so-called "street economy" (*economia del vicolo*) found in the most dilapidated and poorest areas of southern towns is a combination of wages, barter, pawning, street vending, some social assistance, and sometimes illegal activities, where every family member contributes—from children to old people. The street economy may be seen as an imaginative strategy for survival, but it does not offer high degrees of choice and opportunities for planning. At the same time, households that are slightly better off and/or that have a greater interest in social respectability, or that live in new neighborhoods, may be cut off from these kinds of resources, particularly those involving women and children. It has been suggested that one of the consequences of the displacement caused by the earthquake in Naples has been the disruption of the web of relations and way of life that sustained the street economy on which many a household subsistence was based.

THE "THIRD ITALY"

Located mostly in central and northeastern Italy, the "third Italy" is described at the economic and productive levels in terms of "peripheral economy," or "productive decentralization," or by the presence of "industrial districts" (Bagnasco 1977, 1989; Beccattini 1987, 1989). It is made up of small-scale industries, capital-intensive farming, widespread family enterprises, cooperatives, and various types of informal economies ranging from production for self-consumption to semiofficial piecework at home. Traditionally, women work within the family enterprise and contribute unpaid labor or contribute their wages from the formal as well as informal economy to the household economy. Women are a crucial resource both for household economic strategies and for the differentiated demands of the labor markets (Paci et al., 1980; Ardigò and Donati 1976). Family solidarity is also crucial and extends outside the co-resident household; it is expressed through male and female networks, where different kinds of resources and work are shared and exchanged.

At the cultural and political levels, the "third Italy" is characterized by a tradition of strong local homogeneity, be it within the Catholic framework (as in the Veneto Region), or within the Left, Socialist, and especially Communist one (as in Emilia Romagna or Tuscany). This homogeneity contributes to the creation of distinctive social and political cultures with regard to individual and family social needs and responsibilities as well as to public/private boundaries and to the relationship between public and private solidarity. Needs and responsibilities, therefore, may be defined quite differently according to local cultures. At the same time, this cultural homogeneity implies and encourages closer attention to community demands, which, in turn, is favored by smaller-scale, and on average richer, administrative units than those found in the metropolitan areas of the northwest. Although there are great variations, these regions are also generally equipped with fairly widespread and organized social services, often characterized by interesting social innovations. These services constitute a substantial asset in total family resources, together with a continuing tradition of family and kin solidarity and exchange. Social services interact strongly with women's family work (child care, care for the elderly), partly substituting for and partly modifying it (see, for instance, Balbo 1986).

Households in the "third Italy" are usually well protected by kin and social solidarity by a diversification of the labor market that allows the combination of different jobs and provides different sources of income as well as a buffer against the risks of overspecialization. It is, in fact, in this region where we find the cities with the highest per capita income. Specific areas and productive sectors, such as the ceramic industry, have however been severely affected in the past decade. Workers in small-scale industries have been less protected than their colleagues in large-scale production (for example, FIAT or Montedison), where unions have greater power to negotiate unemployment benefits. The very fragmentation and articulation of production typical of industrial districts, therefore, may be both a resource and a risk at the same time.

The household division of labor by sex and age balances out these risks at the household level. For individuals located in the most fragile, least protected sectors, particularly adult women and the young, it might, however, be a restriction when household solidarity becomes too constraining or hard to bear. The household division of labor, in fact, assigns married women both to unpaid family work and to the less secure job positions in the peripheral and informal economy: positions whose flexibility in time and organization may more easily fit into the rhythm and needs of family work (Paci et al., 1980). As has been observed, the family/gender/generation division of labor (in terms of forming a diversified labor pool) is particularly well adapted to a labor market and to a productive organization that need high degrees of labor flexibility, following variations in the demand for goods (see also Saraceno 1989). The "fit" may be also convenient at the household level, while it might be risky for individuals.

This "fit" becomes apparent in old age, particularly for women. Most older women's lifelong employment has been in jobs without social security benefits, being for the most part activities performed within the family economy and enterprise. Their minimum pension benefits may, therefore, be far from adequate if kin and social solidarity are lacking.

The group most exposed both to risks and to lack of adequate buffers in these regions, however, are Third World immigrants. This often unregistered, but substantial group works increasingly in "industrial district" jobs that resident workers refuse to take because they are too fatiguing, dangerous, unskilled, or socially unacceptable (for example, foundries or animal farming). These migrants are often single men whose families have remained behind. Their wages are low, social security protection is often lacking, and extended family or kin networks are nonexistent.

From this brief account it is clear that both exposure to the risks of experiencing an economic crisis, and the alternative options and resources to deal with crisis, depend on the combination of resources and constraints available to households and to families. The crucial elements at the macro level appear to be the structure and articulation of labor demands, social security coverage, and the overall system of social protection, including social services. The geographical differentiation of these elements, even within the same class and/or social strata, determines the degree to which individuals and households are both exposed to and protected from economic crises in Italy.

At the micro level the crucial elements appear more numerous and complicated, especially when they interact with macro factors. First are household size, household structure, and life cycle stage. Large families are more liable to be or become poor than smaller ones. Particularly when children are small (Commissione Povertà 1986), a single wage earner in the family is often inadequate, and it is difficult, if not impossible, for the mother to take on a paid job. Extended households and some forms of the "new extended family" (nuclear families or individuals with separate households, but sharing resources and exchanging services) can be an efficient way of pooling resources. Individually inadequate incomes are pooled together,[5] and the division of labor among women allows some of them to take paid jobs. But this arrangement can also be an economic constraint, for example, when a dependent elderly person prevents his/her daughter or daughter-in-law from holding a job. Dual-earner families are better protected than single-earner families, irrespective of total household income. Households with elderly members may experience an economic strain due to low pensions, which become even lower in the case of survivor pensions for older widows.[6] Separation and divorce also represent a differentiated risk for men and women, particularly if the woman does not have a regular job, and/or if she is the custodial parent. Other important elements are the work culture of individuals and their reference groups, their previous experiences and training, their perception of proper adult and gender roles, their sense of self-worth, and the support they find in their social networks.

As Negri (1990) indicates, although there are many causes that lead an individual or a household into poverty—loss of job, being on welfare, divorce, eviction, foster care, migration—none of them necessarily means remaining in poverty. Rather, at the micro level, the most irreversible entrances into poverty are likely to happen when a particular cause sets up a process that destroys the complex network of material and psychological resources available to a particular individual or household, which, in turn, destroys their abilities, and hopes, to move competently in the social world (what Negri calls "citizenship technologies").

Social policies appear to be crucial elements in counteracting and providing social buffers against these breakages in the sense of personal adequacy. The functioning of informal social networks—particularly of households, extended families, and communities—is crucial as well, although in different ways for men and women as well as for people with or without family responsibilities.

I will now briefly show how some of these micro dimensions interacted in the case of a social policy that acted as a buffer against the immediate economic and social costs of joblessness.

HOUSEHOLD COMPOSITION AND
INDIVIDUAL STRATEGIES:
THE CASE OF CIG WORKERS[7]

The recourse to Cassa Integrazione Guadagni (CIG)[8] at FIAT in Turin during the 1980s was an important social policy intervention: "a large-scale welfare state operation which has no precedents in the history of industrialized countries, given its massive, prolonged, systematic features" (IRES Piedmonte 1987:417). For the first time in history, thousands of people—over 20,000—were put out of work in order to receive (for a periodically negotiated and de facto indefinite period of time) a subsidy that was equivalent to almost 90 percent of their previous salary; only those workers who could prove they held no other job, even in the informal economy, had the right to continue to be defined as "temporarily suspended from work," and therefore entitled to CIG.[9] At the same time, they were encouraged to find a new job. FIAT encouraged this solution through a policy of monetary incentives and publicity concerning the improbability of a recall under the same conditions as before.

State and local government played an important role in this situation. The state subsidized the CIG and favored early retirement for older workers; local government sponsored work and training projects aimed specifically at CIG workers to help them to find new jobs, set up their own enterprises, or organize cooperatives. It must be noted that, although the CIG workers were not officially unemployed, as long as they remained on CIG (which might last for more than one year) they were still part of a job contract.

Although workers on CIG were granted an unprecedented form of social protection from the costs of unemployment, they were subject to ambivalent social and individual perceptions of their status as workers and their right to an income. These perceptions separated them both from "real workers" (that is, those who were not on CIG) and from the unemployed, who did not have the same rights and guaranteed income. It even set them up as possible "unlawful" and "unrightful" competitors for jobs and income in the labor market of the *indotto,* the workshops and small enterprises that—often using a combination of formal and informal workers—work directly for FIAT. The *indotto* were heavily affected by the restructuring processes of FIAT and often laid off employees and/or substituted less costly (because illegal) CIG workers for them.

These ambivalences were an integral part not only of the social image of the *cassintegrati* (CIG workers), but often also of their own self-perceptions, influencing the ways they dealt with this experience and developed strategies to exit from it. At the same time, these self-perceptions and resulting strategic directions varied according to age, sex, family responsibilities, and available options, although all workers involved were "typical representative[s] of the working class of the large Fordist factory in crisis in a situation of deindustrialization" (IRES Piedmonte 1987:119). They were, in fact, mostly poorly qualified, middle-aged workers. The CIG experience, however, acted as a differentiating process, underlining, but also liberating, new and old differences within this class—by sex, age, regional origin, length of time worked in an industrial setting, seniority, and qualifications, which produced different ways of experiencing what appears to be only nominally the "same experience." (Godard [1988] has pointed out an analogous phenomenon in the case of the restructuring processes in the Somme region in France.)

From this perspective the IRES researchers speak of the existence in their sample of "one class, two strata, three generations." The first stratum consists of specialized males. The majority are in their thirties, and most are Piedmonte natives, but in a few cases they belong to the long-established migrant families who migrated from the south to Turin in the 1950s and 1960s. A minority of the total FIAT CIG workers, they made up the majority both of those who were eventually recalled by FIAT and of those who, having chosen to quit, now hold the best jobs (either wage work or self-employment) among the new jobs found by ex-CIG workers. The second stratum is the vast majority of women of all ages, of older men, and of poorly qualified young male workers who had recently migrated from the south and had been hired by FIAT just before the crisis. As for the three generations, the first comprises those hired before 1968 (during the period of economic expansion) and coincides largely with the first stratum; the second comprises those hired between 1968 and 1975; and the third includes those who had been hired just a short time before being put on CIG and who had neither enough seniority to protect them from CIG selection nor experience enough as workers to qualify them for other jobs. The second, and particularly third, generation included more women, tended to be from the south, and was less qualified on average than the first.

Within these differences—particularly those due to gender, geographical origin, time of migration, and entrance into FIAT—household structure, the position of the individual in the household, and life cycle stage appear very important in shaping the strategies used to face the complex CIG experience. These I will analyze in some detail, with reference to the different paths that led to the decision to quit jobs and to the different meanings attached both to the CIG experience and to its outcome.

Research data indicate that those—mostly middle-aged men—who were the main household providers developed a strategy distinct from that of the other workers. They did not take risks by accepting the FIAT offer of a lump sum in exchange for quitting or trying to negotiate for a higher sum.[10] They quit the job contract only when they found a (wage) job that they perceived as secure enough, even if worse paid and requiring less qualifications than the one at FIAT. Conversely, younger male workers who were married but had no children, and especially unmarried ones, risked more: On average, they quit earlier (that is, before the average two years of CIG experience) in exchange for a monetary incentive, even without having yet found a secure job. Among these, there are also the few who used the incentive money to try to launch their own enterprise.

Researchers have pointed out that the positive linkage between family responsibilities and success in a job search is at least ambivalent. Success is mediated for by a restriction of available options as well as the subjective preferences of the job seeker. In the words of one worker, married to a housewife, with a child, "If I was not married probably I would not have considered this job" (IRES Piedmonte 1989:191). Particularly the absence of a second earner in the household, generally the wife, is a strong incentive to follow a conservative strategy. Conversely, when the family has two wage earners, the CIG worker seems to have a greater range of alternatives and is more likely to take some risk. In this case the household is also more likely to invest the incentive money to complete its plans—buying a house, some furniture, and so forth—instead of saving it against possible unemployment risks. Married women's paid work, therefore, represents a resource not only for the family economy but also for their husbands' individual strategies in the labor market.

The reverse is also partly true. Because most married women have a working husband, the CIG for them may not represent an economic threat, even if it can represent, as some of them explicitly declare, a threat to their way of living and organizing outside the home. For many women in the sample the CIG seems, in fact, to represent an opportunity to reverse the balance between paid and family work. This reversal, however, can become permanent out of choice or out of lack of alternatives:[11] Less than half of the women in the sample were working at the time of the interview. Older, mostly Piedmonte-born, women, with a long history of paid work, might be content to quit work permanently and be satisfied with job termination money with the addition of the incentive sum. However, younger women, with a shorter work history (therefore less seniority and little termination money), greater family needs, and for the most part recently immigrated with little local resources, are in effect desperately looking for jobs and accepting any kind of work, under any conditions. Housework for them is a necessity, more than for older women whose families are past the most pressing nurturing needs. It cannot, however, compensate for lost pay, especially in view of the fact that their husbands, too, are on average more exposed than native Piedmontese to unemployment. Moreover, migration was part of a plan for securing a better way of life for themselves and their family. If they cannot secure a job with a regular income, this plan fails. In the words of a woman whose household situation was among the economically worst off (the husband had only a small pension and both their over 18-year-old sons were unemployed), "If I and my sons do not find a job soon, we will go back down to Calabria. Life costs less there, and people help each other."

If housework appears to be flexibly adapted to women's changing availability of time as well as to the household's changing needs and resources in times of high unemployment rates and/or economic stress, its permeability to changes in males' availability of time during the CIG is less clear. About one-third of male respondents in the Turin sample declared that they helped more with housework during the CIG period. Men over forty, who had both greater family responsibilities and greater difficulties in finding a new job, changed their behavior more than younger ones (38 percent compared to less than 20 percent); but younger men in general had a more balanced pattern of sharing housework to start with. From this point of view, the pressure to perform household work directed at middle-aged men seems to indicate a diminishing legitimization in their traditional role as breadwinners, which adds to their self-perception as having "failed." Moreover, their "helping" implies neither a role reversal nor a substantial redefinition of the previous gender balance. Men help out in very specific areas, such as caring for small children and shopping. And their wives, although they expect their husbands' cooperation, tend to dismiss it as almost worthless, given their husbands' "incompetence" (IRES Piedmonte 1987:209–210). In conclusion, a situation of uncertainty in work and economic roles and in social standing seems to be unfavorable to men's changing family roles.

CONCLUSIONS

The case study presented above indicates that income protection such as the CIG can represent not only a needed and equitable subsidization of those who are out of work, but, insofar as it grants both money and time, also a means to work out one's own strategies and life plans on the basis of individual as well as household needs and resources. At the same time, household composition and responsibilities, work biography, and cultural and network resources make a difference in the way this "resource" is experienced and utilized. Therefore, while for some it can be a welcome opportunity (to go back to school, to launch a business, to devote time to family and friends), for others it might represent a psychological wound and also a very concrete social risk if they have no resources to transform it into an opportunity and can rely only on the hope of being eventually recalled by the firm. Gender and individual differences interplay with household composition and age.

If the CIG acts as a differentiating agent on a social group that only appears to be homogeneous, the lack of a similar measure for a large portion of workers, and for all those permanently without regular jobs, produces even greater, socially created differentiations. The most socially important feature of the long-term CIG is not so much its maintaining a formal linkage with a job, as its providing the right to an adequate income with time to think and decide. If it is certain that other measures and services (for example, training and counseling) must be provided in order to make the period on welfare a resource, the lack both of income and of time in the absence of family support makes it impossible for recipients to develop any long- or middle-term strategy. People are forced either to take any job, or to waste their time looking for a job, or to abandon any idea of personal autonomy.

For these reasons, together with debates on the "reform of the CIG" that tend to reduce the scope of its application, proposals are increasingly being advanced and supported in Italy within the unions, political parties, and among experts, concerning the introduction of a form of unemployment benefit that is nearer to actual wages. The benefit would be available to all unemployed, both because they have lost their job and because they cannot find jobs (see, for example, Bettio 1988; Garonna 1989). At the same time a debate is developing, mostly among social policy experts but also within the Communist and Socialist parties and the CGIL (the Social and Communist trade union), around the issue of some form of guaranteed minimum income. The plan could be similar to the French RMI (Revenue Minimum d'Insertion), as partly suggested by the Poverty Commission in its report, or the Basic Income, as in the northern European model. In the latter case, the exclusive linkage between work and income would be definitively severed, insofar as the right to a basic income would become a universal citizenship right.[12] This would certainly not solve the complex problems of the gender division of labor, the organization of work, the place of work in personal identity, or the mix of personal autonomy and interdependence within a household. Some form of basic income, however, would grant individuals some negotiating power not only with regard to labor market demands, but also to family and household demands, changing the framework of gender and generational relationships. At the same time it would protect individuals and households from the economic risks arising from causes other than those linked to the labor market.

NOTES

1. In Italy legal separation must always precede divorce, which now may be obtained three years after a legal separation.

2. The total labor-force participation rate of southern women is 29 percent as compared to 33 percent for all Italy. At the same time, a recent study by the Office of Census (ISTAT) and the Italian Sociological Association (AIS) found that there are one and a half million women aged 14–29, mostly living in the south, who are neither in school nor in the labor force. This means that, given the high unemployment rate both for women and for the young in the south, young women in this area are discouraged both from studying and from entering the labor market, therefore preparing for a life of economic dependency and/or work in the underground economy. See AIS-ISTAT 1988; Pugliese 1989. On the national, gender, and geographical characteristics of contemporary Italian unemployment see also Accornero and Carmignani (1986); on trends in women's employment see IRES Piedmonte 1989.

3. Studies indicate that some form of coverage such as the Cassa Integrazione Guadagni (CIG) was utilized proportionately more to protect workers in the south than in the center-north, although in absolute terms the higher number of *cassintegrati*, that is, of workers covered by the CIG, was to be found in the Milan and Turin provinces. (See Schenkel and Zenezini 1986; Schenkel 1989.) People who are looking for a job but cannot prove they have held a job contract for at least one year in the two years preceding unemployment are not entitled to these benefits. This particularly affects youths and adult women who are looking for a job after having devoted themselves to family work. (On the Institute of CIG see also Romani 1987.)

4. They represented 11 percent of all families in Italy, but 18.5 percent in the south and 7.8 percent in the center-north. See Commissione Povertà 1986.

5. From this perspective the Italian family has been defined as an "income clearing house" (CENSIS 1978) or as an "extended family" because it provides for its members into adulthood. The pooling of various family resources was first pointed out by Balbo 1977.

6. Here, too, a gender difference shows: Older women living alone are thought to be more self-sufficient and less in need of extra services because of their ability to perform housework; older widowed men are perceived as more in need. Data on institutionalization of the elderly in old-age homes by sex indicate this to be the case. More men are institutionalized, notwithstanding their lower incidence in the total older population.

7. In this section I rely heavily on a study undertaken by IRES, the research institute of the Piedmonte Region, on a sample of 90 workers who had been put on CIG and who eventually dissolved their job contracts with FIAT. The sample studied was taken from a list of 6,547 people who had been put on CIG between 1980 and 1981 and who in 1985 still belonged to the so-called "mobility list," that is, to the list of workers whom FIAT did not think it would need in the near future. From these, a subgroup of about 30 percent of workers who had either resigned or had been dismissed or retired early was drawn out. Thirty percent of the sample was composed of women, corresponding to the percentage of women on the list. On the CIG experience in Piedmonte and particularly at FIAT, and its consequences on workers and on the labor market, see also ISFOL 1983; Regione Piedmonte 1986; qualitative studies in other regions have been carried out by Camusi 1986; Regione Toscana 1986.

8. The Cassa Integrazione Guadagni (CIG) was instituted in the 1940s and revised in the 1950s and 1960s to pay to workers the hours lost due to technical changes in plant production or a temporary market crisis. In the early 1980s, when the crisis of the automobile industry and of other industrial sectors provoked mass redundancy and reconversion needs, the CIG was extended to cover situations of workers' redundancy.

9. This does not mean that many CIG workers, especially males, did not work for pay in the informal economy. Many workers had worked in the informal economy before being put on CIG (Gallino 1982). Women mostly worked in unpaid family work, although there are examples of women who worked in the paid informal economy of housecleaning, babysitting, workshop jobs, or piece-work at home. Given the importance of FIAT in the Turin area, the automobile crisis had long-range negative effects on the whole local labor market, at the formal as well as at the informal level (see also Bianchi and Saraceno 1988), reducing the traditional work and income options available to individuals and families.

10. This, too, was a gamble, insofar as the FIAT offer varied over time, and many workers eventually had to quit without any extra money because it was clear that they would not be needed by FIAT and that the CIG would not be renewed.

11. Two older women in their late forties and early fifties, with a long work history, grown children, and under no economic pressure due to their CIG

experience and "forced" job termination decision, well express these two different experiences: "Before having to retire, I had thought I would not stay home all the time; I would find myself a small, part-time job to keep busy. But now I feel I am happy at home, and have changed my mind." "O.K., there is housework. But I am organized by now. What I want is a job."

12. The debate on the Basic Income is quite rich and diversified; it has been promoted by BIEN—Basic Income European Network—located in Belgium. Among the main spokespersons of this network are Offe, Standing, and Van Parjis. Proposals have been advanced also by Meade in England and by Darhendorf. For the Italian debate see the November and December 1988 and January, February, March, and June 1989 issues of the journal *Politica ed Economia*. The study center of the CGIL union—IRES/CGIL—in Rome has been among the promoters of this debate, organizing an international seminar in May 1989 whose conclusions have been partly published in the CGIL weekly magazine, *Rassegna Sindacale*, July 29, 1989.

REFERENCES

Accornero, A. 1987. "La Novità è l'Inoccupazione di Massa." *Rivista Trimestrale* 1–2.

Accornero, A., and F. Carmignani. 1986. *I Paradossi della Disoccupazione.* Bologna: Il Mulino.

AIS-ISTAT (Associazione Italiana di Sociologia–Istituto Italiano di Statistica) 1988. *Immagini della Società Italiana.* Roma: ISTAT (see particularly Ch.5, "Il Lavoro").

Ardigò, A., and P. Donati. 1976. *Famiglia e Industrializzazione.* Milano: F. Angeli.

Artoni, R., and E. Ranci Ortigosa (eds.). 1989. *La Spesa Pubblica per l'Assistenza in Italie.* Milano: F. Angeli.

Bagnasco, A. 1977. *Le Tre Italie.* Bologna: Il Mulino.

———. 1989. "Développement Régional, Sociéé Locale et Economie Diffuse." Pp. 287–296 in M. Maruani, E. Reynaud, and C. Romani (eds.), *La Flexibilité en Italie.* Paris: Syros Alternative.

Balbo, L. 1977. "Un Caso di Capitalismo Assistenziale: La Società Italiana." *Inchiesta* 7.

———. 1986. "Forme Familiari e Strategie di Organizzazione della Vita Quotidiana." Pp. 201–216 in *Atti del Convegno La Famiglia in Italia, Annali di Statistica.* Roma: Istituto Italiano di Statistica (ISTAT).

Barile, G. (ed.). 1984. *Lavoro Femminile, Sviluppo Tecnologico e Segregazione Occupazionale.* Milano: F. Angeli.

Beccattini, G. (ed.). 1987. *Mercato del Lavoro e Forze Locali. Il Distretto Industriale.* Bologna: Il Mulino.

———. 1989. "Les Districts Industriels." Pp. 261–270 in M. Maruani, E. Reynaud, and C. Romani (eds.), *La Flexibilité en Italie.* Paris: Syros Alternative.

Becchi Collidà, A. 1979. *Politiche del Lavoro e Garanzie del Reddito in Italia.* Bologna: Il Mulino.

Bettio, F. 1988. *The Sexual Division of Labour: The Italian Case*. Oxford: Clarendon Press.

Bianchi, M., and C. Saraceno. 1988. "Changes in Labour Market Regulations: Three Italian Case Studies." Pp. 97–132 in A. Evers and H. Wintersberger (eds.), *Shifts in the Welfare Mix: Their Impact on Work, Social Services and Welfare Policies*. Wien: Eurosocial.

Camusi, M. P. 1986. "L'identità del Disoccupato in Provincia di Ancona," *CENSIS. Quindicinale di Note e Commenti* 22 (13–14): 3–21.

CENSIS. 1978. *Rapporto Sulla Situazione del Paese*. Milano: F. Angeli.

Commissione Povertà. 1986. *La Povertà in Italia*. Roma: Poligrafico dello Stato.

Federici, N. 1984. *Procreazione, Famiglia, Lavoro della Donna*. Torino: Loescher.

Gallino, L. 1982. *Occupati e Bioccupati*. Bologna: Il Mulino.

Garonna, P. 1984a. *L'Economia della CIG*. Padova: Cleup Editore.

———. 1984b. *Nuove Povertà e Sviluppo Economico*. Padova: Cleup Editore.

———. 1989. "La CIG: Instrument de Politique Industrielle ou Sociale?" Pp. 131–142 in M. Maruani, E. Reynaud, and C. Romani (eds.), *La Flexibilité en Italie*. Paris: Syros Alternative.

Godard, F., with P. Bouffartigue. 1988. *D'une Generation Ouvrière à l'Autre*. Paris: Syros Alternative.

Inchiesta. 1986. Special issue on "Economia Informale, Strategie Familiari e Mezzogiorno," edited by E. Mingioni. *Inchiesta* 74.

IRES Piedmonte. 1987. *L'Espulsione Tutelata*. Torino: *Quaderni di Ricerca IRES* (Instituto Regionale per la Ricerca Economico-Sociale) 48.

———. 1989. *L'Occupazione Femminile dal Declino alla Crescita*. Torino: Rosenberg & Sellier.

ISFOL (Instituto por la Formazione dei Lavoratorio). 1983. "Caratteristiche e Comportamenti degli Operai FIAT in Mobilità." *Quaderni ISFOL* 3 (May-June).

Maggioni, G., V. Pocar, and P. Ronfani. 1988. *La Separazione Senza Giudice*. Milano: F. Angeli.

Negri, N., and W. Santagata. 1984. "Distribuzione del Reddito e Ineguaglianza in un'Area Urbana." *Economia & Lavoro* 3.

Negri, N., G. Ortona, and W. Santagata. 1986. "Inflazione a Misura di Famiglia." *Politica ed Economia* 5 (May).

Negri, N. (ed.). 1990. "Introduzione: La Povertà, una Crisi di Cittadinanza?" *Povertà nella Transformazione dello Stato Sociale in Europa*. Milano: F. Angeli.

Paci, M. 1980. *Famiglia e Mercato del Lavoro in un'Economia Periferica*. Milano: F. Angeli.

Pugliese, E. 1989. "Jeunes et Marchés de Travail." Pp. 87–96 in M. Maruani, E. Reynaud, and C. Romani (eds.), *La Flexibilité en Italie*. Paris: Syros Alternative.

Regione Piedmonte. 1986. "I Lavoratori in CIGS e le Forme della Cassa Integrazione." *Osservatorio sul Mercato del Lavoro* (June).

Regione Toscana. 1986. Osservatorio sul Mercato del Lavoro, "Cassintegrati in Toscana. Ricerca sui Lavoratori in Cassa Integrazione Guadagni Straordinaria a Zero Ore e in Disoccupazione Speciale." *Flash Lavoro Quaderni* 6 (June).

Romani, C. 1987. *La Cassa Integrazione Guadagni. Réalités Juridiques, Economiques et Sociales d'une Institution.* Aix-en-Provence: LEST.

Saraceno, C. 1981. "Modelli di Famiglia." In S. Acquaviva et al. (eds.), *Ritratto di Famiglia degli Anni Ottanta.* Bari: Laterza.

——. 1987. "Between State Intervention, the Social Sphere and Private Life: Changes in the Family Role." Pp. 60–78 in A. Evers et al. (eds.), *The Changing Face of Welfare.* Aldershot: Gower Press.

——. 1989. "Stratégies Familiales sur les Marchées de Travail." Pp. 113–121 in M. Maruani, E. Reynaud, and C. Romani (eds.), *La Flexibilité en Italie.* Paris: Syros Alternative.

——. 1990. "Nuove Povertà o Nuovi Rischi di Povertà?" In N. Negri (ed.), *Povertà nella Transformazione dello Stato Sociale in Europa.* Milano: F. Angeli.

Schenkel, M. 1989. "La CIG: Instrument de Réduction du Temps de Travail?" Pp. 143–153 in M. Maruani, E. Reynaud, and C. Romani (eds.), *La Flexibilité en Italie.* Paris: Syros Alternative.

Schenkel, M., and M. Zenezini. 1986. "Alcuni Aspetti della Cassa Integrazione Guadagni: un'Analisi Empirica." Pp. 87–112 in *Rivista Internazionale di Scienze Sociali* 94.

SVIMEZ (Instituto per lo Sviluppo del Mezzogiorno). 1989. *Rapporto Annuale Sull'Economia Meridionale.* Roma: 1989.

Zanuso, L. 1984. "La Segregazione Occupazionale: I Dati di Lungo Periodo." Pp. 24–90 in G. Barile (ed.), *Lavoro Femminile, Sviluppo Tecnologico e Segregazione Occupazionale.* Milano: F. Angeli.

10

Economic Crisis & Women in Nicaragua

❧ PAOLA PÉREZ-ALEMÁN

During the 1980s, all Latin American countries faced a deep economic crisis; thus the decade was called "the lost decade." For Central America, that period saw the merging of a political/military crisis with an economic crisis. In the specific case of Nicaragua, the economic crisis must be examined within a context of revolutionary transformation aimed at meeting the strategic demands of the majority of the population. In addition, the effects of the "low-intensity" war on the country must be taken into account.[1] Since 1983, the covert war promoted by the United States made Nicaragua's economy increasingly precarious. The main objective of this war was to destroy the economy and to force the country to shift its resources to military defense, away from programs designed to improve the living standards of the majority.

This chapter analyzes the role women have played in the coping processes generated at the household level to confront the crisis. The chapter is organized in four parts: The first identifies the key factors behind the Nicaraguan economic crisis and describes the adjustment policies implemented by the Sandinista government. The second part examines the adjustments at the household level to deal with the crisis, emphasizing women's role in this process. In the third part, attention is given to the collective organizational strategies developed during this period that have contributed to challenging oppressive gender relations. Finally, the last section examines the new challenges brought about by the newly elected Chamorro government.

KEY FACTORS BEHIND THE ECONOMIC CRISIS
AND ADJUSTMENT POLICIES

The economic crisis that Nicaragua faced during the 1980s was the result of structural as well as circumstantial factors. Nicaragua inherited a structurally weak economy from the Somoza era, which depended on the export of only a few agricultural products. For example, by the end of 1970, four export crops accounted for 60 percent of foreign earnings: coffee (31 percent), cotton (22 percent), meat (11 percent), and sugar (3 percent) (Gibson 1987). The modern agroexport sector coexisted with a traditional agricultural sector, mainly small peasant families who produced basic food items. Moreover, the export sector characteristically generated unstable employment opportunities. In the mid-1970s, half of the rural economically active population (EAP) consisted of seasonal agricultural workers who worked the cotton harvest. The majority did not have stable work during the rest of the year (Arana, Stalher, and Timossi 1987).

Agriculture provided foreign exchange to a small industrial sector principally oriented toward the manufacture of nondurable consumer goods. This industrial model, promoted since the 1960s with the formation of the Central American Common Market, was characterized by its dependence on imported inputs and its inability to generate much employment. One study shows that in 1974, 96 percent of inputs needed for the plastics industry and 85 percent of those required for metal production had to be imported (Brundenius 1985). The entire industrial sector employed only 15 percent of the work force (Barraclough et al. 1988).

In 1979, Nicaragua began a transformation of this dependent economy with the victory of the Sandinista Revolution. The four basic objectives of the new development policies were: (1) to improve the population's standard of living through the provision of basic services in health, education, food, and housing; (2) to develop an economic model based on a mixed economy involving cooperation between diverse forms of state and private property (incorporating both large and small landowners) and including the implementation of a major agrarian reform; (3) to reorganize foreign trade in order to reduce dependency, along with a parallel reorganization of the financial system to gain control over the country's surplus and channel it toward social investment; and (4) to increase popular participation in the power structure through mass organizations, as part of a process to create a democratic system. Although these objectives remained constant throughout the first decade of the revolution, there were distinct phases and contradictions within the model of transformation, the most recent being characterized by the economic crisis.

Initially, major shifts in public expenditures had to be made to satisfy the Sandinista government's priority of meeting the basic needs of the population. Between 1980 and 1983, the state used its control over the financial system and international trade to expand the country's social services. Using the philosophy of the "logic of the majority" to guide the state's economic policies meant placing an emphasis on social spending in areas such as health and education. For example, in 1980, 39 percent of state spending went into the combined sectors of health, education, and housing. Likewise, since 1980, workers' real incomes were protected by significant government subsidies of basic goods, transportation, health, and education services.[2] Specifically, 40 percent of the urban population benefited from the state's housing policy in some way. Drinking water availability was extended to most of Managua's housing settlements, thereby increasing the percentage of the city's population with drinking water to 80 percent, up from 50 percent in 1979 (IHCA 1988a).

In addition, the expansion of health and education services during this period was significant. The number of teachers grew by two-thirds; the literacy rate increased from 50 percent to 88 percent (Vilas 1989). In the area of public health, massive vaccination campaigns virtually eradicated several serious endemic diseases, such as poliomyelitis; and the number of health centers increased twelvefold—from 43 to 532 between 1978 and 1983 (Vilas 1989). Thus, in the period prior to 1983, with no military aggression and therefore low levels of defense spending, the average Nicaraguan enjoyed a reasonable and improving standard of living.

During the same period (1980–1983), Nicaragua faced enormous constraints. With an economy so heavily dependent on agroexport crop production, the country suffered a serious deterioration (a 31 percent decrease) in its international terms of trade, resulting in a significant foreign trade gap (IHCA [September] 1986).[3] In addition, the foreign debt inherited from the Somoza period (US$1.6 billion), high interest rates, and the financial commitments made during the first years of the revolution resulted in a significant foreign debt. By 1984, Nicaragua's external debt amounted to US$4 billion, equivalent to 185 percent of the gross domestic product (GDP) for that year, and the debt servicing amounted to 35.3 percent of exports (INIES [June] 1988).

Some of the government's economic policies up until 1985 also contributed to the deterioration of the country's finances, resulting in a growing fiscal deficit. In particular, the implementation of a national economic project that concentrated major investments and foreign aid subsidies into state-owned agricultural development contributed to this trend (Stahler-Sholk 1988). The multiple policies of providing subsidies to producers through very favorable exchange rates, the extension of credit at virtually "give away" rates, and price controls distorted Nicaragua's economy in relation to the world market. The domestic gap (income versus government spending) was financed by an endless creation of the national currency (the cordoba).

The war of aggression that was simultaneously being waged against Nicaragua since 1982 had an even more profound effect on the national economy, marking a new phase in the country's economic development. Estimates of the economic impact of the war between 1980 and 1984 indicate that direct material damages and losses were some US$305 million, and indirect costs totaled some US$2.24 billion (Fitzgerald 1987a). By May 1986, the total economic costs of the war due to material losses, lost credit and trade, amounted to almost US$3 billion—roughly the equivalent of ten years revenue (Barraclough, Utting, and Gariazzo 1988). By 1988, 62 percent of the national budget was being consumed by the defense effort, leaving only 24 percent for health and education and 14 percent to sustain the economy (IHCA [April] 1988a).

A significant gap in the balance of payments, a considerable fiscal deficit, and an uncontrollable spiral of inflation from 1984 onward resulted from these factors. By 1984, the fiscal deficit had risen to one-third of the GDP and was a key factor sparking the inflationary situation in the country (Arana, Stalher, and Timossi 1987). By the end of 1987, the rate of inflation had reached an alarming annual equivalent of almost 5,000 percent, only to worsen by 1988, to 33,000 percent per annum, which was one of this century's ten highest levels reached by any country (IHCA 1990b). Inflation in Nicaragua had been fueled primarily by the war, but also by the government's investment and credit policies.

The major impact of the crisis on the entire working population was a drastic drop in real incomes. For example, the real value of salaries in the formal sector in 1985 dropped to 54 percent of what it had been in 1980 (INIES 1988). In the period after 1985, the economic crisis took on even more acute dimensions; inflation continued to rise and workers' salaries could not keep pace. Official prices rose 400 percent whereas salaries rose only 200 percent (IHCA 1988b). By 1986, the real value of formal sector wages was only 21 percent of the 1980 level and by 1987, this proportion declined to a mere 6 percent, turning the salary into a mere symbolic concept (INIES 1988).

In this context, poverty levels increased significantly. Whereas in 1980 two-thirds of the population was in absolute poverty, by 1988 the level was estimated to be 80 percent (Garcia and Gomariz 1989). The deterioration in formal sector wages contributed significantly to that trend. As the proportion of formal wage workers had increased during the first half of the 1980s, the subsequent dramatic fall in real wages brought poverty to more families.[4]

In the face of the deteriorating economic situation, the government was forced to implement a severe economic adjustment program beginning in 1988 and furthered in 1989 in an attempt to restore stability. Initially, a monetary reform in February 1988 devalued the cordoba by 3,000 percent—seven times more than similar devaluations in Argentina and Brazil (IHCA [April] 1988a). Secondly, the reform measures included the elimination of consumer and producer subsidies, staff cutbacks in the public sector (30,000 employees), and reduction of government spending on social programs (from 35 percent of the national budget in 1981 to 19 percent in 1988).

In the face of the continued hyperinflationary situation, the central pivot of the Economic Program for 1989 was the battle against inflation by way of further reducing the fiscal deficit. Emphasis was also put on the production of exports to generate foreign exchange. Salary policies were oriented at making agroexport production more profitable. Additionally, the state reduced its intervention in the economy, opening more space to the private sector and market relations in the assignment of resources (that is, price controls were eliminated and the marketing of nontraditional exports did not have to go through the channels of the foreign trade ministry).

This package of measures had to be implemented against the background of an acute shortage of foreign currency as the country did not have the usual IMF and World Bank loans to back the adjustment process. Moreover, foreign aid had dropped from US$772 million in 1984 to US$384 million in 1987 and less arrived in the form of cash (IHCA 1990a). The Nicaraguan economic adjustment was likened by some to "an operation without anaesthetic" (IHCA 1988b). Attempting to restore some measure of economic stability meant paying a very high price.

The program was not without its successes, however. The deficit, more than 20 percent of the GDP in 1988, was reduced to 7 percent in 1989 and for the first time since 1983, exports rose by 25 percent (IHCA 1990a). However, only the export-oriented sector (namely, large producers) prospered, while those with lesser resources lost income and faced unemployment or underemployment along with the advancing consequences of impoverishment. When viewed in this context, it is not surprising that the Sandinista Party was defeated in the elections of February 1990.

WOMEN AND ADJUSTMENTS
AT THE HOUSEHOLD LEVEL

In the face of the economic crisis, the Nicaraguan population has been continually making adjustments in an effort to avert sharp drops in their living standard. One of the most widespread responses to the crisis has been the increased labor-market participation and the diversification of the sources of household income (Vilas 1989; Alemán et al. 1986). In particular, the reduction of real wages in the formal sector was countered by an increase in the number of household members participating in the labor market in order to enhance family income. One study of 45 families in Managua's lower-income neighborhoods discovered that in each household where the members were primarily employed in the formal sector, an average of five separate incomes was necessary to meet the family's basic subsistence needs (Alemán et al. 1986).

In this process, women and younger members of the family are most affected. According to national surveys, women's labor force participation has increased during the 1980s. Whereas in 1977 women constituted 29.8 percent of the EAP, by 1985 they were 35.3 percent (OEDEC 1979; INEC 1989). Women's labor-force participation rate showed a steady increase from 26.7 percent in 1977 to 32 percent in 1985. Comparing it to men's participation rate, which was constant between 1977 and 1985 at 68 percent, it is evident that more women were occupied with paid work.

The increased participation of women in the labor force was expressed by the rapid growth in the number of women who were seeking work for the first time. In 1971, 1.8 percent of women and 1.0 percent of men were newcomers into the labor force. By 1985, the number of new women workers had increased both in relative terms (1.6 percent compared to 0.5 percent for men) as well as in absolute terms (5.8 thousand women compared to 3.4 thousand men) (INEC 1985).

As a consequence of formal-sector wage decline, the growth of informal employment provided increasing numbers of families with a means for obtaining their income in the face of the crisis. Owing to the impact of inflationary pressures, increasing numbers of people gave up formal salaried employment and entered the informal sector where wages and incomes were considerably higher (Vilas 1986).[5] The most current research conducted in Managua has indicated that 48 percent of those currently in the informal sector (IS) had previously worked in formal employment (INEC 1990).

The growth in the IS has been most notable since 1983. For example, between 1980 and 1985, the economically active population in that sector increased by 66 percent, whereas, by contrast, there was a 6 percent drop in the formal (nonagricultural) sector (Fitzgerald 1987b). National surveys indicate that the proportion of EAP in this sector grew from 43.6 percent in 1970 to 52 percent in 1985 (INEC 1990).

Women have been significantly represented in this coping process, as indicated by their higher proportion in the informal sector. In 1985, 60 percent of the women in the EAP were occupied in the IS in comparison with 49 percent for male EAP (INEC 1985). The data for Managua indicate that women represent 51 percent of those self-employed in the IS and 41 percent of microenterprisers (INEC 1989).[6] By comparison, women comprise 30 percent of Managua's formal salaried workers and 39 percent in the public sector. One reason for women's high entrance to the informal sector is their ability to combine domestic and remunerated work. This situation is also related to the high proportion of female heads of households (45 percent in Managua) as a result of the war and the economic crisis.

Contrary to what is commonly accepted, the informal sector attracts primary, not secondary, household earners. In addition, there is a high proportion of heads of households in this sector. For example, 66 percent of microenterprisers, 52 percent of the self-employed, and 40 percent of microenterprise employees are heads of households. This situation contrasts significantly with their presence in the formal sector where only 37 percent of government workers and 47 percent of enterprise workers are heads of households (INEC 1990).

THE REVERSAL OF THE FORMAL/INFORMAL CONTRIBUTION TO SURVIVAL

The above data indicate a pattern where informal sector income became primary to household survival, whereas formal income took a complementary role. Households in Nicaragua have dealt with the crisis by employing some members in the formal sector, as a means of obtaining additional state-supplied benefits and goods in kind, and have integrated others in the IS in order to obtain better income.[7] For example, women factory workers often sold items (materials, clothes, or food) made available to them at subsidized prices as a means of increasing their total level of income (Pérez-Alemán, Martinez, and Widmaier 1989).

In the agricultural sector, women's participation rate as agricultural wage workers also increased significantly. The combined effects of the escalation of the war led to a "feminization" of the salaried work force in the rural sector (CIERA 1987). For every man mobilized in the Sandinista government defense effort or to the counterrevolutionary army ("the Contras"), there was a woman who became primarily responsible for the household's subsistence. A sample of 800 female agricultural wage workers revealed that 36 percent of them were heads of households without direct access to land (CIERA 1987). Women became an integral part of the agricultural labor force, the cooperatives, and other collective organizations in order to face this situation. Thus, in 1985, women constituted 40 percent of permanent salaried agricultural workers (48 percent of tobacco workers, 36 percent of cotton, and 35 percent of coffee workers). During harvest time, their presence was even higher: 70 percent in tobacco and coffee, and 60 percent in cotton. Prior to this period, women represented only 20 percent of total coffee workers.

For many heads of households, integration into cooperatives was a response to the household's survival needs. One survey showed that 40.5 percent of female cooperative members in three regions of Nicaragua were heads of households (Pérez-Alemán 1990). A consequence of the war was that women became primarily responsible for household maintenance as well as agricultural production. Women sought collective organization as a way to confront the crisis. As a woman who became a member of a cooperative when her husband was kidnapped by the Contras describes it:[8]

> I lived with my mother-in-law during eight months after he disappeared. But then I began to struggle alone. Sometimes I have had to work like a man in the field, but I do it for my children. We have survived. You see how I look after the corn, I install the motor. I work hard now that I am alone. Before I did not like to be organized, I saw it as a waste of time, going here and there. But when I was left alone I saw the need to become organized. Then I joined the Cooperativa Otto Casco.

In urban areas women sought collective ways to secure food supply by growing their own vegetables. These coping strategies were often promoted by AMNLAE, the Nicaraguan Women's Organization. In the city of Leon, a neighborhood organized a communal garden because, as one member put it:[9]

> Growing one's own food is another way of helping to make ends meet. What we are trying to do at the moment is survive, so if you can cook up a meal using your own vegetables that's something; you feel the inflation a little less.

The crisis has affected women differently than men. One of the major problems for women in Nicaragua has been underemployment accompanied by lower wages for women than for men. According to a national survey, the rate of underemployment in 1985 was 37.6 percent for women and 28.6 percent for men (INEC 1985). Though more recent figures are not available, this gap is likely to have increased.

In addition, there was a marked distinction between the position of men and women in the informal sector, which is primarily manifested by pay differentials. Traditional men's jobs, like craftsmanship, electrical repair, and construction, pay much better than the domestic work traditionally done by women (Alemán et al. 1986). Also, men tend to be more represented than women among microenterprisers, whose income is much higher in comparison to the self-employed (see Note 4). As a result of this form of sexual segregation, women are also disproportionately affected by reductions in income during a crisis situation.

Similarly, access to land tends to be highly differentiated by sex in rural areas. After the Agrarian Reform implemented by the Sandinista government, women represented only 8 percent of total cooperative members and received only 7 percent of individual land titles that were assigned as part of the agrarian reform program (CIERA 1989). In February 1989, at their First National Congress, peasant women expressed that "many of us request land, but nobody pays attention to our demands, neither government nor the UNAG (Small Farmers' Union); we are the last to receive titles, credit and technical assistance" (UNAG 1989).

Migration

Another strategy for coping with the economic crisis and the war was migration. During the 1980s, emigration (mainly to the United States, Canada, and Mexico) was significantly higher than in other periods. Whereas during the 1960s only 30,000 Nicaraguans migrated abroad, in the period 1980–1985 (only five years) the figure rose to nearly 100,000 (Garcia and Gomariz 1989). During the second half of the 1980s these high levels were maintained, given the worsening economic situation. Men constituted the majority of the migrants, which in turn contributed to the rise of females as heads of households. The decision to migrate was considered a mechanism to increase family income as those who moved would (might) send cash to the families left behind. At the same time, male migration was the best way to avoid the obligatory military draft imposed by the government as part of its strategy to fight against the Contras.

During the period of the crisis, the practice of receiving cash from relatives living abroad became an important means of supplementing household income. In Managua, during 1989, 10 percent of poor-strata households and 20 percent of medium strata received some cash from relatives who lived abroad (SPP 1989). Moreover, women have played an important role in this response as the main recipients and administrators of these funds; relatives abroad feel they can be trusted more than men to make the "right" use of the money (CEPAL 1988).

However, not all those who migrate carry out their promise to send money to the family left behind. As a single mother of three children put it:[10]

> He left. He went to another country because he said he did not have a job here. He told me that by working abroad he could send me money for the kids; but after a short while he stopped sending money. Then I had to look for a job to support the children.

Thus, male migration has meant an increased burden for women, who in the process have become heads of households.

Women have assumed a primary role in family survival strategies by allocating all of their earnings to support family members. Even though men's work is usually better paid, men typically contribute relatively less than women to the household expenses. For example, in a study of garment and textile industry workers, it was found that 67 percent of women contributed all of their salary to maintain the household, and among female heads of households the proportion was even greater. By comparison, only 35 percent of the husbands contributed all their salary to family maintenance, while 43 percent contributed half or less (Pérez-Alemán, Martinez, and Widmaier 1989).

Given their roles as organizers and providers of daily consumption, women must compensate for decreasing household income: What to feed children? How should the money be spent? How to get the cheapest prices? How much to purchase? Their administrative role increases in order to cope with the crisis, and domestic work is intensified. For instance, purchasing patterns change. As one woman described the process: "We buy food on a daily basis; but we were able to buy some food reserves with the extra money I made during Easter time."[11]

However, the increase in domestic labor is not distributed equally among all family members. In the majority of families much of the burden falls on women. One case study indicated that women contributed most of their time to household maintenance: 67 percent versus 5 percent for men. Women perform most of the labor for maintaining and developing human resources as well as being active in remunerated work. The study concluded that the adult woman dedicates 92 percent of her time to survival activities—paid and nonpaid (Guerrero and Guerrero 1986). As seen in the case of Mercedes, a garment worker, head of household, with three children, ages nine, eight and twenty months:[12]

> I have to get up at 3 a.m. At that time I heat up the food and prepare the baby's meal for the day. Then I get ready and wake up the older children who take care of the youngest. I wash every day. When I finished cleaning

the house I leave for the bus stop at 5 a.m. My two older kids help with the baby's care: the oldest goes to school in the morning and the girl goes in the afternoon; they take turns. But I leave everything ready for them so they don't run into problems. I get out of work at 5 p.m. At that time I go to buy the food and then cook it for the children. Sometimes I would like to go home directly to bed, but I can't. I have to do the housework, cooking, washing, see the baby. After I finish all that I go to bed around 10:30 p.m.

Similarly, research on female agricultural and industrial wage workers has shown that domestic activities for household maintenance continue to be overwhelmingly performed by women, with only minor tasks performed by men (CIERA 1987; Pérez-Alemán, Martinez, and Widmaier 1989). The result is increased demands on women's time as they simultaneously participate in salaried work while also being exclusively responsible for carrying out the tasks required for household maintenance. In many cases, the double burden is lessened when a grandmother lives with the family as she will usually look after small children and cook, while children in the seven-to-twelve age range also assume certain responsibilities.

Given the still recent implementation of the adjustment program, there are no studies on its impact on Nicaraguan women, but some consequences are clearly visible. For instance, the need to reduce public expenditures has meant significant staff reduction in public services since February 1988. Employees with the least skills, such as secretaries, cleaners, and other support staff, were among the first to go. The vast majority of these were women.

Budgets for social services such as health, education, housing, and transportation were cut, which created shortages, as the same facilities had to support the same or growing population with less and less resources. Under these new conditions, women's workloads and work time increased as a result of having to spend more time buying food, caring for the sick at home, and having to wait longer at the public health centers and bus stops.

The reduction in social spending also resulted in the closure of many child care centers. This had a particularly negative effect on working women and increased the burden of their double workday. Under these circumstances, more domestic responsibility fell upon other members of the family, especially children.

On the other hand, the shortage of foreign exchange and material inputs hit hard the supply of basic inputs for informal food and clothing production where significant numbers of women are employed. As a matter of state policy, most inputs were assigned to the large private and state enterprises, further marginalizing the small industry and artisan production. In addition, the credit policies, which were based on high interest rates and increased taxation, both increased the debts of the small family enterprises and left them with no working capital.

As a result, employment and income became highly unstable, affecting women in particular given their high participation in informal production. Many workshops were forced to close and the lack of capital for the purchase of basic inputs allowed them to purchase only enough to operate for one week each month, which considerably limited their monthly income (Pérez-Alemán, Martinez, and Widmaier 1989). In the short term, the most serious problem was the reduction of employment alternatives for women whose educational level was low and whose only skills were in sewing and processing foods.

WOMEN ORGANIZING: BETWEEN SURVIVAL AND TRANSFORMATION

The consequences of the economic crisis meant that women faced greater demands on their time and were forced to confront more contradictions in their lives. They now had to face the tensions generated by combining increased labor-force participation with their daily household responsibilities and the reality of oppressive gender relations in the public and private realms. Yet, the crisis also allowed possibilities for change. It contributed to the raising of women's individual and collective gender consciousness and to increasing their desire to organize in order to confront oppressive gender relations.

Significantly, agriculture has been one of the sectors where women have been most organized and outspoken about their gender problems. In the organization of the Agricultural Workers Union (ATC), women constituted 40 percent of members in 1985 (CIERA 1987). In 1986, more than 8,000 female wage workers began discussions about their specific problems and demanded that their union make women's rights a priority. For instance, they argued that because the burden of parallel domestic/employment responsibilities was one of their biggest obstacles, the union should attempt to change that situation. As a result of these demands, the ATC proposed major actions (that is, better provision of child care, training women for nontraditional occupations, increased female quotas for leadership positions, and the initiation of sexual education). For example, with resources from local employees and international solidarity groups, the ATC was able to build 69 rural child-care centers in 1988 and 39 in 1989 (Murguialday 1990). Women now hold 35 percent of leadership positions, and gender-specific issues such as paid maternity leave and provision for laundry and child care services were incorporated in the union's contract negotiations.

Women industrial workers also began collective discussions about their problems and interests within the Urban Workers Union, or CST, where they constituted 37 percent of members (Chamorro 1989). In 1986, 200 women met in Managua to discuss work and personal issues ranging from prime material shortages to domestic violence. The conclusions included demands to eliminate pregnancy test requirements for employment and to have access to technical and organizational training as well as sexual education.

At the same time, peasant women have increasingly organized around gender demands within a traditionally male organization, UNAG, where they represent 12 percent of affiliates (UNAG 1989). Their integration into cooperatives and their limited access to land exposed common problems they share as women. At the First National Congress of Peasant Women in February 1989, they pressed for land titles to be written in the name of the family and not simply the men's; they complained that some cooperatives paid women less than men; they criticized machismo within their own organization; and they denounced the daily violence they confronted at home. As a leader of peasant women said:[13]

> We did not have an idea of the relevance of our specific problems. We have organizational, political and economic problems we share with men. But as women we have specific problems. For instance, wife-battering is not suffered by men; child care should be a communal problem, but it is not; the fact that a woman with ten or fifteen children has to request permission from her husband to become sterilized; the little experience we women have to speak in public. All these issues must be discussed together by women.

The economic crisis also promoted the development of different organizational forms at the neighborhood level to confront the crisis. Many groups have been organized around how to lower food costs; how to clean up the neighborhood; and how to maintain the schools. It is mainly women who participate in these neighborhood organizations, making up 67 percent of their members (Chamorro 1989).

The prevailing force behind these community initiatives has been what Maxine Molyneux (1987) called "practical gender interests." They are motivated by the need to respond to their immediate needs, as opposed to serving as a means of promoting more general and long-term strategic objectives, such as the emancipation of women.

Practical gender interests that have mobilized women into these "subsistence" groups have "not always been converted into the negation of alienation" (Molyneux 1987). Immediate, survival-related interests have not challenged consciously the mechanisms of women's subordination and, as such, have not been translated in the majority of cases into concrete struggles for the transformation of gender relations. Although AMNLAE played an important role in these groups, it has been slow to link these actions with women's demands against their oppression and against the existing sexual division of labor. Until 1987, AMNLAE emphasized the mobilization around immediate problems (nutrition, vaccination, and food supply), leaving aside strategic gender issues. This was in part due to AMNLAE's fear to assume a strategy that prioritized gender issues. The women often saw a dichotomy between production and defense (seen as priority issues) and women's demands (seen as secondary). For instance, the issue that these activities often meant an added burden on women's time was never linked to questioning why reproductive tasks are women's tasks. Similarly, it was never questioned why self-help mobilization for health and nutrition was mostly female and it did not attempt to engage men in these activities. In many Nicaraguan women's organizations, gender interests that implicitly underlie their daily activities have not surfaced at a conscious level.

Although these groups are organized around women's traditional roles, they provide opportunity for communication and solidarity among members. Often in their informal discussions women share common family problems, such as their partner's irresponsibility (drunkenness, philandering), and conflicts (that is, battering) due to their participation in the group. Often they discover that these problems are not just their individual experiences, but a common situation.

Similarly, women's increased participation in local action groups and their interest in organizing has created tension between couples. A central theme of many disputes is the differences in perception of the "proper" role of women. A study of women's food collectives found that women faced strong resistance from their husbands and were up against the pressures of housework in an atmosphere of acute conflict (Pérez-Alemán 1988). Thus, this development is also inextricably linked to the strategic interests of women.[14]

> My husband did not accept that I be out when he comes home. Food has to be ready when he wants it. It has to be hot and I have to serve it. It is hard to change his mind. He also fights with me because he says I have abandoned the children.

Under conditions of war and economic crisis, women from diverse sectors began to discuss their subordination and to make public a formulation of gender-specific issues—such as domestic violence, discrimination at work and in unions, reproductive choices—thus beginning a process of collective strategies to achieve gender equality. In those groups, like the ATC and UNAG, where discussions on gender inequalities and women's needs have been part of a conscious strategy within the organization, it has proved to be very effective in raising women's gender consciousness and in moving them from individual survival strategies to "transformation strategies" (see Elson in this volume) within a context of economic crisis.

It is significant that, as a result of the increased gender demands made by diverse sectors of women, in 1987 AMNLAE incorporated various proposals into its national plan of action. Although it continued to prioritize general and immediate interests, it began to raise issues more directly related to strategic demands. Its 1987 plan made explicit its commitment to struggle for gender equality, thus opening possibilities for gender transformation in the future at a wider (organized) level.

In a sense, the major role played by women in production during this period called attention to their oppressive conditions. Although the Sandinista discourse that promoted participation and equality was a significant factor in promoting women's organizations, this was so as a consequence of women's actions in various sectors. As a result, the struggle for gender equality achieved legitimacy at the national level and women's demands were integrated as a priority. Thus in 1987 the Sandinista Party (FSLN) took a clearer position on the struggle against gender inequality. This was spelled out in a public statement by the FSLN, which acknowledged that women have specific gender-based demands that are a function of their subordinate position in society. In contrast to other revolutionary thinking, the FSLN stated that class, gender, and ethnic struggles are interrelated; in principle it did not subordinate women's emancipation to economic development.

The FSLN statement was translated into several actions, such as legal reforms, institutional struggle to eliminate discrimination against women, and educational campaigns. In practice, however, the FSLN leadership often overreacted when AMNLAE leadership did try to push for a more feminist direction, as evidenced in 1988 when it forced a change of AMNLAE's leadership toward a more gender-conscious and feminist agenda. AMNLAE was not able to overcome its lack of party autonomy, which would have been a prerequisite for leading women toward more transformative type strategies.

A NEW PHASE OF CHALLENGES: THE 1990s

With the change of leadership brought by the newly elected Chamorro government, the Nicaraguan economy is facing a new round of profound adjustments. The present period is characterized by qualitative advancements in women's consciousness and organization, but at the same time, by the deepening of the economic crisis and by the many "reforms" that have eroded gains achieved during the past decade. In May 1990, the new government devalued the national currency by 180 percent; the monthly rate of inflation rose over 150 percent; formal sector workers' salaries fell by one-third; and it announced plans to perform massive cutbacks of jobs in the public sector (IHCA 1990b).

The recent adjustments, however, have further intensified the contradiction faced by women between immediate and strategic gender needs. Women have been especially receptive to the political discourse that offers immediate solutions to economic problems, as demonstrated by the hopes put on the government of Violeta Chamorro. In other words, as the crisis raised the cost for the majority, wearing them down, it also increased their desire for *immediate survival,* while undermining, at least for the moment, their desire for *transformation.* This dichotomy might pose difficulties for the formulation of strategic demands in the immediate future, resulting in a setback for the goal of achieving gender equality.

In this context, the women's movement must develop a new strategy within the new political environment to continue promoting the consciousness raising necessary to transform gender relations, particularly in the domestic sphere where the changes have been the slowest (Chamorro 1989; Murguialday 1990).

The challenge is how women's immediate interests can be articulated and politicized, as Molyneux argues, as part of a conscious battle for the promotion of their strategic interests within the new political regime. How can the kind of energy mobilized for women's initiatives to confront the economic crisis be directed to promote initiatives that will effect transformative strategies? How can strategies be developed that consciously and explicitly transform gender relations while at the same time satisfy both practical and strategic gender demands? These are difficult questions without easy answers.

Some priorities deserve mention. It is necessary to develop a national strategy for truly democratizing politics. As a consequence of the Sandinista revolution, the building of an authentic representative and participatory democracy has gained a primary place in Nicaragua's political agenda. For the future, the challenge is that this process continues and that it includes all levels of society: the state, political parties, popular organizations, and the family. It is fundamental that women be able to create the mechanisms necessary to be represented and participate actively at all levels. In this process, gender awareness of women's subordinated position is crucial.

The questioning of gender subordination should be promoted from different points of departure, taking into account the different everyday contexts in which women live. This means that, as Vargas argues, the gender awareness necessary in order to lead to "transformation" strategies does not imply "that the only way of developing this process is through overt feminist stands, or by placing gender issues as the first and foremost. On the contrary, what we must visualize is that everything relating to women's interests within the family and society includes gender subordination" (Vargas 1990).

It is necessary to develop linkages with feedback mechanisms between the diverse women's groups and with different organizations. At the same time, it will be necessary for women's demands for equality to be no longer considered postponable or of secondary nature. Toward this, it is important that organizations such as AMNLAE develop autonomy, with their own agenda of initiatives and an independent vision.

Policies and organizational strategies must be developed to preserve and protect women's jobs in every sector—agriculture, modernized industry, small-scale informal industry, and rural cooperatives. Some policies may entail assigning resources such as credit, training, and inputs to the informal sector. Parallel to this, a nontraditional occupational training program must be implemented to raise women's qualifications and thereby allow them access to employment outside of the usual informal and services sector occupations.

For the Nicaraguan women's movement, the present challenge in the context of economic crisis and adjustment is to continue leading women toward a conscious questioning of their gender subordination. More than ever, it is important to mobilize women in order to ensure that their needs and demands are not subordinated to other "priority" issues. The dilemma facing the women's movement in Nicaragua closely parallels the one facing women's movements throughout Latin America. As Virginia Vargas has pointed out, "it has not been easy to find the right balance between women's short-term demands for immediate and visible conquests and the longer-term demand for a more subversive feminist project. We have oscillated between the risk of distancing ourselves from the most immediate and urgent needs and demands and the equal risk of being subsumed by them" (Vargas 1988).

NOTES

1. The term "low-intensity war" has been used to describe the new strategy implemented by the United States that prioritizes economic, political, and ideological confrontation over military confrontation. The objective is "to dele-

gitimize and to isolate the enemy until it is no longer considered a possible or stable political alternative" (Barry 1986).

2. Roberto Pizarro, "La Nueva política económica: Un reajuste necessario." Unpublished paper, 1985, Managua, Nicaragua.

3. This figure is based on the value of 1980 index prices according to the National Central Bank of Nicaragua.

4. For example, the number of public sector employees in Managua doubled between 1981 and 1984 (Molero 1988).

5. Wages and incomes were higher in the informal than in the formal sector, even for skilled workers. In August 1989, real income in microenterprises (US$428) was higher than in the highest level occupation in the formal sector (US$360). Similarly, the self-employed earned US$318, twice the average salary of a public sector worker (US$164) (INEC 1989). Even with the system of subsidies, incentives, and other social benefits that formal sector workers enjoyed, the total was insufficient to cope with the crisis.

6. These data are based on a representative survey of Managua's households; the sample includes 1,500 households (INEC 1989).

7. The Sandinista government distributed subsidized food packages to complement the low salaries of state workers. These included rice, beans, sugar, oil, and dry milk.

8. Testimony of Marina collected in *La Vida Cotidiana de la Mujer Campesina* (CIERA 1989). Original in Spanish. Translation by the author.

9. Neighborhood leader. Testimony collected in *Women and Revolution in Nicaragua* (Collison 1990).

10. Textile factory worker. Interview conducted by the author in 1987.

11. Street-seller. Interview published in *GENTE*, No. 23, Managua, June 1, 1990.

12. Mercedes, garment worker. Interview conducted by the author. Published in *Industria*, genero y mujer en Nicaragua, Instituto, Nicaraguense de la Mujer (INIM), Managua, 1988.

13. Marta Valle. Peasant leader in Matagalpa. Interview published in *Pensamiento Propio*, No. 60, Managua, May 1989.

14. Communal organization member in Managua. Interview published in *Envío*, IHCA, Managua, April 1984.

REFERENCES

Alemán, M., et al. 1986. "La Estrategia de Sobrevivencia de los Sectores Populares de Managua y el Impacto del Mensaje Económico Gubernamental." *Encuentro* (Managua), September–December.

Arana, Mario, Richard Stalher, and Gerardo Timossi. 1987. *Deuda, Estabilización y Ajuste: La Transformación en Nicaragua, 1979–1986.* Managua: Coordinadora Regional de Investigaciones Económicas y Sociales (CRIES).

Banco Central de Nicaragua. 1974. Censo 1971, Managua.

Barraclough, Solon, Peter Utting, and Alicia Gariazzo. 1988. *Aid that Counts: The Western Contribution to Development and Survival in Nicaragua.* Amsterdam: Transnational Institute.

Barry, Deborah. 1986. *Aproximación al Conflicto Centroamericano desde la Perspectiva de la Guerra de Baja Intensidad.* Mangua: c.

Brundenius, Claes. 1985. "Estrategia del Desarrollo Industrial en Nicaragua, 1979–1984." *Cuadernos de Pensamiento Propio.* Managua: Instituto Nicaraguense de Investigaciones y Estudios Sociales (INIES)/Coordinadora Regional de Investigaciones Económicos y Sociales (CRIES).

CEPAL (Comisión Económica Para América Latina). 1988. "Las Remesas, la Economia Familiar y el Papel de la Mujer." Document presented at the Fourth Regional Conference on Women's Integration to Social and Economic Development, Guatemala City.

Chamorro, Amalia. 1989. "La Mujer: Logros y Limites en 10 Años de Revolucion." *Cuadernos de Sociologia* (Managua), no. 9–10, January–August 1989.

CIERA (Centro de Investigaciones y Estudios de la Reforma Agraria). 1987. *ATC, CETRA, Mujer y Agroexportación en Nicaragua.* Managua: Instituto Nicarguense de la Mujer.

———. 1989. *La Vida Cotidiana de la Mujer Campesina.* Managua: CIERA.

Collison, Helen (ed.). 1990. *Women and Revolution in Nicaragua.* London: Zed Books.

Fitzgerald, E.V.K. 1987a. "An Evaluation of the Economic Costs to Nicaragua of U.S. Aggression: 1980–1984." In Rose J. Spalding (ed.), *The Political Economy of Revolutionary Nicaragua.* Boston: Allen & Unwin.

———. 1987b. "Notas sobre la Fuerza de Trabajo y la Estructura de Clases en Nicaragua." *Revista Nicaraguense de Ciencias Sociales* (Managua), Vol. 2 (2) (March).

Garcia, Ana Isabel, and Enrique Gomariz. 1989. *Mujeres Centroamericanas ante la Crisis, la Guerra y el Proceso de Paz.* FLACSO (Facultad Latinoamericana de Ciencias Sociales, San Jose, Costa Rica), Vols. 1–2.

Gibson, Bill. 1987. "A Structural Overview of the Nicaraguan Economy." In Rose J. Spalding (ed.), *The Political Economy of Revolutionary Nicaragua.* Boston: Allen and Unwin.

Guerrero, L., and G. Guerrero. 1986. "Las Estrategias de Sobrevivencia y el Papel de la Mujer." Paper presented at the Asociación Nicaraguense de Ciencias Sociales (ANICS), Managua, October.

IHCA (Instituto Historico Centroamericano). 1986. *Envío* (Managua), September-December.

———. 1988a. *Envío,* no. 82, April–May.

———. 1988b. *Envío,* no. 85, July–August.

———. 1989. *Envío,* no. 92, March.

———. 1990a. *Envío,* no. 104, Special Edition, May.

———. 1990b. *Envío,* no. 105–106, June.

INEC (Instituto Nicaraguense de Estadisticas y Censos). 1985. Encuesta Sociodemografica de Nicaragua (ESDENIC), Managua.

———. 1989. Encuesta de Coyuntura de Managua, Managua, August.

———. 1990. "Analisis Preliminar sobre el Sector Informal," elaborated by Carlos Becerra, Managua, unpublished.

INIES (Instituto Nicaraguense de Investigaciones y Estudios Sociales). 1988. *Boletin Socioeconomico* (Managua), No. 7 (May) and No. 8 (June–July).

Molero, Maria. 1988. Nicaragua Sandinista: Del Sueño a la Realidad. Madrid: Coordinadora Regional de Investigaciones Económicos y Sociales (CRIES)/ Instituto de Estudios Politicos para America Latina y Africa (IEPALA).

Molyneux, Maxine. 1987. "Movilización sin Emancipación? Intereses de la Mujer, el Estado y la Revolución: El Caso de Nicaragua." In J. L. Coraggio and C. D. Deere (eds.), *La Transición Difícil*. Managua: Editorial Vanguardia.

Murguialday, Clara. 1990. *Nicaragua: Revolución y Feminismo*. Madrid: Editorial Revolución, S.A.L.

OEDEC (Organización de Estudios Demograficos y Censos). 1979. *Encuesta demografica nacional EDENIC 1976–1978*. Managua: OEDEC.

Pérez-Alemán, Paola. 1988. *Movimiento de Mujeres, Crisis y la Alimentacion: El Caso De Nicaragua*. Managua: INIM.

———. 1990. *Organización, Identidad y Cambio: las Campesinas en Nicaragua*. Managua: Editorial Vanguardia.

Pérez-Alemán, Paola, Diana Martinez, and Christa Widmaier. 1989. *Industria, Genero y Mujer en Nicaragua*. Managua: INIM.

SPP (Secretaria de Planificación y Presupuesto). 1989. "Ajuste Economico y Situacion de los Hogares en la Ciudad de Managua." Managua: SPP.

Stahler-Sholk, Richard. 1988. "Ajuste y Estabilización en Nicaragua." *Boletín Socioeconómico* (INIES, Managua), May.

UNAG (Union Nacional de Agricultores y Ganaderos). 1989. Plan de Lucha de las Mujeres Campesinas. Managua: UNAG.

Vargas, Virginia. 1988. *El Aporte de la Rebeldia de las Mujeres*. Santo Domingo, Dominican Republic: Centro de Investigación para la Acción Femenina.

———. 1990. "The Women's Movement in Peru: Streams, Spaces and Knots." Paper presented at the Development Alternatives with Women for a New Era (DAWN) meeting in Rio de Janeiro, May.

Vilas, Carlos. 1989. *Transición desde el Subdesarrollo: Revolución y Reforma en la Periferia*. Caracas, Venezuela: Editorial Nueva Sociedad.

Acronyms

ADEMI	Association for the Development of Microenterprises (Dominican Republic)
ADN	Acción Democratica Nacional (Bolivia)
AIS	Italian Sociological Association
AMNLAE	Nicaraguan Women's Organization
ANICS	Asociación Nicaraguense de Ciencias Sociales
APEC	Asociación Pro Educación y Cultura (Dominican Republic)
ASSA	American Social Science Association
ATC	Agricultural Workers Union (Nicaragua)
BIAG	Bangladesh International Action Group
BIEN	Basic Income European Network
BNP	Bangladesh Nationalist Party
CBI	Caribbean Basin Initiative
CELADE	Centro Latinoamericano de Demografía (Costa Rica)
CEPAL	Comisión Económica Para América Latina
CEPROMIN	Centro de Promoción Minero (Bolivia)
CERES	Centro de Estudios de Realidad Económica (Bolivia)
CGIL	Social and Communist trade union (Italy)
CIDA	Canadian International Development Agency
CIESAS	Centro de Investigaciones y Estudios Superiores en Antropología Social (Mexico)
CIG	Cassa Integrazione Guadagni (Italy)
CIPAF	Centro de Investigación para la Acción Femenina (Dominican Republic)
COB	Canasta Obrera Básica (Mexico)
COB	Central Workers Union (Bolivia)
COI	Canasta Obrera Indispensable (Mexico)
COMIBOL	Nationalized Tin Company (Bolivia)
CST	Urban Workers' Union (Nicaragua)
DAWN	Development Alternatives with Women for a New Era
EAP	economically active population
ECA	Economic Commission for Africa
ECLA	Economic Commission for Latin America
ECLAC	Economic Commission for Latin America and the Caribbean
EGS	Employment Guarantee Scheme (India)
EPZ	export-processing zones
ERP	Economic Recovery Programme (Tanzania)

ESCAP	Economic and Social Commission for Asia and the Pacific
FAO	Food and Agriculture Organization of the United Nations
FDI	foreign direct investments
FIAT	Fabbrica Italiana Automobili Torino
FLACSO	Facultad Latinoamericana de Ciencias Sociales (Costa Rica)
FLPRS	female labor-force participation rates
FSLN	Sandinista Front of National Liberation (Nicaragua)
FSTMB	Federated Syndicate of Mining Workers (Bolivia)
GDP	gross domestic product
GNP	gross national product
ICHD	International Conference on Human Development
IDSS	Instituto Dominicano de Seguridad Social (Dominican Republic)
IFC	International Finance Corporation
IHCA	Instituto Histórico Centroamericano (Nicaragua)
ILO	International Labour Organisation
IMF	International Monetary Fund
INEC	Instituto Nicaraguense de Estadísticas y Censos
INIES	Instituto Nicaraguense de Investigaciones y Estudios Sociales
INSTRAW	International Research and Training Institute for the Advancement of Women (an agency of the United Nations)
INTEC	Instituto Tecnológico de Santo Domingo (Dominican Republic)
IRES/CGIL	study center of the CGIL union (Italy)
ISTAT	Italian Office of Census
ITC	International Tin Cartel
MIR	Leftist Revolutionary Movement (Bolivia)
MNR	National Revolutionary Movement (Bolivia)
MNRI	Leftist National Revolutionary Movement (Bolivia)
NEP	New Economic Policy (Bolivia)
NGO	nongovernmental organization
NIC	newly industrializing country
NIP	New Industrial Policy (Bangladesh)
ODI	Overseas Development Institute
ONAPLAN	Oficina Nacional de Planificación (Dominican Republic)
PCB	Bolivian Communist Party
PIDW	Program on International Development and Women at Cornell University
PRD	Partido Revolucionario Dominicano (Dominican Republic)
PREALC	Programa Regional de Empleo para América Latina y el Caribe (Dominican Republic)
RMI	Revenue Minimum d'Insertion (France)
SAP	structural adjustment policies
SEF	Social Emergency Fund
SEWA	Self-Employed Women's Association (India)
SIDA	Swedish International Development Agency
SPP	Secretaria de Planificación y Presupuesto (Mexico)
STATIN	Statistical Index Labour Force Survey (Jamaica)
UDP	Popular Democratic Union (Bolivia)

UK	United Kingdom
UNAG	Small Farmers' Union (Nicaragua)
UNDP	United Nations Development Programme
UNICEF	United Nations International Children's Emergency Fund
UNRISD	United Nations Research Institute for Social Development
URPE	Union for Radical Political Economics
USAID	United States Agency for International Development
VCs	village commons (Bangladesh)
YWCA	Young Women's Christian Association

About the Book & Editors

The debt crisis and global economic changes of the past decade have caused Third World nations to restructure economic policies, community resources, the labor market, and intrahousehold divisions of labor. These changes have swelled the ranks of the unemployed, the poor, and the malnourished. Women, in particular, have been affected negatively by processes of structural adjustment because they represent a disproportionate share of the world's poor, are increasingly represented among low-wage workers, and are forced to balance wage work with subsistence and domestic production in meeting household needs.

Using country-based studies, this text offers new perspectives on the consequences of economic crisis in terms of changing state practices and household and family work. Throughout, the contributors raise two critical questions: For what segments of the population do austerity measures mean more limited access to food, social services, and unemployment? For whom do they create increased access to credit and new incentives to expand production, thus increasing accumulation and profit-making opportunities? The field-based investigations of crisis and poverty also emphasize the salience of gender relations and embrace a view of the household and its diverse organizational forms and relations as a contradictory institution in which conflict and cooperation create the complex dynamic of daily survival.

Lourdes Benería is professor of city and regional planning and director of the Program on International Development and Women at Cornell University. **Shelley Feldman** is assistant professor of rural sociology and associate director of the Program on International Development and Women at Cornell University.

About the Contributors

Bina Agarwal is professor of agricultural economics at the Institute of Economic Growth, Delhi University. Currently she is a fellow at the Bunting Institute, Radcliffe/Harvard University (1989–1991), and member of the Harvard Center for Population and Development Studies. She is author of *Cold Hearths and Barren Slope: The Woodfuel Crisis in the Third World* (1986) and *Mechanisation in Indian Agriculture* (1983) and has edited *Structures of Patriarchy: State, Community and Household in Modernising Asia* (1988) and *Women, Poverty and Ideology in Asia* (1989). At present, she is completing a book on gender and land rights in South Asia.

Peggy Antrobus is tutor/coordinator of the Women and Development Unit (WAND) as well as the general coordinator of a Third World feminist network—Development Alternatives with Women for a New Era (DAWN), which was launched in 1984. DAWN's secretariat moves periodically to different regions and will be located in Barbados for the next four years.

Lourdes Benería is professor of city and regional planning and women's studies at Cornell University where she is also the director of the Program on International Development and Women. She has worked at the Geneva office of the International Labor Organization and as a consultant with several of the UN branches. An economist, her work has dealt with issues related to women's work, gender, and development. She is the editor of *Women and Development: The Sexual Division of Labor in Rural Societies* and coauthor (with Martha Roldán) of *The Crossroads of Class and Gender: Homework, Subcontracting and Household Dynamics in Mexico City*. Her writings have also appeared in edited volumes and scholarly journals.

Diane Elson is a lecturer in the Department of Economics, University of Manchester. She has written widely on the implications of recent economic trends for women in both developed and developing countries and acted as consultant on gender and structural adjustment in the Commonwealth Secretariat, the Food and Agriculture Organization of the United Nations (FAO), and the Swedish International Development Agency (SIDA). She is active in fostering international links between women workers through a nongovernmental organization called Women Working Worldwide. Her latest book is *Male Bias in the Development Process*, 1991.

Shelley Feldman is a sociologist who has carried out research on both rural and urban Bangladeshi women as well as on the political economy of Bangladesh. She has written extensively on these themes and is currently completing a coauthored volume with Florence E. McCarthy, *The Gender and Development Matrix: Development Policy in Bangladesh*. She presently combines these interests with those concerning social regulation, the gender division of labor, and household food production systems. She teaches in the Department of Rural Sociology, Cornell University.

Wendy McFarren is completing her doctorate in city and regional planning from Cornell University. She is conducting her research in La Paz, Bolivia, on changing policy toward the microenterprise sector and the women who comprise it. In particular, she is concerned with understanding the effects of the debt crisis and structural adjustment on policy toward sectors previously considered "marginal" and that are now the center of policy support. She is also working for the Quipus Cultural Foundation planning a national craft promotion program directed especially toward women and for the City of La Paz developing a microenterprise support program.

Paola Pérez-Alemán is a graduate of the University of California at Berkeley in development economics. She has been involved in research and policy action in the area of women's employment and income problems in Nicaragua. She was founder and director of the Research Department at the Nicaraguan Institute for Women as well as adviser to urban and rural women's grass-roots associations. Her publications include *Industria, Género y Mujer en Nicaragua* and *Organización, Identidad y Cambio: Las Campesinas en Nicaragua*.

Helen I. Safa is the author of *The Urban Poor of Puerto Rico* and the editor of *Migration and Development, Women and Change in Latin America, Toward a Political Economy of Urbanization in Third World Countries* and other books. Her articles and reviews on migration, housing, race, ethnicity, education, and women and national development have appeared in a variety of scholarly journals and periodicals. She has served as a consultant on immigration and urban planning and women and development in the United States and abroad, particularly Latin America.

She has taught at Syracuse University and Rutgers University and was former director of the Center for Latin American Studies at the University of Florida, where she is currently professor of anthropology and Latin American studies. She is past president of the Latin American Studies Association and former chair of the Advisory Committee for the American Republics, Council for International Exchange of Scholars (Fulbright). She also served on the selection committee of the Doctoral Fellowship Committee of the Inter-American Foundation.

Chiara Saraceno is professor of sociology at the University of Turin, Italy, Faculty of Political Sciences. She has researched and published extensively on family, gender, and social policies; some of her work is published in English. She has served on the Poverty Commission and on the Social Impact Commission at the prime minister's office in Italy.

Aili Mari Tripp is an assistant professor of political science and women's studies at the University of Wisconsin–Madison. She worked as a research associate with the Program on Peace and International Cooperation, John D. and Catherine T. MacArthur Foundation (1989–1991). Her research interests include: political economy and gender in developing countries, particularly Africa; the politics and social impact of structural adjustment programs in developing countries; and the relationship between informal economies and states in comparative perspective. Her publications include: "Local Organizations, Participation and the State in Urban Tanzania" in M. Bratton and G. Hyden (eds.), *Governance in Africa* (1991), and "Women and the Changing Household Economy in Urban Tanzania" in the *Journal of Modern African Studies* (1989).

Index